P9-DFZ-963

The Depression and New Deal

A History in Documents

The Depression and New Deal
A History in Documents

Robert S. McElvaine

Oxford University Press
New York • Oxford

For John Lee and in memory of Anna Lee, who lived through the Great Depression and later created the love of my life.

OXFORD
UNIVERSITY PRESS

Oxford New York

Athens Auckland Bangkok Bogotá Buenos Aries Calcutta Cape Town
Chennai Dar es Salaam Delhi Florence Hong Kong Istanbul Karachi
Kuala Lumpur Madrid Melbourne Mexico City Mumbai Nairobi
Paris São Paulo Singapore Taipei Tokyo Toronto Warsaw

and associated companies in
Berlin Ibadan

Copyright © 2000 by Robert S. McElvaine

Design: Sandy Kaufman
Layout: Loraine Machlin

Published by Oxford University Press, Inc.,
198 Madison Avenue, New York, New York 10016
www.oup.com

Library of Congress Cataloging-in-Publication Data
McElvaine, Robert S.
The Depression and New Deal: a history in documents/
by Robert S. McElvaine.
p. cm. — (Pages from history)
Includes index.
1. United States—History—1933–1945 Sources. 2. United States—
Social conditions—1933–1945 Sources. 3. United States—
Social life and customs—1918–1945 Sources. 4. Depressions—
1929—United States Sources. 5. New Deal, 1933–1939 Sources.
I. Title. II. Series.
E806.M43   1999
973.91—dc21
99-36644
CIP

ISBN 0-19-510493-5

1 3 5 7 9 8 6 4 2

Printed in the United States of America
on acid-free paper

General Editors

Sarah Deutsch
Associate Professor of History
Clark University

Carol Karlsen
Professor of History
University of Michigan

Robert G. Moeller
Professor of History
University of California, Irvine

Board of Advisors

Steven Goldberg
Social Studies Supervisor
New Rochelle, N.Y., Public Schools

John Pyne
Social Studies Supervisor
West Milford, N.J., Public Schools

George Sanchez
Professor of History
University of Southern California

Cover: *Unemployed men lined up outside a depression soup kitchen that was opened in Chicago by gangster Al Capone.*

Frontispiece: *An advertisement for one of Franklin D. Roosevelt's New Deal programs, the Social Security Act of 1935.*

Title page: *The two Presidents who presided over the United States government during the depression, Herbert Hoover and Franklin D. Roosevelt, en route to Roosevelt's inauguration on March 4, 1933.*

Contents

As if the distress caused by the collapse of the free-market economy, which most economists and businessmen had insisted was "natural," were not difficult enough for the people of the United States in the 1930s, nature itself turned savage. A huge drought transformed most of the Great Plains into a vast dust bowl, destroying farms and resulting in the sort of wind erosion seen in this photograph taken in Rosebud County, South Dakota, in 1935.

What Is a Document?

To the historian, a document is, quite simply, any sort of historical evidence. It is a primary source, the raw material of history. A document may be more than the expected government paperwork, such as a treaty or passport. It is also a letter, diary, will, grocery list, newspaper article, recipe, memoir, oral history, school yearbook, map, chart, architectural plan, poster, musical score, play script, novel, political cartoon, painting, photograph—even an object.

Using primary sources allows us not just to read *about* history, but to read history itself. It allows us to immerse ourselves in the look and feel of an era gone by, to understand its people and their language, whether verbal or visual. And it allows us to take an active, hands-on role in (re)constructing history.

Using primary sources requires us to use our powers of detection to ferret out the relevant facts and to draw conclusions from them; just as Agatha Christie uses the scores in a bridge game to determine the identity of a murderer, the historian uses facts from a variety of sources—some, perhaps, seemingly inconsequential—to build a historical case.

The poet W. H. Auden wrote that history was the study of questions. Primary sources force us to ask questions—and then, by answering them, to construct a narrative or an argument that makes sense to us. Moreover, as we draw on the many sources from "the dust-bin of history," we can endow that narrative with character, personality, and texture—all the elements that make history so endlessly intriguing.

Cartoon
This political cartoon addresses the issue of church and state. It illustrates the Supreme Court's role in balancing the demands of the First Amendment of the Constitution and the desires of the religious population.

Illustration
Illustrations from children's books, such as this alphabet from the New England Primer, tell us how children were educated, and also what the religious and moral values of the time were.

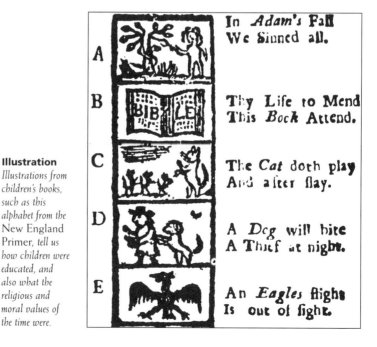

In *Adam's* Fall
We Sinned all.

Thy Life to Mend
This *Book* Attend.

The *Cat* doth play
And after slay.

A *Dog* will bite
A Thief at night.

An *Eagles* flight
Is out of sight.

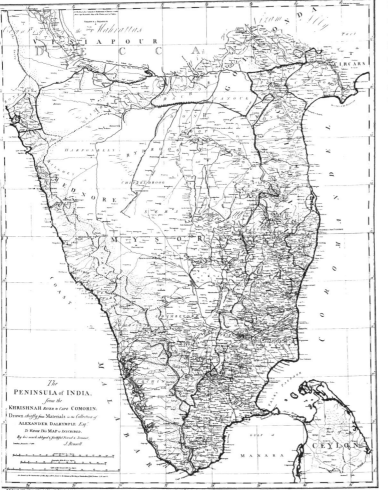

Treaty
A government document such as this 1805 treaty can reveal not only the details of government policy, but information about the people who signed it. Here, the Indians' names were written in English transliteration by U.S. officials; the Indians added pictographs to the right of their names.

Map
A 1788 British map of India shows the region prior to British colonization, an indication of the kingdoms and provinces whose ethnic divisions would resurface later in India's history.

Literature
The first written version of the Old English epic Beowulf, from the late 10th century, is physical evidence of the transition from oral to written history. Charred by fire, it is also a physical record of the wear and tear of history.

How to Read a Document

During the depression and New Deal, one overarching condition so dominated people's lives that almost every document in the book is in some way related to it: the most total collapse of the economy that the United States has ever experienced

The backgrounds of the Americans affected by that collapse—their sex, class, age, ethnicity, region, political affiliation, income, and educational level—influenced the way they responded to the crisis. As a result, when reading documents from this period, we need to consider who produced them and for whom they were intended.

For example, during the depression, political allegiance was linked to economic class. A vast majority of the poor and most of the middle class rejected the Republican party (largely because they made the same associations with it that the cartoon on the facing page portrays). Most people from these economic levels held Franklin Roosevelt and the New Deal in high esteem.

The cartoon and photograph on the opposite page represent two types of documents that were prevalent in the depression era. Cartoons always seek to "say" something, usually from a particular point of view. They generally use symbolism and humor in making their points. Both pro- and anti–New Deal attitudes were common, and cartoons proved an effective vehicle for expressing the conflicting views of the time.

Whereas a painting or cartoon is obviously composed by the artist in order to achieve certain effects, a photograph gives the impression of providing objective evidence about its subject matter. But in the formal choices a photographer makes, he or she may elicit certain responses in the viewer. Most of the photos in this book were taken under the auspices of a government agency, the Farm Security Administration. They were intended to document social conditions, but also to build support for New Deal programs. Thus, the images must be read for the ways in which they serve their various purposes: documentary, artistic, and persuasive.

Text

Text in a cartoon is used in different ways. Sometimes the main caption indicates what the characters are saying or thinking; in other cases, as here, it is the voice of the cartoonist, commenting on the characters or situation presented.

Text elsewhere in the cartoon—in this case, on the signs—is often in the voice of characters whose ideas the cartoonist is ridiculing and is therefore meant to be read ironically.

Caricature

Cartoonists frequently depict people with exaggerated features or outlandish appearance. The large figure in the center of this cartoon represents the G.O.P. (Republican party). The cartoonist uses such features as a very aged face and a bloated stomach to suggest that the party's ideas are out-of-date and its supporters are those who are overfed in an era when many are going hungry.

Symbolic figures

By placing figures symbolizing different groups together, a cartoonist can send a message to his or her audience. In this one, the smaller figures representing "Rugged Individualism" and "Wall Street" cling to the coattails of the Republican party, indicating the close ties between the party and an idea and institution that were widely discredited during the depression. The poses of the symbolic figures support the stereotypes associated with the groups they represent.

Orientation of figures

Notice that the two women, both clearly showing great worry in their faces, are looking away from each other. The photo would convey a different meaning if they were looking at each other, perhaps speaking. The actual orientation of the women gives the viewer a message about the need for depression victims to come together, to communicate and cooperate

Categories of people

The impact this photograph has on viewers and the meaning they take from it would be different if the people pictured were men instead of women. In a society in which men have traditionally been providers for women, there is something very wrong if women have to wait outside a government relief station. It is also significant that one of the women is old and the other young. It can readily be seen that the economic problems are so severe that they have left women of all ages vulnerable and, as is evident in their faces, desperate.

Rollin Kirby cartoon from 1934

Waiting Outside Relief Station, Urbana, Ohio *by Ben Shahn*

Unemployment and the hardships, both physical and psychological, that followed in its wake posed the central problem of the depression–New Deal era. Many socially conscious artists in the United States sought to depict with sympathy the desperate lives of those who had been struck by the economic calamity. Isaac Soyer's Employment Agency (1937) captures the mood of the time and the diversity of the victims of the depression.

Introduction

"My father he staying home. All the time he's crying because he can't find work. I told him why are you crying daddy, and daddy said why shouldn't I cry when there is nothing in the house. I feel sorry for him."

These words from a letter a 12-year-old Chicago boy wrote to President Franklin D. Roosevelt and his wife, Eleanor, in 1936 capture the personal impact of the Great Depression. The full text of the letter may be found in chapter 8.

The Great Depression was not simply one of the major historical events of the 20th century. It was, of course, an unprecedented economic crisis, but it cannot be understood in economic terms alone. Rather, it was a personal tragedy for millions of individuals of all ages. Its cost must be counted not just in diminished stock prices and lost wages but in feelings of hunger, despair, and self-doubt. As Cabell Phillips stated in his book *From the Crash to the Blitz, 1929–1939,* "Mass unemployment is both a statistic and an empty feeling in the stomach. To fully comprehend it, you have to both see the figures and feel the emptiness." The documents collected in these pages are intended to provide readers with some of that feeling.

The Great Depression was the deepest and longest economic collapse in American history. It ranks with World War II (1939–45) as one of the two most important events in the shaping of the 20th-century United States. The only period in the nation's history that had as great an impact on the thoughts, feelings, and political life of Americans was the Civil War.

What caused such a massive upheaval?

From the late 19th century onward, the ways in which people live have been fundamentally transformed by the development of mass-production industries. Mass production requires mass consumption, if demand is to match supply and the economy kept on an even keel. This fact has led to a remarkable shift in values. By the 1920s, such new (or relatively new) items as radios, automobiles, and household appliances were rolling off assembly lines in huge numbers. Businesses (and thus the economy as a whole) became dependent on the ability of advertisers to persuade consumers to abandon the traditional virtues of the work ethic, such as thrift and community, and replace them with the new habits and values of what might be called the "consumption ethic." Americans were now called upon to think first of themselves and of their day-to-day ease and enjoyment, and the way to do that was to buy the latest products. Instead of saving for the future, people were urged to borrow in order to purchase consumer goods right away.

Through the late 1920s, advertising and "credit" buying kept afloat an economy that was fundamentally unsound due to gross inequities in the distribution of income. (In simple terms, the mass of people who were expected to buy consumer goods did not receive a large enough share of the national income to do so.) By the summer of 1929, this imbalance was catching up with the economy. Businesses that could not sell all that they were manufacturing laid off workers. Individuals who lost their jobs had to cut back on their own spending, and a downward spiral was underway. The stock market crash of October 1929 reflected this underlying problem in the economy. Rather than causing the depression, the crash signaled its beginning.

There had been several earlier economic collapses—usually called "panics"—in U.S. history, before President Herbert Hoover substituted the seemingly less alarming word *depression* for the crisis that began during his administration. But the economic disaster of the 1930s was much worse than any previous period of "hard times." One reason for the increasingly harsh effects of U.S. business slumps was the steady migration from the farms to the cities. In 1880, 43.8 percent of Americans had lived on farms; by 1930, the percentage had fallen to 24.9 percent. No longer having a ready means of feeding themselves and, often, not owning their homes, Americans in the 1930s were totally dependent upon their jobs. Thus unemployment now meant almost immediate hardship for workers and their families. During the Great Depression, unemployment reached levels never before seen in a nation that prided itself on being a land of plenty. By early 1933, one-quarter of the U.S. workforce was jobless.

The impact of this hardship was severe but varied. As many of the documents in this book show, people's experiences of and reactions to the depression differed substantially. In general terms (although not, in every particular case), the economic collapse affected women somewhat differently than men, children differently than adults, and various ethnic and racial groups differently than others. There were also different effects based on region and type of economic activity. Agriculture, for example, had already been in depression throughout the generally prosperous 1920s.

One of the most striking alterations brought about by the Great Depression was a move away from the consumption-oriented values of the marketplace that had become so prominent in the twenties—and which revived and increased in the second half of the 20th century. The depression-era swing away from extreme individualism and materialism toward the more cooperative values of an earlier day can be seen in everything from politics to paintings, from literature to labor unions.

The persona of Franklin D. Roosevelt came to dominate much of the Depression Decade, and his importance can hardly be overstated. But his New Deal was as popular as it was because it fit so well with the community values to which so many Americans returned in the face of economic deprivation.

In responding to the popular will, the New Deal dramatically changed the relationship between U.S. citizens and their government. Starting with the idea that had emerged in the Progressive Era at the century's beginning—that government in a democracy can be used as a tool to advance the well-being of the people—FDR and his administration set about the threefold task of easing the hardship of the depression, trying to revive the economy, and enacting reforms that would make another depression less likely (and less severe, should it happen).

Homelessness was widespread during the depression. People who lived in cities generally did not own their own homes and were forced onto the streets when they lost their jobs and could not pay the rent. Many farm families met the same fate when the drought or low prices left them unable to sell enough produce to meet payments on loans. People without homes had to make do for shelter in any way they could: tents, shacks, even wooden or cardboard boxes.

During his election campaign in 1932, Roosevelt said that the American people were demanding "bold, persistent experimentation." As President, FDR was certainly persistent in his experimentation, but never as bold as he might have been and needed to be. The New Deal was highly successful in its first objective of easing the pain of the depression. But it never quite managed to bring about the full recovery it sought, largely because Roosevelt declined to be sufficiently bold in calling for the sort of massive government spending in peacetime that would be readily accepted in war. As a result, the depression did not end until 1941, when U.S. entry into World War II necessitated the level of spending needed to stimulate the economy.

Many of the issues and programs that emerged during the Great Depression remain very much current well over a half century later. Questions about the propriety of a welfare state; the proper role and size of the federal government; the mutual obligations of citizens; individualism versus community; the place of labor unions in U.S. society; and the viability of the Social Security system are among the legacies of the 1930s that reverberate daily in the nation's political, social, and economic life today.

Americans will continue to live in the shadows of the Great Depression, as they do those of the Civil War, for years to come. The documents that follow will put the reader in touch with some of the events and ideas that cast those shadows.

BLUE SKIES

Words and Music by
IRVING BERLIN

Chapter One

The New Era and Its Undertaker

The Twenties, the Crash, and Herbert Hoover

The dominant mood, attitude, or spirit of an era (customarily called by the German term Zeitgeist) is often reflected in popular culture, such as music. No song better captures the outlook of the 1920s than Irving Berlin's 1927 composition "Blue Skies." This song remained popular during the depression, when it became a lyric of hope for the future.

There are many names for the 1920s, including the Roaring Twenties, the Prosperity Decade, and the New Era. The last of these is the most revealing. Many Americans, especially those involved in business, argued that the nation had entered an era of eternal prosperity. The basis of this economic miracle was mass production of consumer goods, most notably automobiles, radios, and a host of newly developed household appliances.

Mass production required mass consumption, which in turn required an alteration in such traditional values as saving, avoiding debt, and living with the future in mind. Advertising and purchases on credit became major features of American life in the twenties, as they assisted in the task of selling all that the economy was producing. (By the end of the decade, nearly 15 percent of all retail sales in the United States were made on the basis of installment purchase.)

But these institutions could not forever keep afloat a fundamentally imbalanced economy, in which the bulk of the people did not receive a large enough share of the national income to buy all the products coming off the assembly lines. Wages were simply too low to provide the purchasing power demanded by the economy. By the late summer of 1929, unsold goods were beginning to pile up in warehouses. This necessitated cutbacks in production; workers were laid off, leading to an even greater decline in buying and creating a downward spiral that would suck the entire economy into a deepening whirlpool later that year.

The great bulk of the things consumed by American families is no longer made in the home and efforts of family members are focused instead on buying a living. Buying by husbands, wives, bachelors, single women and children constitutes the neck of the bottle through which the varied output of America's industrial machinery must somehow flow to provide acceptable standards of health, possessions and happiness.

—Robert S. Lynd, "The People as Consumers" (1933)

Advertising became a major "industry" in the decade preceding the depression. This advertisement for advertising, which appeared in Printers' Ink *in 1926, reflects the sole purpose of advertising: "Making us want."*

GO AHEAD AND MAKE US WANT

MRS CONSUMER says I'm a little lazy, anyway

Sometimes I get mighty mad at advertising—tempting me all the time I wish it would leave me be. If it weren't for advertising, I wouldn't know what I was missing

If it hadn't been for radiator advertising we'd still have stoves and base burners in our house instead of steam heat. Bath room ads gave Mrs Consumer a bee for a fancy bath room. (All foolishness!)

Gosh, I had to hump myself to pay for that heating plant and bath room. Had to work hard for a spell. I was sore

Still, it's nice not to have to stoke a lot of stoves, and a real-estate man

told me I had doubled the sales value of my house with that boiler and bath. So, I'm 'way ahead financially

I begin to see it's advertising that makes America hum. It gives ginks like me a goal. Makes us want something. And the world is so much the better for our heaving a little harder

Looking at the ads makes me think I've GOT to succeed. *Every advertisement is an advertisement for success*

I guess one reason there's so much success in America is because there's so much advertising—of things to want—things to work for.

Keep the Consumer Dissatisfied

The following article, which appeared in *Nation's Business* just 10 months before the stock market crash in 1929, was written by Charles Kettering, the director of the General Motors Research Laboratories. It reflects the new view of stimulating consumption as a basis for continuing prosperity that many U.S. business leaders adopted in the 1920s.

Not long ago one of the great bankers of the country said to me:

"The trouble with you fellows is that you are all the time changing automobiles and depreciating old cars, and you are doing it at a time when people have three or four payments to make on the cars they already have.

"Yesterday I got an engraved invitation from one of your companies to see a new model. Out of curiosity I went. I darn near bought one. I didn't because you people wouldn't allow me enough money for my old car."

A few weeks later I was again talking with this banker. He appeared to be greatly disgruntled.

"I bought the new model," he barked. "But it was a rotten shame that I had to accept so much depreciation on my old car. You are the fellow who is to blame. You, with all your changes and refinements, made me dissatisfied with the old model."

He paused, then added, mournfully, "And that old car ran like new."

I told him I thought it was worth what he paid—that is, the difference between the old and the new model—to have his mind changed.

He didn't argue over that but he did say something to the general effect that "the only reason for research is to keep your customers reasonably dissatisfied with what they already have."

I might observe, here and now, that he was right. . . .

"You research people are always disrupting things. You cause us more trouble than any other group. I, as a banker, will make a loan to a firm and am apt to discover, in a few days, that you fellows have put this concern out of business. All because your research methods have found different ways for doing things. Perhaps they are better ways, but what of it? The old ways were satisfactory."

This banker was thoughtless.

Prosperity has nothing to do with dollars in the bank or with bank clearances. Prosperity is measured by the tonnage of useful materials going through the channels of trade. That is what makes prosperity. This is what makes busy workshops and busy railroads. That is what makes everybody happy. . . .

There are no places where anyone can sit and rest in an industrial situation. It is a question of change, change, change, all the time—and it is always going to be that way. It must always be that way for the world only goes along one road, the road to progress. Nations and industries that have become satisfied with themselves and their ways of doing things, don't last. While they are sitting back and admiring themselves other nations and other concerns have forgotten the looking-glasses and have been moving ahead. . . .

The younger generation—and by that I mean the generation that is always coming—knows what it wants and it will get what it wants. This is what makes for change. It brings about improvements in old things and developments in new things.

You can't stop people being born. You can't stop the thing we call progress. You can't stop the thing we call change. But you can get in tune with it. Change is never waste—it is improvement, all down the line. Because I have no further need of my automobile doesn't mean that that automobile is destroyed. It goes to someone who has need for it and, to get it, he disposes of something that is unnecessary to his happiness. And so on to the end where the thing that is actually thrown away is of no further use to anyone. By this method living standards, all around, are raised. . . .

If automobile owners could not dispose of their cars to a lower buying strata they would have to wear out their cars with a consequent tremendous cutting in the yearly demand for automobiles, a certain increase in production costs, and the natural passing along of these costs to the buyer.

If every one were satisfied, no one would buy the new thing because no one would want it. The ore wouldn't be mined; timber wouldn't be cut. Almost immediately hard times would be upon us.

You must accept this reasonable dissatisfaction with what you have and buy the new thing, or accept hard times. You can have your choice.

The prosperity of the 1920s rode in by automobile and was fueled by advertising and installment buying. "New lower prices" such as that trumpeted for the 1929 Oldsmobile in this ad were not sufficient to make up for the fully-extended credit of many prospective purchasers, and demand fell behind supply as the decade neared its end.

Between 1909 and 1929 periodical advertising rose, according to the Census of Manufacturers, from $54,000,000 to $320,000,000, and newspaper advertising from $149,000,000 to $792,000,000. If we add the estimate of $75,000,000 for radio advertising in 1929, and Copeland's 1927 estimates in *Recent Economic Changes* (probably all of them conservative for 1929) of $400,000,000 for direct advertising, $20,000,000 for street car advertising, $75,000,000 for outdoor advertising, $75,000,000 for business papers, and $25,000,000 for premiums, programs and directories, we get a total of $1,782,000,000 for 1929. In current advertising we are therefore viewing commercial consumer stimulation on the greatest scale attempted, totaling in 1929 about 2 percent of the national income or nearly $15 per capita.

—Robert S. Lynd, "The People as Consumers" (1933)

Herbert Hoover's Optimism

Herbert Clark Hoover (1874–1964)

Born to Quaker parents and orphaned at the age of nine, Herbert Hoover became a millionaire through his work in mining enterprises around the world. Once he had become rich and internationally famous, Hoover devoted himself to the Quaker ideal of service to others. His work as the head of the Commission for the Relief of Belgium during World War I and his leadership of the effort to prevent starvation in Europe at the war's end gave Hoover the reputation of being both a brilliant organizer and a great humanitarian.

Contrary to popular impression, Hoover was not an advocate of "rugged individualism." He believed instead in what he termed "voluntarism." He wanted people to help one another but to do so voluntarily, through private charity, rather than by government action. His experience in business, which was—a few setbacks notwithstanding—enormously successful, did not equip him well for the task of leading a nation caught in a depression. Here he manages a rare public smile as he throws out the first ball of the 1930 World Series.

In his speech on August 11, 1928, accepting the Republican Presidential nomination, Herbert Hoover reviewed what he saw as the great successes of the 1920s and his party's role in those accomplishments. He gave no hint of what was to happen little more than a year later. On the contrary, he asserted, in a statement that was to come back to haunt him during the depression, "We in America today are nearer to the final triumph over poverty than ever before in the history of any land."

On the other hand, Hoover's emphasis on "spiritual progress," "charity," and "moral progress" mark him as a man with more progressive instincts than his frequently sour public demeanor indicated.

Our problems of the past seven years have been problems of reconstruction; our problems of the future are problems of construction. They are problems of progress. New and gigantic forces have come into our national life. The Great War [World War I (1914–18)] released ideas of government in conflict with our principles. We have grown to financial and physical power which compels us into a new setting among nations. Science has given us new tools and a thousand inventions. Through them have come to each of us wider relationships, more neighbors, more leisure, broader vision, higher ambitions, greater problems. To insure that these tools shall not be used to limit liberty has brought a vast array of questions in government.

The points of contact between the Government and the people are constantly multiplying. Every year wise governmental policies become more vital in ordinary life. As our problems grow so do our temptations grow to venture away from those principles upon which our Republic was founded and upon which it has grown to greatness. Moreover, we must direct economic progress in support of moral and spiritual progress.

Our party platform deals mainly with economic problems, but our nation is not an agglomeration of railroads, of ships, of factories, of dynamos, or statistics. It is a nation of homes, a nation of men, of women, of children. Every man has a right to ask of us whether the United States is a better place for him, his wife, and his children to live in, because the Republican Party has conducted the Government for nearly eight years. Every woman has a right to ask whether her life, her home, her man's job, her hopes, her happiness will be better assured by the continuance of the Republican Party in power. I propose to discuss the questions before me in that light. . . .

Nor have our people been selfish. They have met with a full hand the most sacred obligation of man—charity. The gifts of America to churches, to hospitals, and institutions for the care of the afflicted, and to relief from great disasters have surpassed by hundreds of millions any totals for any similar period in all human record.

One of the oldest and perhaps the noblest of human aspirations has been the abolition of poverty. By poverty I mean the grinding by undernourishment, cold, and ignorance, and fear of old age of those who have the will to work. We in America today are nearer to the final triumph over poverty than ever before in the history of any land. The poorhouse is vanishing from among us. We have not yet reached the goal, but, given a chance to go forward with the policies of the last eight years, we shall soon with the help of God be in sight of the day when poverty will be banished from this Nation. There is no guarantee against poverty equal to a job for every man. That is the primary purpose of the economic policies we advocate. . . .

Economic advancement is not an end in itself. Successful democracy rests wholly upon the moral and spiritual quality of its people. Our growth in spiritual achievements must keep pace with our growth in physical accomplishments. Material prosperity and moral progress must march together if we would make the United States that commonwealth so grandly conceived by its founders. Our government, to match the expectations of our people, must have constant regard for those human values that give dignity and nobility to life. Generosity of impulse, cultivation of mind, willingness to sacrifice, spaciousness of spirit—those are the qualities whereby America, growing bigger and richer and more powerful, may become America great and noble. A people or government to which these values are not real, because they are not tangible, is in peril. Size, wealth, and power alone cannot fulfill the promise of America's opportunity. . . .

The Presidency is more than an administrative office. It must be the symbol of American ideals. The high and the lowly must be seen with the same eyes, met in the same spirit. It must be the instrument by which national conscience is livened and it must under the guidance of the Almighty interpret and follow that conscience.

The fundamental business of the country, that is the production and distribution of commodities, is on a sound and prosperous basis. The best evidence is that although production and consumption are at high levels, the average prices of commodities as a whole have not increased and there have been no appreciable increases in the stocks of manufactured goods. Moreover, there has been a tendency of wages to increase, the output per worker in many industries again shows an increase, all of which indicates a healthy condition.

The construction and building material industries have been to some extent affected by the high interest rates induced by stock speculation and there has been some seasonal decrease in one or two industries, but these movements are of secondary character when considered in the whole situation.

—President Hoover, replying to reporters' questions on the business situation, October 25, 1929

Cartoonists had a field day with the stock market crash. This one by O. Soglow seems to show little sympathy for Wall Street tycoons who had lost their paper fortunes.

The trading floor of the New York Stock Exchange was an altered setting following the 1929 crash. The same space that had been the magical money-making playground of prosperity in the preceding years was suddenly turned into its graveyard.

Collapse

The following article from the *New York Times* of October 30, 1929, recounts the nearly complete collapse of the stock market on Black Tuesday, October 29, 1929, the worst of the several days of disaster on Wall Street that fall.

STOCKS COLLAPSE IN 16,410,030–SHARE DAY, BUT RALLY AT CLOSE CHEERS BROKERS

Stock prices virtually collapsed yesterday, swept downward with gigantic losses in the most disastrous trading day in the stock market's history. Billions of dollars in open market values were wiped out as prices crumbled under the pressure of liquidation of securities which had to be sold at any price. . . .

Efforts to estimate yesterday's market losses in dollars are futile because of the vast number of securities quoted over the counter and on out-of-town exchanges on which no calculations are possible. However, it was estimated that 880 issues, on the New York Stock Exchange, lost between $8,000,000,000 and $9,000,000,000 yesterday. Added to that loss is to be reckoned the depreciation on issues on the Curb Market, in the over the counter market and on other exchanges. . . .

Banking support, which would have been impressive and successful under ordinary circumstances, was swept violently aside, as block after block of stock, tremendous in proportions, deluged the market. Bid prices placed by bankers, industrial leaders and brokers trying to halt the decline were crashed through violently, their orders were filled, and quotations plunged downward in a day of disorganization, confusion and financial impotence. . . .

Groups of men, with here and there a woman, stood about inverted glass bowls all over the city yesterday watching spools of ticker tape unwind and as the tenuous paper with its cryptic numerals grew longer at their feet their fortunes shrank. Others sat stolidly on tilted chairs in the customers' rooms of brokerage houses and watched a motion picture of waning wealth as the day's quotations moved silently across a screen.

It was among such groups as these, feeling the pulse of a fever-ish financial world whose heart is the Stock Exchange, that drama and perhaps tragedy were to be found . . . the crowds about the ticker tape, like friends around the bedside of a stricken friend, reflected in their faces the story the tape was telling. There were no smiles. There were no tears either. Just the camaraderie of fellow-sufferers. Everybody wanted to tell his neighbor how much he had lost. Nobody wanted to listen. It was too repetitious a tale.

"When a Horse Balks"

From the start of the depression there was a small number of economists who argued that the solution was to have the government stimulate the economy by spending large amounts of money, borrowing what tax revenues would not cover. This belief that massive deficit spending, such as the country might undertake during a war, would give the economy the boost it needed to get back on track later came to be associated mainly with British economist John Maynard Keynes. In the early 1930s it was most forcefully advocated in the United States by William Trufant Foster and Waddill Catchings. Foster presents the essence of their argument in this 1932 article.

. . . As a matter of fact, we possess in this country now—and have possessed throughout the depression—every material requirement for sustaining trade and employment; indeed, every material requirement for abolishing poverty. No physical necessity is lacking: everything is at hand now which was at hand in the heights of our prosperity. We have the men, machines, mines, materials, money. We have the land, the electrical power, the research laboratories, the ships, trucks and railroads, the banking institutions, the telegraph lines, the shops, warehouses and office buildings. What is lacking? All over the United States, for the past two years, I have been putting this challenge to men and women: What material means of sustaining prosperity did we possess in 1929 which we do not now possess? Not once have I received an answer to that question. There is no answer. Since, therefore, there is no physical deficiency the trouble must be psychological. . . .

. . . [T]he Administration had no plan to offer, except futile reliance on rugged individuals. In place of the disappearing dollars, it put into circulation nothing but cheering words. . . .The country was in a monetary depression, but no monetary measures

In his lithograph, Oct. 29, Dies Irae, *James N. Rosenberg depicts the buildings of Wall Street falling on the investors, symbolizing the massive economic earthquake that rocked the financial world.* Dies irae *is Latin for "day of wrath."*

were taken to stop it. Under these conditions, reliance on Pollyanna bulletins was stupid. The time soon came when each new word of cheer from Washington was followed by an immediate sinking of the stock market. Still the bulletins came forth. Everybody seemed to understand the mental aspects of the situation except those on whom the country relied for leadership.

Since that time the Government has made one psychological blunder after another. Witness the way in which the balancing of the budget has been handled. Unless the country thinks otherwise, it matters little whether or not the budget is balanced in any particular year. The Government has the power to achieve that purpose at any time. It has no net indebtedness to the rest of the world. It can not go bankrupt. It has behind it a proved capacity for a yearly output of wealth in excess of a hundred billion dollars. It has demonstrated that prosperity is possible with a national debt six billion dollars in excess of the present debt. It has proved that the national debt can be paid off at the rate of about a billion dollars a year, even in moderately good years, without hurting business. It has far less reason to be concerned over its finances than the strongest private corporation. Yet no private corporation becomes hysterical merely because, in any one year, its balance sheet shows a deficit. The Speaker of the House of Representatives, on the other hand, did become hysterical. He announced to the world that dire calamity would descend upon us if we did not balance our budget immediately. He and other irresponsible talkers created the necessity. It is not economic. It is psychological. . . .

Mental states have far more to do with this depression than physical facts. Frozen courage hampers business far more than frozen loans. The fear of bank failures ties up more currency and credit than the occurrence of bank failures. The dread of unemployment cuts down the buying of more men than unemployment itself. Anxiety lest Congress may do something foolish hurts business far more than anything which Congress actually does. The way the rest of the world affects our state of mind hurts business more than the way it affects our markets. In short, nothing is very bad in business as a whole, except as bad thinking has made it so.

It is bad thinking which has prompted so much talk in Congress about doles. The unemployed do not want doles: they want jobs. They resent even talk about doles. Charity, public or private, undermines confidence. Employment builds confidence. Nothing would do so much for the mental hygiene of the country as to put five million discouraged men and women to work: to work on anything. The more prudently the projects are chosen, the better; but the important thing is that some kind of work begin and talk about doles cease. The longer the bread-lines, the longer the faces of everybody—the employed as well as the unemployed. . . .

But is it possible to create jobs for so many workers? Not quite yet. It will not be possible until we think it is.

If any one still doubts that our economic troubles are mainly mental, let him consider what would happen if the United States declared war today. Everybody knows what would happen. Congress would immediately stop this interminable talk and appropriate three billion dollars—five billion—ten billion—any necessary amount. Where would the money come from? Precisely where it is now. Orders would be rushed from coast to coast; idle mills would start running; furnaces would go into blast; railroads would come back to life; and every man and woman who wanted a job would get one. What would the nation possess wherewith to perform this miracle which it does not possess today? Absolutely nothing except a new state of mind.

Some day we shall realize that if money is available for a blood-and-bullets war, just as much money is available for a food-and-famine war. We shall see that if it is fitting to use collective action on a large scale to kill men abroad, it is fitting to use collective action on an equally large scale to save men at home. But that will require a change of mental attitude.

Speaking of the present condition of the United States, Herbert N. Casson, a London editor, said, "When a horse balks, the balk is in his head, not in his legs. He goes ahead whenever he decides to go ahead."

"I'll see it through if you will!"

THEY tell me there's five or six million of us—out of jobs.

"I know that's not your fault, any more than it is mine.

"But that doesn't change the fact that some of us right now are in a pretty tough spot—with families to worry about—and a workless winter ahead.

"Understand, we're not begging. We'd rather have a job than anything else you can give us.

"We're not scared, either. If you think the good old U. S. A. is in a bad way more than temporarily, just try to figure out some other place you'd rather be.

"But, until times do loosen up, we've got to have a little help.

"So I'm asking *you* to give us a lift, just as I would give one to you if I stood in your shoes and you in mine.

"Now don't send me any money—that isn't the idea. Don't even send any to the Committee which signs this appeal.

"The best way to help us is to give as generously as you can to your local welfare and charity organizations, your community chest or your emergency relief committee if you have one.

"That's my story, the rest is up to you.

"I'll see it through—if *you* will".

—*Unemployed, 1931*

THE PRESIDENT'S ORGANIZATION ON UNEMPLOYMENT RELIEF
Walter S. Gifford
Director

COMMITTEE ON MOBILIZATION OF RELIEF RESOURCES
Owen D. Young
Chairman

The President's Organization on Unemployment Relief is non-political and non-sectarian. Its purpose is to aid local welfare and relief agencies everywhere to provide for local needs. All facilities for the nation-wide program, including this advertisement, have been furnished to the Committee without cost.
This advertisement is printed without charge by the Clayton Magazines.

President Hoover kept insisting that all that was needed to bring about recovery from the depression was a restoration of confidence. While he steadfastly refused to consider providing federal relief to the unemployed, he did establish committees to gather ideas and promote optimism. One such agency was the President's Organization on Unemployment Relief, which placed ads like this one in popular magazines.

Chapter Two

Stormy Weather

Depression Life

The effects of the Great Depression on the lives of Americans were extremely varied. The harsh conditions described in many of the documents in this chapter were not experienced by everyone. A majority of Americans kept their jobs during the thirties. But unemployment reached levels never seen in the United States, before or since. When the depression hit rock bottom in early 1933, one-quarter of the American workforce was unemployed.

By the early thirties, the "Blue Skies" of the preceding decade had given way to "Stormy Weather," and popular music reflected the change. (Blues songs had been popular among many blacks and some whites in the 1920s, but this genre spoke to a far larger audience after the depression hit.) The lyrics to this 1933 song were written by Ted Koehler, with music by Harold Arlen.

Stormy Weather

Don't know why there's no sun up in the sky,
Stormy Weather,
Since my man and I ain't together.
Keeps rainin' all the time.

Life is bare, gloom and mis'ry ev'rywhere.
Stormy Weather,
Just can't get my poor self together,
I'm weary all the time, the time,
So weary all the time.

During the depression, as the man-made institutions of the economy were failing, it seemed that nature had joined the forces working against human success. In broad regions of the United States—across the Great Plains and into the South—immense dust storms such as this one over Spearman, Texas, in April 1935, literally blackened the formerly blue skies.

The 1932nd Psalm

Hoover is my shepherd, I am in want,
He maketh me to lie down on park benches,
He leadeth me by still factories,
He restoreth my doubt in the
Republican Party.
He guided me in the path of the
Unemployed for his party's sake,
Yea, though I walk through the alley
  of soup kitchens,
I am hungry.
I do not fear evil, for thou art against me;
Thy Cabinet and thy Senate, they do discomfort
  me;
Thou didst prepare a reduction in my wages;
In the presence of my creditors thou anointed
  my income with taxes,
So my expense overruneth my income.
Surely poverty and hard times will follow me
All the days of the Republican administration.
And I shall dwell in a rented house forever.
Amen.

—E. J. Sullivan

*Under the impact of the economic
collapse, the subject matter of
many artists shifted—as did the
values of a majority of people.
This oil painting by Harry Gottlieb,* Home Sweet Home *or*
Their Only Roof *(1935–
36), portrays residents of a
Hooverville.*

When he went away, the blues walked in and met me,
If he stays away, old rockin' chair will get me.
All I do is pray the Lord above will let me
Walk in the sun once more.

Can't go on, ev'rything I had is gone,
Stormy Weather,
Since my man and I ain't together,
Keeps rainin' all the time,
Keeps rainin' all the time.

Hooverville

In part, the Great Depression had a heavier impact than previous economic collapses because far more people were living in cities than had been the case during earlier eras. Compared to farmers, urban residents were less likely to own their homes, and most had no means of growing their own food. When they lost their jobs and could not pay the rent, they faced eviction. With no way of paying for shelter, large numbers of Americans—sometimes women and children as well as men—were reduced in the early thirties to living in makeshift shacks on unoccupied land in or near cities. Everywhere in the country, the name for these colonies of homeless people was the same: "Hooverville." The conditions of life in such shantytowns were described by Charles Walker in 1932.

A few weeks ago I visited the incinerator and public dump at Youngstown, Ohio. Back of the garbage house there are at least three acres of waste land, humpy with ash heaps and junk. The area is not on the outskirts but in the middle of the steel mill district with furnaces nearby, and the tube mills and factory stacks of Youngstown. The dump is a kind of valley with a railroad embankment flanking it. As you approach from the garbage house, certain excrescences compete in vision with the ash humps and junk. They appear more organized than the rest of the place, but one is not sure. When, however, you come close, there is no doubt but the dump is inhabited.

The place is indeed a shanty town, or rather a collection of shanty hamlets, for the separate blotches are not all in one place but break out at intervals from the dump. Some of them are caves with tin roofs, but all of them blend with the place, for they are constructed out of it. From 150 to 200 men live in the shanties. The place is called by its inhabitants Hooverville. I went forward and talked to the men; they showed me their houses. These vary greatly from mere caves covered with a piece of tin, to weather-proof shanties built of packing boxes and equipped with a stolen window-frame or an improved door. Some have beds and one or two a kitchen stove rescued from the junk heap, though most of the men cook in communal fashion over a fire shielded by bricks in the open.

The inhabitants were not, as one might expect, outcasts or "untouchables," or even hoboes in the American sense; they were men without jobs. Life is sustained by begging, eating at the city soup kitchens, or earning a quarter by polishing an automobile—enough to bring home bacon and bread. Eating "at home" is preferred. The location of the town also has its commissary advantage; men take part of their food from the garbage house. This I entered; the stench of decaying food is appalling. Here I found that there were more women than men—gathering food for their families. In Hooverville there are no women.

This pitiable village would be of little significance if it existed only in Youngstown, but nearly every town in the United States has its shanty town for the unemployed, and the same instinct has named them all "Hooverville." . . . The largest Hooverville in the United States is in St. Louis, with a hovel population of 1200. Chicago had a flourishing one, but it was felt to be an affront to municipal pride and was ordered burned. The inhabitants were summarily told to get out, and thirty minutes later the "homes" were in ashes.

In the Hooverville of Ambridge, Pennsylvania, I met a man with whom I talked a long time. He was a Slav who had come to this country thirty years ago, and who had grown sons somewhere, though he had lost touch with them. As a veteran worker, he reminisced over many jobs, skilled and unskilled, in the Amer-

Shantytowns, tent cities, cardboard shacks, lean-tos—whatever means of shelter homeless people could find—they all went by the same name: "Hooverville." It was a bitter irony for a President whose name had been given to streets in several European cities after World War I, to honor him for his work in relieving economic distress.

← Chicago burned

ican mills. But he had now lost his last one. Standing in front of the huts and clasping the fist of one hand with the other, he said to me, "If you had told me, when I come to this country that now I live here like dis, I shot you dead."

City Breadlines

Many women found themselves without means of support during the depression. They joined men on the breadlines. In the following 1932 article from the Communist periodical *New Masses*, writer Meridel Le Sueur of Minneapolis provides a look into their desperate situation. The Communist editors of the magazine considered the article too "defeatist" and added an editorial note saying so.

I am sitting in the city free employment bureau. It's the woman's section. We have been sitting here now for four hours. We sit here every day, waiting for a job. There are no jobs. Most of us have had no breakfast. Some have had scant rations for over a year. Hunger makes a human being lapse into a state of lethargy, especially city hunger. Is there any place else in the world where a human being is supposed to go hungry amidst plenty without an outcry, without protest, where only the boldest steal or kill for bread, and the timid crawl the streets, hunger like the beak of a terrible bird at the vitals?

We sit looking at the floor. No one dares think of the coming winter. There are only a few more days of summer. Everyone is anxious to get work to lay up something for that long siege of bitter cold. But there is no work. Sitting in the room we all know it. That is why we don't talk much. We look at the floor dreading to see that knowledge in each other's eyes. There is a kind of humiliation in it. We look away from each other. We look at the floor. It's too terrible to see this animal terror in each other's eyes. . . . This is a domestic employment bureau. Most of the women who come here are middle-aged, some have families, some have raised their families and are now alone, some have men who are out of work. Hard times and the man leaves to hunt for work. He doesn't find it. He drifts on. The woman probably doesn't hear from him for a long time. She expects it. She isn't surprised. She struggles alone to feed the many mouths. Sometimes she gets help from the charities. If she's clever she can get herself a good living from the charities, if she's naturally a lick-spittle, naturally a little docile and cunning. If she's proud then she starves silently, leaving

Picturing an Era

The New Deal's Resettlement Administration, which was replaced by the Farm Security Administration (FSA) in 1937, included a Historical Section that was charged with photographically documenting conditions of life and land in the United States. Some of the best photographers of the era, including Walker Evans, Carl Mydans, Dorothea Lange, Ben Shahn, Marion Post Wolcott, Arthur Rothstein, and Russell Lee, were hired to carry out the assignment. The resulting collection of some 270,000 photographs, known by the FSA label, is one of the great national treasures. FSA photographs appear at many points in this book. They are, in fact, the images that first come to mind when most people think of the depression.

her children to find work, coming home after a day's searching to wrestle with her house, her children. Some such story is written on the faces of all these women.

There are young girls too, fresh from the country. Some are made brazen too soon by the city. There is a great exodus of girls from the farms into the city now. Thousands of farms have been vacated completely in Minnesota. The girls are trying to get work. The prettier ones can get jobs in the stores when there are any, or waiting on table, but these jobs are only for the attractive and the adroit, the others, the real peasants, have a more difficult time.

Bernice sits next me. She is a large Polish woman of thirty-five. She has been working in people's kitchens for fifteen years or more. She is large, her great body in mounds, her face brightly scrubbed. She has a peasant mind and finds it hard even yet to understand the maze of the city where trickery is worth more than brawn. . . .

Although the Hoovervilles were generally populated by men, women of all ages also faced the terrible prospect (and, often, reality) of hunger and deprivation. Artist and photographer Ben Shahn captured some of the anxiety in the faces of these women outside a relief station in Urbana, Ohio.

She came to the city a young girl from a Wisconsin farm. The first thing that happened to her a charlatan dentist took out all her good shining teeth and the fifty dollars she had saved working in a canning factory. After that she met men in the park who told her how to look out for herself, corrupting her peasant mind, teaching her to mistrust everyone. Sometimes now she forgets to mistrust everyone and gets taken in. They taught her to get what she could for nothing, to count her change, to go back if she found herself cheated, to demand her rights. . . . She wants to get married but she sees what happens to her married friends, being left with children to support, worn out before their time. So she stays single. She is virtuous. She is slightly deaf from hanging out clothes in winter. She has done people's washing and cooking for fifteen years and in that time she saved thirty dollars. Now she hasn't worked steady for a year and she has spent the thirty dollars. She dreamed of having a little house or a houseboat perhaps with a spot of ground for a few chickens. This dream she will never realize.

She has lost all her furniture now along with the dream. A married friend whose husband is gone gives her a bed for which she pays by doing a great deal of work for the woman. She comes here every day now sitting bewildered, her pudgy hands folded in her lap. She is hungry. Her great flesh has begun to hang in folds. She has been living on crackers. Sometimes a box of crackers lasts a week. She has a friend who's a baker and he sometimes steals the stale loaves and brings them to her. . . .

A Lady's Request

Philadelphia Pa.
Feb'y 19, 1935.

Dear Mrs. Roosevelt:

After Seeing So many of your pictures in the Magazines and papers, and seeing that you always look so well dressed, a thought came to me. that you may have a few old discarded dresses among the ones that you have tired of that you would like to get rid of, and do some one good at the same time. I have waited and waited for work until every thing I had is about finished. I can sew and would only be too glad to take two old things and put them to gether and make a new one. I don't care what it is, any thing from an old bunch of stockings to an old Sport Suit or an old after-noon dress, in fact. Anything a lady 40 years of age can wear. I will await an early reply.

Thanking you in advance.

Mrs. E. T.
Phila. Pa.

A scrub woman whose hips are bent forward from stooping with hands gnarled like water soaked branches clicks her tongue in disgust. No one saves their money, she says, a little money and these foolish young things buy a hat; a dollar for breakfast, a bright scarf. And they do. If you've ever been without money, or food, something very strange happens when you get a bit of money, a kind of madness. You don't care. You can't remember that you had no money before, that the money will be gone. You can remember nothing but that there is the money for which you have been suffering. Now here it is. A lust takes hold of you. You see food in the windows. In imagination you eat hugely; you taste a thousand meals. You look in windows. Colours are brighter; you buy something to dress up in. An excitement takes hold of you. You know it is suicide but you can't help it. You must have food, dainty, splendid food and a bright hat so once again you feel blithe, rid of that ratty gnawing shame.

"I guess she'll go on the street now," a thin woman says faintly and no one takes the trouble to comment further. Like every commodity now the body is difficult to sell and the girls say you're lucky if you get fifty cents.

It's very difficult and humiliating to sell one's body. Perhaps it would make it clear if one were to imagine having to go out on the street to sell, say, one's overcoat. Suppose you have to sell your coat so you can have breakfast and a place to sleep, say, for fifty cents. You decide to sell your only coat. You take it off and put it on your arm. The street, that has before been just a street, now becomes a mart, something entirely different. You must approach someone now and admit you are destitute and are now selling your clothes, your most intimate possessions. Everyone will watch you talking to the stranger showing him your overcoat, what a good coat it is. People will stop and watch curiously. You will be quite naked on the street.

It is even harder to try and sell one's self, more humiliating. It is even humiliating to try and sell one's labour. When there is no buyer. . . .

It's one of the great mysteries of the city where women go when they are out of work and hungry. There are not many women in the bread line. There are no flop houses for women as there are for men, where a bed can be had for a quarter or less. You don't see women lying on the floor at the mission in the free flops. They obviously don't sleep in the jungle or under newspapers in the park. There is no law I suppose against their being in these places but the fact is they rarely are.

Yet there must be as many women out of jobs in cities and suffering extreme poverty as there are men. What happens to them? Where do they go? Try to get into the Y.W. without any money or looking down at heel. Charities take care of very few and only those that are called "deserving." The lone girl is under suspicion by the virgin women who dispense charity. I've lived in cities for many months broke, without help, too timid to get in bread lines. I've known many women to live like this until they simply faint on the street from privations, without saying a word to anyone. A woman will shut herself up in a room until it is taken away from her, and eat a cracker a day and be as quiet as a mouse so there are no social statistics concerning her.

I don't know why it is, but a woman will do this unless she has dependents, will go for weeks verging on starvation, crawling in some hole, going through the streets ashamed, sitting in libraries, parks, going for days without speaking to a living soul like some exiled beast, keeping the runs mended in her stockings, shut up in terror in her own misery, until she becomes too supersensitive and timid to even ask for a job. . . .

It's no wonder these young girls refuse to marry, refuse to rear children. They are like certain savage tribes, who, when they have been conquered refuse to breed. . . .

The young ones know though. I don't want to marry. I don't want any children. So they all say. No children. No marriage. They arm themselves alone, keep up alone. The man is helpless now. He cannot provide. If he propagates he cannot take care of his young. The means are not in his hands. So they live alone. Get what fun they can. The life risk is too horrible now. Defeat is too clearly written on it.

So we sit in this room like cattle, waiting for a nonexistent job, willing to work to the farthest atom of energy, unable to work, unable to get food and lodging, unable to bear children; here we must sit in this shame looking at the floor, worse than beasts at a slaughter.

It is appalling to think that these women sitting so listless in the room may work as hard as it is possible for a human being to work, may labour night and day, . . . wash street cars from midnight to dawn and offices in the early evening, scrubbing for fourteen and fifteen hours a day, sleeping only five hours or so, doing this their whole lives, and never earn one day of security, having always before them the pit of the future. The endless labour, the bending back, the water soaked hands, earning never more than a week's wages, never having in their hands more life than that.

**HOMELESS WOMEN
SLEEP IN CHICAGO PARKS**

CHICAGO, SEPT. 19 (AP). Several hundred homeless unemployed women sleep nightly in Chicago's parks, Mrs. Elizabeth A. Conkey, Commissioner of Public Welfare, reported today. She learned of the situation, she said, when women of good character appealed for shelter and protection, having nowhere to sleep but in the parks, where they feared that they would be molested.

"We are informed that no fewer than 200 women are sleeping in Grant and Lincoln Parks, on the lake front, to say nothing of those in the other parks," said Mrs. Conkey. "I made a personal investigation, driving from park to park, at night, and verified the reports."

The commissioner said the approach of winter made the problem more serious, with only one free women's lodging house existing, accommodating 100.

—*New York Times*, September 20, 1931

It's not the suffering, not birth, death, love that the young reject, but the suffering of endless labour without dream, eating the spare bread in bitterness, a slave without the security of a slave.

Editorial Note: This presentation of the plight of the unemployed woman, able as it is, and informative, is defeatist in attitude, lacking in revolutionary spirit and direction which characterize the usual contribution to *New Masses*. We feel it our duty to add, that there is a place for the unemployed woman, as well as man, in the ranks of the unemployed councils and in all branches of the organized revolutionary movement. Fight for your class, read *The Working Woman*, join the Communist Party.

The appearance of the following poem by Florence Converse in the highly respectable *Atlantic Monthly* reflects how deeply the depression had affected U.S. social thought by the winter of 1931–32.

Bread Line

WHAT's the meaning of this queue,
Tailing down the avenue,
Full of eyes that will not meet
The other eyes that throng the street—
The questing eyes, the curious eyes,
Scornful, popping with surprise
To see a living line of men
As long as round the block, and then
As long again? The statisticians
Estimate that these conditions
Have not reached their apogee.
All lines end eventually;
Except of course in theory.

Breadlines became as much a symbol of the impact of the depression as Hoovervilles were. The symbolism of waiting in line for hours to be fed perfectly expressed the defeat and degradation felt by men who had lost their traditional role as breadwinners and now had to beg for their bread. Artist Reginald Marsh worked on this theme several times, as in this 1932 drawing.

THE BREAD LINE   Reginald Marsh

This one has an end somewhere.
End in what?-Pause, there.
What's the meaning in these faces
Modern industry displaces,
Emptying the factory
To set the men so tidily
Along the pavement in a row?
Now and then they take a slow
Shuffling step, straight ahead,
As if a dead march said:
"Beware! I'm not dead."
Now and then an unaverted
Eye bespells the disconcerted
Passer-by; a profile now
And then will lift a beaten brow,—
Waiting what?—The Comforter?
The Pentecostal Visitor?
If by fasting visions come,
Why not to a hungry bum?
Idle, shamed, and underfed,
Waiting for his dole of bread,
What if he should find his head
A candle of the Holy Ghost?
A dim and starveling spark, at most,
But yet a spark? It needs but one.
A spark can creep, a spark can run;
Suddenly a spark can wink
And send us down destruction's brink.
It needs but one to make a star,
Or light a Russian samovar.
One to start a funeral pyre,
One to cleanse a world by fire.
What if our bread line should be
The long slow-match of destiny?
What if even now the Holy
Ghost should be advancing slowly
Down the line, a kindling flame,
Kissing foreheads bowed with shame?
Creep, my ember! Blaze, my brand!
The end of all things is at hand.
Idlers in the market place,
Make an end to your disgrace!
Here's a fair day's work for you,—

*"Soup kitchens" served the same func-
tion as breadlines. The soup was
invariably thin at these charitable
institutions, but when this photo was
taken in 1932 there was no federal relief
and thin soup was better than none.*

Brother, Can You Spare a Dime?

They used to tell me I was building a dream,
And so I followed the mob—
When there was earth to plough or guns to
  bear—
I was always there—right there on the job.

They used to tell me I was building a dream
With peace and glory ahead—
Why should I be standing in line
just waiting for bread?

Once I built a railroad, made it run,—
Made it race against time.
Once I built a railroad,
Now it's done—
Brother, can you spare a dime?

Once I built a tower, to the sun.—
Brick and rivet and lime,
Once I built a tower,
Now it's done,
Brother, can you spare a dime?

Once in khaki suits
Gee, we looked swell
Full of that Yankee Doodle-de-dum.

Half a million boots went sloggin' thru Hell,
I was the kid—with the drum.—
Say don't you remember, they called me Al—
It was Al—all the time.

Say, don't you remember I'm your Pal!
Buddy, can you spare a dime?

—Lyrics by E. Y. Harburg, music by
  Jay Gorney (1932)

To build a world all over new.
What if our slow-match have caught
Fire from a burning thought?
What if we should be destroyed
By our patient unemployed?
Some of us with much to lose
By conflagration will refuse
To hallow arson in the name
Of Pentecost. We'd rather blame
The Devil, who can always find
For idle hand or empty mind
Work to do at Devil's hire.
The Devil loves to play with fire.
We'd rather blame him,—ah, but this
May be just our prejudice.

Rural Hardship

Conditions were every bit as bad in many rural areas during the depression as they were in cities. In some locales, life for many was worsened by the policies of major employers, who often completely dominated the towns and counties in which they were located. One of the most notorious examples of such domination prevailed in the mining region of Harlan County, Kentucky. The following letter from a Kentucky miner was written in 1932 to Arthur Garfield Hays.

Arthur Garfield Hays, who made a courageous trip to Kentucky a while ago, was the recipient of a letter which the Drifter would like to be able to quote in full. It explains in convincing detail what life is like in the coal fields, and although the material is not new it has never been more dramatically presented. The first paragraph follows:

After reading about you and your party being Bars from Bell and Harlan Counties I am force to write and tell you as a Citizen of Kentucky. I regrets very much to read such and account I am going to tell you as a Miner of Harlan Count some facts why you outsiders are Bars—1st the conditions in Harlan County among the miners and their family are bad. We are force to take all cuts the company make regardless. 2nd We are half fed because we can'nt feed ourselves and family's with what we make. and we can'nt go to a Cut rate Store and buy food because most all the company forbids such tradeing. If you got the cash. But now we have no cash. And the companies keeps their food stuffs at high prices at all time. So you can not clear enough to go anywhere. and if you do go some where and buy food you are subjects to be canned under the one man "Law" and kick off the Company Proptery or thrown off. And now we are coward down. Can't tell the boss we are dissatisfied with conditions.

We have been eating wild greens since January this year. Such as Polk salad. Violet tops, wild onions, forget me not wild lettuce and such weeds as cows eat as a cow wont eat a poison weeds. Mr. Hayes our family are in bad shake childrens need milk women need nourishments food shoes and dresses—that we cannot get. and there at least 10,000 hungry people in Harlan County daily. I know because I am one off them. these people would welcome you to come to their shacks but the company forbid it. The Black Mountain Coal Corp. last year fired a man because he was talking to a "Lady" writer from Pittsburgh, Penn. he had a wife and five childrens. and was force to vacate in twenty four hours. . . . I would leave Harlan County if I had only $6 to send my wife and boy to Bristol, Va. and I could walk away—But I can't clear a dollar per month that why I am here. that why hundreds are here they can't ship their family's home. but I am Glad we can find a few wild greens to eat. . . .

Many artists sought to capture the depression experience. The following excerpt from Stephen Vincent Benét's 1935 poem is one of the most successful attempts. In it, Benét uses the device of having Walt Whitman come back, four decades after his death, to inquire about the condition of the American nation.

Ode to Walt Whitman

"Is it well with These States?"
"We have made many, fine new toys.
We—
There is a rust on the land.
A rust and a creeping blight and a scaled evil,
For six years eating, yet deeper than those six years,
Men labor to master it but it is not mastered.

Desperate times require desperate measures, as the saying has it. Farm Security Administration photographer John Vachon captured a depression-era scene that was, unfortunately, not uncommon. In this 1940 picture, a man forages for food at the Dubuque, Iowa, city dump. Hungry people could collect semi-rotten but still edible fruit and vegetables discarded by produce houses and stores.

Hard Time Blues

Well, the time is so hard, the birds refuse to sing,
And no matter how I try, I can't get a doggone thing.

Lord, I walked, and I walked, but I cannot find no job,
Lord, I can't 'fford to borrow no money, and I sure don't wanna rob.

Lord, my woman is hard to get along with, as a sitting hen,
And she ain't cooked me a square meal, honey, in God knows when.

Everybody cryin': "Depression," I just found out what it means,
It means a man ain't got no money, he can't find no big money tree.

—Charlie Spand (1931)

There is the soft, grey, foul tent of the
    hatching worm
Shrouding the elm, the chestnut, the
Southern cypress.
There is shadow in the bright sun,
    there is shadow upon the streets.
They burn the grain in the furnac
    while men go hungry.
They pile the cloth of the looms while
    men go ragged.
We walk naked in our plenty."

        "My tan-faced children?"

"These are your tan-faced children.
These skilled men, idle, with the holes
in their shoes.

*"Riding the rails" was a way of life
that came to extend far beyond the
usual small number of hobos. Men—
and boys, along with much smaller
numbers of girls and women—used
this mode of transportation to get
around the country in their quest for
work and food.*

These drifters from State to State, these wolvish,
    bewildered boys
Who ride the blinds and the box-cars from jail to jail,
Burnt in their youth like cinders of hot smokestacks,
Learning the thief's crouch and the cadger's whine,
Dishonored, abandoned, disinherited.
These, dying in the bright sunlight they cannot eat,
Or the strong men, sitting at home, their hands clasping
    nothing,
Looking at their lost hands.
These are your tan-faced children, the parched young,
The old man rooting in waste-heaps, the family rotting
In the flat, before eviction,
With the toys of plenty about them,
The shiny toys making ice and music and light,
But no price for the shiny toys and the last can empty.
The sleepers in blind corners of the night.
The women with dry breasts and phantom eyes.
The walkers upon nothing, the four million.
These are your tan-faced children."

        "But the land?"

"Over the great plains of the buffalo-land,
The dust-storm blows, the choking, sifting, Small dust.
The skin of that land is ploughed by the dry, fierce wind
And blown away, like a torrent;

It drifts foot-high above the young sprouts of grain
And the water fouls, the horses stumble and sicken,
The wash-board cattle stagger and die of drought.
We tore the buffalo's pasture with the steel blade.
We made the waste land blossom and it has blossomed.
That was our fate; now that land takes its own revenge,
And the giant dust-flower blooms above five States."
"But the gains of the years, who got them?"

                                 "Many, great gains.

Many yet few; they robbed us in the broad daylight,
Saving, Give us this and that; we are kings and titans;
We know the ropes: we are solid; we are hard-headed;
We will build you cities and railroads.-as if they built
   them!
They, the preying men, the men whose hearts were like
   engines,
Gouging the hills for gold, laying waste the timber,
The men like band-saws, moving over the land.
And, after them, the others,
Soft-bodied, lacking even the pirate's candor,
Men of paper, robbing by paper, with paper faces,
Rustling like frightened paper when the storm broke.
The men with the jaws of moth and aphid and beetle,
Boring the dusty, secret hole in the corn,
Fixed, sucking the land, with neither wish nor pride
But the wish to suck and continue.
They have been sprayed, a little.
But they say they will have the land back again, these
   men."

"There were many such in my time.
I have seen the rich arrogant and the poor oppressed.
I have seen democracy, also. I have seen
The good man slain, the knave and the fool in power,
The democratic vista botched by the people,
Yet not despaired, loving the giant land,
Though I prophesied to these States."

"Now they say we must have one tyranny or another
And a dark bell rings in our hearts."
"Was the blood spilt for nothing, then?"

Beans, Bacon, and Gravy

I was born long ago, in 1894,
And I've seen many a panic, I will own;
I've been hungry, I've been cold,
And now I'm growing old,
But the worst I've seen is 1932.

Refrain: Oh, those beans, bacon, and gravy,
They almost drive me crazy,
I eat them till I see them in my dreams,
In my dreams;
When I wake up in the morning,
And another day is dawning,
Yes, I know I'll have another mess of beans.

We congregate each morning
At the county barn at dawning,
And everyone is happy, so it seems;
But when our work is done
We file in one by one,
And thank the Lord for one more mess of beans.

We have Hooverized on butter,
For milk we've only water,
And I haven't seen a steak in many a day;
As for pies, cakes, and jellies,
We substitute sow-bellies,
For which we work the county road each day.
If there ever comes a time
When I have more than a dime
They will have to put me under lock and key;
For they've had me broke so long
I can only sing this song,
Of the workers and their misery.

—American folksong

Even those who retained some income would find prices such as those displayed in this storefront window in Greensboro, Alabama, during the summer of 1936, difficult to deal with. The unemployed or those on work relief might as well walk on by.

Chapter Three

"A War Against the Emergency"

The New Deal

Posters such as this one were produced by artists working for the Federal Art Project under the major New Deal work relief program, the WPA. It portrays the mission and results of the Civilian Conservation Corps in glowing terms. The CCC, which took unemployed young men into the wilderness to work on conservation and park-construction projects, was one of the most popular of New Deal programs.

In the 1932 election, voters repudiated both the Republican Party and the let-big-business-do-whatever-it-wants attitude of the 1920s. The instrument of this repudiation was Franklin D. Roosevelt, who had an opportunity beginning in March 1933 to reconstruct the American economy and society. The massive amount of legislation proposed by President Roosevelt and enacted by Congress during the first hundred days of the new administration was unprecedented in U.S. history. It still ranks ahead of the only similar fusillades of reform legislation, those of the Second New Deal in 1935 and Lyndon Johnson's Great Society bills in 1964–65. In a period of a few months, the New Deal completely altered the prevailing idea of the federal government's role in the lives of U.S. citizens.

Prompted in part by the "thunder on the left" (see chapters 6 and 7) of 1934 and 1935 and the prospect of facing the voters again in 1936, President Roosevelt launched a series of new initiatives in 1935. Collectively known as the Second New Deal, the measures of 1935 include those that have most defined the legacy of the Roosevelt years: Social Security, the Works Progress Administration (WPA), and the National Labor Relations Act (Wagner Act). It is plain that much of the Second New Deal was a response to the popular demand for such objectives as old-age pensions, tax reform, and a fair chance for unions; these demands had been made evident by (respectively) Dr. Townsend, Huey Long, and the labor uprisings of 1934 (see chapters 5–7).

Franklin D. Roosevelt's First Inaugural Address

Among Franklin Roosevelt's many notable speeches, his first inaugural address, made on March 4, 1933, is probably the one for which he is most remembered. In assuring the nation that "the only thing we have to fear is fear itself," FDR accomplished what Hoover had so long tried to do: restore a degree of confidence. The radiant optimism of Roosevelt's speech was such a contrast to Hoover's uninspiring pronouncements that it became infectious. The new President spoke against the ways of the twenties and advocated more traditional, community-oriented values when he condemned "a generation of self-seekers" and "the mad chase of evanescent profits" and declared that "we now realize as we have never realized before our interdependence on each other."

I am certain that my fellow Americans expect that on my induction into the Presidency I will address them with a candor and a decision which the present situation of our Nation impels. This is preeminently the time to speak the truth, the whole truth, frankly and boldly. Nor need we shrink from honestly facing conditions in our country today. This great Nation will endure as it has endured, will revive and will prosper. So, first of all, let me assert my firm belief that the only thing we have to fear is fear itself—nameless, unreasoning, unjustified terror which paralyzes needed efforts to convert retreat into advance. In every dark hour of our national life a leadership of frankness and vigor has met with that understanding and support of the people themselves which is essential to victory. I am convinced that you will again give that support to leadership in these critical days.

In such a spirit on my part and on yours we face our common difficulties. They concern, thank God, only material things. Values have shrunken to fantastic levels; taxes have risen; our ability to pay has fallen; government of all kinds is faced by serious curtailment of income; the means of exchange are frozen in the currents of trade; the withered leaves of industrial enterprise lie on every side; farmers find no markets for their produce; the savings of many years in thousands of families are gone.

More important, a host of unemployed citizens face the grim problem of existence, and an equally great number toil with little

Happy Days Are Here Again

So long, sad times!
Go 'long, bad times!
We are rid of you at last.

Howdy, gay times!
Cloudy gray times,
You are now a thing of the past.
'Cause happy days are here again!

The skies above are clear again.
Let us sing a song of cheer again
Happy days are here again!

Altogether about it now!
There's no one who can doubt it now,
So let's tell the world about it now
Happy days are here again!

Your cares and troubles are gone;
There'll be no more from now on.
Happy days are here again;
The skies above are clear again;
Let us sing a song of cheer again
Happy days are here again!

—music by Milton Ager, lyrics by Jack Yellen (1929)

ROOSEVELT INAUGURATED, ACTS TO END THE NATIONAL BANKING CRISIS QUICKLY; WILL ASK WAR-TIME POWERS IF NEEDED

(newspaper front page — headlines including:)

PLAN TO USE SCRIP HERE — Bankers Ready to Issue Clearing House Paper at End of Holiday.

WILL MEET WOODIN TODAY — Eastern Financiers to Join Parley at Capital on Plans to Permit Reopenings.

STOCK EXCHANGES CLOSED

VICTORY FOR HITLER IS EXPECTED TODAY

READY TO CALL CONGRESS — President Probably Will Summon Extra Session for Wednesday.

THE NEW PRESIDENT TAKING THE OATH OF OFFICE.

100,000 AT INAUGURATION — President, Grim, Terse, Pledges 'Adequate but Sound Currency.'

HOOVER, AS CITIZEN, HERE ON WAY HOME

Text of the Inaugural Address; President for Vigorous Action

500,000 IN STREETS CHEER ROOSEVELT

(Caption:) The front page of the New York Times the day after Roosevelt's inauguration reflects the mood of hope inspired by the new President's pledge of "action, and action now." In other front-page news: "Victory for Hitler is Expected Today."

return. Only a foolish optimist can deny the dark realities of the moment.

Yet our distress comes from no failure of substance. We are stricken by no plague of locusts. Compared with the perils which our forefathers conquered because they believed and were not afraid, we have still much to be thankful for. Nature still offers her bounty and human efforts have multiplied it. Plenty is at our doorstep, but a generous use of it languishes in the very sight of the supply. Primarily this is because rulers of the exchange of mankind's goods have failed through their own stubbornness and their own incompetence, have admitted their failure, and have abdicated. Practices of the unscrupulous money changers stand indicted in the court of public opinion, rejected by the hearts and minds of men.

True they have tried, but their efforts have been cast in the pattern of an outworn tradition. Faced by failure of credit they have proposed only the lending of more money. Stripped of the lure of profit by which to induce our people to follow their false leadership, they have resorted to exhortations, pleading tearfully for restored confidence. They know only the rules of a generation of self-seekers. They have no vision, and when there is no vision the people perish.

The money changers have fled from their high seats in the temple of our civilization. We may now restore that temple to the ancient truths. The measure of the restoration lies in the extent to which we apply social values more noble than mere monetary profit.

Happiness lies not in the mere possession of money; it lies in the joy of achievement, in the thrill of creative effort. The joy and moral stimulation of work no longer must be forgotten in the mad chase of evanescent profits. These dark days will be worth all they cost us if they teach us that our true destiny is not to be ministered unto but to minister to ourselves and to our fellow men.

Recognition of the falsity of material wealth as the standard of success goes hand in hand with the abandonment of the of false belief that public office and high political position are to be valued only by the standards of pride of place and personal profit; and there must be an end to a conduct in banking and business which too often has given to a sacred trust the likeness of callous and selfish wrongdoing. Small wonder that confidence languishes, for it thrives only on honesty, on honor, the sacredness of obligations, on faithful protection, on unselfish performance; without them it cannot live.

Restoration calls, however, not for changes in ethics alone.

This nation asks for action, and action now. . . .

If I read the temper of our people correctly, we now realize as we have never realized before our interdependence on each other; that we cannot merely take but we must give as well; that if we are to go forward, we must move as a trained and loyal army willing to sacrifice for the good of a common discipline, because without such discipline no progress is made, no leadership becomes effective. We are, I know, ready and willing to submit our lives and property to such discipline, because it makes possible a leadership which aims at a larger good. This I propose to offer, pledging that the larger purposes will bind upon us all as a sacred obligation with a unity of duty hitherto evoked only in time of armed strife.

With this pledge taken, I assume unhesitatingly the leadership of this great army of our people dedicated to a disciplined attack upon our common problems. . . .

It is to be hoped that the normal balance of Executive and Legislative authority may be wholly adequate to meet the unprecedented task before us. But it may be that an unprecedented demand and need for undelayed action may call for temporary departure from that normal balance of public procedure.

I am prepared under my constitutional duty to recommend measures that a stricken Nation in the midst of a stricken world may require. These measures, or such other measures as the Congress may build out of its experience and wisdom, I shall seek in my constitutional authority, to bring to speedy adoption.

But in the event that the Congress shall fail to take one of these two courses, and in the event that the national emergency is still critical, I shall not evade the clear course of duty that will then confront me. I shall ask the Congress for the one remaining instrument to meet the crisis—broad Executive power to wage a war against the emergency, as great as the power that would be given to me if we were in fact invaded by a foreign foe. . . .

We do not distrust the future of essential democracy. The people of the United States have not failed. In their need they have registered a mandate that they want direct, vigorous action. They have asked for discipline and direction under leadership. They have made me the present instrument of their wishes. In the spirit of the gift I take it.

The First Fireside Chat

One of Franklin Roosevelt's most remarkable political talents was his ability to speak over the radio in a manner that made listeners feel as if he was talking personally to them. It was, indeed, as if the President was right in their living room conversing with them. This quality of FDR's radio talks led them to be dubbed "fireside chats."

What follows is the first of these "intimate talks," on March 12, 1933, explaining the closing of the nation's banks and the conditions under which they would be reopened in the coming days. Roosevelt's reassurances were so successful that many of the same people who had rushed to withdraw their funds from banks in the closing days of the Hoover Administration went back as the banks reopened and deposited their money once more.

I want to talk for a few minutes with the people of the United States about banking—with the comparatively few who understand the mechanics of banking but more particularly with the overwhelming majority who use banks for the making of deposits and the drawing of checks. I want to tell you what has been done in the last few days, why it was done, and what the next steps are going to be. I recognize that the many proclamations from State

Although the highly conservative Walt Disney was anything but a promoter of the New Deal, the release of his animated feature The Three Little Pigs *in the spring of 1933 inadvertently provided an anthem for Americans buoyed by the dramatic measures Roosevelt was proposing. The song "Who's Afraid of the Big Bad Wolf?," composed for the film, captured the new feeling of optimism as the New Deal was launched.*

In the closing weeks of the Hoover administration in 1932 and early 1933, the nation's banking system had collapsed. There was no insurance for deposits and panic set in as banks with insufficient cash reserves found themselves unable to meet their depositors' demands to withdraw the funds in their accounts. "Bank holidays"—a more pleasant-sounding name for closing banks so that panicky depositors could not withdraw their money—had been declared in states around the country to put a temporary halt to the runs on banks.

capitols and from Washington, the legislation, the Treasury regulations, etc., couched for the most part in banking and legal terms, should be explained for the benefit of the average citizen. I owe this in particular because of the fortitude and good temper with which everybody has accepted the inconvenience and hardships of the banking holiday. I know that when you understand what we in Washington have been about I shall continue to have your cooperation as fully as I have had your sympathy and help during the past week.

First of all, let me state the simple fact that when you deposit money in a bank the bank does not put the money into a safe deposit vault. It invests your money in many different forms of credit-bonds, commercial paper, mortgages and many other kinds of loans. In other words, the bank puts your money to work to keep the wheels of industry and of agriculture turning around. A comparatively small part of the money you put into the bank is kept in currency—an amount which in normal times is wholly sufficient to cover the cash needs of the average citizen. In other words, the total amount of all the currency in the country is only a small fraction of the total deposits in all of the banks.

What, then, happened during the last few days of February and the first few days of March? Because of undermined confidence on the part of the public, there was a general rush by a large portion of our population to turn bank deposits into currency or gold—a rush so great that the soundest banks could not get enough currency to meet the demand. The reason for this was that on the spur of the moment it was, of course, impossible to sell perfectly sound assets of a bank and convert them into cash except at panic prices far below their real value.

By the afternoon of March 3d scarcely a bank in the country was open to do business. Proclamations temporarily closing them in whole or in part had been issued by the Governors in almost all the States.

It was then that I issued the proclamation providing for the nationwide bank holiday, and this was the first step in the Govern- ment's reconstruction of our financial and economic fabric.

The second step was the legislation promptly and patriotically passed by the Congress confirming my proclamation and broadening my powers so that it became possible in view of the requirement of time to extend the holiday and lift the ban of that holiday gradually. This law also gave authority to develop a program of rehabilitation of our banking facilities. I want to tell our citizens in every part of the Nation that the national Congress—Republicans and Democrats alike—showed by this action a devotion to public welfare and a realization of the emergency and the necessity for speed that it is difficult to match in our history. . . .

A question you will ask is this: why are all the banks not to be reopened at the same time? The answer is simple. Your Government does not intend that the history of the past few years shall be repeated. We do not want and will not have another epidemic of bank failures. . . .

It is possible that when the banks resume a very few people who have not recovered from their fear may again begin withdrawals. Let me make it clear that the banks will take care of all needs—and it is my belief that hoarding during the past week has become an exceedingly unfashionable pastime. It needs no prophet to tell you that when the people find that they can get their money—that they can get it when they want it for all legitimate purposes—the phantom of fear will soon be laid. People will again be glad to have their money where it will be safely taken care of and where they can use it conveniently at any time. I can assure you that it is safer to keep your money in a reopened bank than under the mattress.

The success of our whole great national program depends, of course, upon the cooperation of the public—on its intelligent support and use of a reliable system. . . .

I hope you can see from this elemental recital of what your Government is doing that there is nothing complex, or radical, in the process.

We had a bad banking situation. Some of our bankers had shown themselves either incompetent or dishonest in their handling of the people's funds. They had used the money entrusted to them in speculations and unwise loans. This was, of course, not true in the vast majority of our banks, but it was true in enough of them to shock the people for a time into a sense of insecurity and to put them into a frame of mind where they did not differentiate, but seemed to assume that the acts of a comparative few had tainted them all. It was the Government's job to straighten out this situation and do it as quickly as possible. And the job is being performed.

America hasn't been as happy in three years as they are today. No money, no banks, no work, no nothing, but they know they got a man in there who is wise to Congress and wise to our so-called big men.

The whole country is with him. Even if what he does is wrong they are with him. Just so he does something. If he burned down the Capitol we would cheer and say, "Well, he at least got a fire started, anyhow."

Yours,
WILL ROGERS.

—*New York Times*, March 6, 1933.

I do not promise you that every bank will be reopened or that individual losses will not be suffered, but there will be no losses that possibly could be avoided; and there would have been more and greater losses had we continued to drift. I can even promise you salvation for some at least of the sorely pressed banks. We shall be engaged not merely in reopening sound banks but in the creation of sound banks through reorganization.

It has been wonderful to me to catch the note of confidence from all over the country. . . .

After all, there is an element in the readjustment of our financial system more important than currency, more important than gold, and that is the confidence of the people. Confidence and courage are the essentials of success in carrying out our plan. You people must have faith; you must not be stampeded by rumors or guesses. Let us unite in banishing fear. We have provided the machinery to restore our financial system; it is up to you to support and make it work.

It is your problem no less than it is mine. Together we cannot fail.

"The Social Economics of the New Deal"

One of the innovations of Roosevelt's 1932 campaign had been the establishment of a group of academics from Columbia University to advise the candidate on policy matters. The leading figures in what came to be known as FDR's Brain Trust were Raymond Moley, Rexford G. Tugwell, and Adolf A. Berle, Jr. They, along with a host of other intellectuals, helped to shape the New Deal. In the process they cemented an alliance between a substantial majority of the academic community and Democratic liberalism.

In the article that follows, written in 1933 about six months after Roosevelt took office, Berle provides an excellent summary of the meaning of the early New Deal.

There is no mystery about the economics of the New Deal. For several generations, governments ran their affairs on the theory that natural economic forces balance themselves out. The law of supply and demand would regulate prices. When there was too little supply, the price would go up, and this would automatically increase the supply. When there was too much, the price would go down, and this would automatically decrease the supply. The efficient producer would succeed, the inefficient would fail, and this would keep the productive capacity of the country about in line with the needs for consumption. When credit was needed, bankers would supply it; when too much credit had been extended, there was a period of general inflation cutting down the debt. All this was comprehended in the governmental theory of the time which was really based on the classical economics of Adam Smith.

A tremendous force came into the world in the middle of the nineteenth century. It is usually tied up with what is called the industrial revolution and the advent of large-scale production. But we know now that the actual forces released ran further than that. The power and force of organization had come into economics. Originally this collected around great investments of capital in huge plants, such as railroads, steel companies and the like. But as the economic machinery adapted itself to the idea of great organizations to run these plants, it became possible to have great organizations only partly dependent upon such plants.

This has led to a revision in some of our economic thinking. No longer can we rely on the economics of balance to take care of human needs. The effect of organization will distort and delay the forces leading to a balance to a degree as yet unmeasured. . . .

The old economic forces still work and they do produce a balance after a while. But they take so long to do it and they crush so many men in the process that the strain on the social system becomes intolerable. Leaving economic forces to work themselves out as they now stand will produce an economic balance, but in the course of it you may have half of the entire country begging in the streets or starving to death.

The New Deal may be said to be merely a recognition of the fact that human beings cannot indefinitely be sacrificed by millions to the operation of economic forces accentuated by this factor of organization. Further, the mere process of organization which could create the economic mechanism can be invoked to prevent the shocking toll on life and health and happiness which readjustment under modern conditions demands.

Whatever the outcome, President Roosevelt will live in history as a great President if only for this one fact. He not only appreciated the situation, but had the courage to grapple with the cardinal economic problem of modern life. And he did so not in the spirit of

Bank failures made a mockery of the traditional value of saving for the future. This late 1932 Chicago Tribune cartoon by John Tinney McCutchen reflects how the defects in the economic system harmed even people who had resisted the new consumption ethic of the 20s and tried to "save for a rainy day."

hatred manifested by the red revolutionary or the black Fascist abroad, but in the typical American spirit of great generosity and great recognition that individual life and individual homes are the precious possessions; all else is merely machinery for the attainment of a full life. . . .

Now distribution of the national income is something more than a problem in social welfare. America, in a most intense form, is struggling with a problem that is common to all countries which are highly developed industrially. This is the fact that no industrial civilization can function at all unless there is a tremendous body of people able and willing to buy the products of industry.

The very process of building big factories means that there is a great output of goods which were formerly called luxuries, but which become necessities as the standard of living rises. In order to keep these plants going at all there have to be customers. Which means, when you carry it one step further, that there have to be people whose wages are high enough and steady enough to enable them to buy these goods. In the economist's jargon, it means that the national income has to be widely diffused. A national income of, say, eighty millions will not support an industrial civilization if 5 per cent of the country has most of it and 95 per cent divides the remnant. We got into exactly that position— we are there yet, for that matter—and it is one of the great obstacles to recovery.

This is, in political thinking, a new approach to the problem of wealth. The Communist has talked about having no property at all and distributing goods and services currently, because he thought of it in terms of social justice. Sociologists have talked about an evenly distributed income, on the theory that a large middle class, or rather, a nation of people of moderate means, formed the basis for a healthier national life. It remained for the hard-boiled student to work out the simple equation that unless the national income was pretty widely diffused there were not enough customers to keep the plants going; and as the plants shut down the wages shut down, too, and you became engaged in a vicious spiral in which there was less production, hence less wages, hence less income, hence still fewer customers, still less production, and so on down the scale.

We hit the bottom of that mad spiral some time last February, at which point roughly 40 per cent of all wage-earners were out of a job. At that time, as a necessary result, no factories had orders enough to carry on with; only a few railroads had traffic enough to pay their current bills, and the whole machinery threatened to

fall into absolute collapse. To this problem the incoming administration addressed itself.

It was conceived that by mobilizing industry through the
National Recovery Administration and requiring it to meet the
responsibilities of an income distributing group, much could be
done toward achieving the balance and distribution of income
which is required to keep a system like ours afloat. When people
talk of "creating purchasing power" what they really mean is that
the national income goes not into stagnant pools of unneeded
investment but into the hands of people who need goods. . . .

Will this gigantic attempt to mold an individualist, capitalist
system into a directed economic effort produce the result? . . .

A question has been asked which has not yet been answered.
Every one is familiar with it. Why is it that with more food, more
clothing, more housing, more luxuries, than we know what to do
with, there are some 25,000,000 people in the United States who
are hungry, naked, living most precariously, and with little more
than the bare necessities of subsistence? Every civilized human
being is asking that question; and the fact that there are millions
of people to whom civilization offers nothing just now means that
the question will go right on being asked until an answer is found.

Now there is an answer possible. If, let us say, the government
of the United States, forgetting all about the Constitution, were
to commandeer everything and every one tomorrow afternoon, it
could make a program . . . .

I can imagine an American Government doing this if it had
to—but only if it had to. If there is a general breakdown, it will
have to do, temporarily at least, something very like this; but it is
the last resort; a counsel of despair; an indication that we cannot
run our private lives effectively enough to solve the situation.
Moreover, under the stress of that kind of experiment, a great deal
of the grace of life and human values, which we all of us hold dear,
might very easily go out. Complicated and difficult as it may seem
to manipulate private industry and private economic processes,
this is still preferable to attempting a wholesale solution, so long
as there is any hope of success.

This is why the experiment of the Roosevelt administration not
only is historic, but why it must succeed. This is why the only intelligent attitude to take is one of cooperation. This is why, though all
of us will undoubtedly have moments of discouragement at the
slowness of it, we build more strongly than we might were we either
to attempt a wholesale revolution, or to plunge back into the chaos
which was failing dismally only a few months ago.

The N.R.A. Prosperity March

Join the good old N.R.A., Boys, and we will
 end this awful strife.
Join it with the spirit that will give the Eagle
 life.
Join it, folks, then push and pull, many millions
 strong,
While we go marching to Prosperity.

How the Nation shouted when they heard the
 joyful news!
We're going back to work again, and that
 means bread
and shoes.

Folks begin to smile again. They are happy and
 at ease,
While we go marching to Prosperity

*The National Recovery Administration
attempted to use symbols (the blue eagle),
songs, parades, and other techniques that
had been developed to build public enthusiasm for World War I to make its
program for economic recovery work.*

. . . In a world in which revolutions just now are coming easily, the New Deal chose the more difficult course of moderation and rebuilding. This, in a word, is the social economics—the political economics, in the old phrase—of the New Deal.

An Open Letter to President Roosevelt

Although Roosevelt never accepted the doctrine of deficit spending associated with British economist John Maynard Keynes (as well as with Americans William T. Foster and Waddill Catchings), Keynes realized that the President was more open to experimentation than was almost any other important leader. In the following open letter to the President, written at the end of 1933 and published in the *New York Times*, Keynes assesses the early New Deal.

Dear Mr. President:

You have made yourself the trustee for those in every country who seek to mend the evils of our condition by reasoned experiment within the framework of the existing social system.

If you fail, rational change will be gravely prejudiced throughout the world, leaving orthodoxy and revolution to fight it out.

But if you succeed, new and bolder methods will be tried everywhere, and we may date the first chapter of a new economic era from your accession to office. . . .

The Present Task.

You are engaged on a double task, recovery and reform—recovery from the slump, and the passage of those business and social reforms which are long overdue. For the first, speed and quick results are essential. The second may be urgent, too, but haste will be injurious, and wisdom of long-range purpose is more necessary than immediate achievement. It will be through raising high the prestige of your administration by success in short-range recovery that you will have the driving force to accomplish long-range reform.

On the other hand, even wise and necessary reform may, in some respects, impede and complicate recovery. For it will upset the confidence of the business world and weaken its existing motives to action before you have had time to put other motives in their place. It may overtask your bureaucratic machine, which the traditional individualism of the United States and the old "spoils system" have left none too strong. And it will confuse the thought and aim of yourself and your administration by giving you too much to think about all at once.

NRA Aims and Results.

Now I am not clear, looking back over the last nine months, that the order of urgency between measures of recovery and measures of reform has been duly observed, or that the latter has not sometimes been mistaken for the former. In particular, though its social gains are considerable, I cannot detect any material aid to recovery in the NRA. The driving force which has been put behind the vast administrative task set by this act has seemed to represent a wrong choice in the order of urgencies. The act is on the statue book: a considerable amount has been done toward implementing it; but it might be better for the present to allow experience to accumulate before trying to force through all its details. . . .

I do not mean to impugn the social justice and social expediency of the redistribution of incomes aimed at by the NRA and by the various schemes for agricultural restriction. The latter, in particular, I should strongly support in principle. But too much emphasis on the remedial value of a higher price-level as an object in itself may lead to serious misapprehension of the part prices can play in the technique of recovery. The stimulation of output by increasing aggregate purchasing power is the right way to get prices up and not the other way around.

Thus, as the prime mover in the first stage of the technique of recovery, I lay overwhelming emphasis on the increase of national purchasing power resulting from governmental expenditure which is financed by loans and is not merely a transfer through taxation, from existing incomes. Nothing else counts in comparison with this.

Boom, Slump and War.

In a boom, inflation can be caused by allowing unlimited credit to support the excited enthusiasm of business speculators. But in a slump governmental loan expenditure is the only sure means of obtaining quickly a rising output of rising prices. That is why a war has always caused intense industrial activity. In the past, orthodox finance has regarded a war as the only legitimate excuse for creating employment by government expenditure. You, Mr. President, having cast off such fetters, are free to engage in the interests of peace and prosperity the technique which hitherto has only been allowed to serve the purposes of war and destruction. . . .

You may be feeling by now, Mr. President, that my criticism is more obvious than my sympathy. Yet truly that is not so. You

C.W.A. Blues

C.W.A., look what you done for me:
You brought my good gal back, and lifted
    Depression off-a-me.

I was hungry and broke, because I wasn't drawing
    any pay,
But in stepped President Roosevelt, Lord, with
    his mighty C.W.A.

I don't need no woman now, nor no place to stay,
Because I'm makin' my own living, now with the
    C.W.A.
You didn't ever think, woman, some day things
    would come my way,
And especially, baby, in the form of the C.W.A.

So you go your way, I don't want you anymore,
I made a very great change, in Nineteen and
    Thirty-Four.

C.W.A., you're the best pal we ever knew,
You're killing old man Depression, and the bread-
    lines too.

—Joe Pulliam (1934)

*With this poster, the government attempted
to build support for its Social Security
programs by promising to help support
family members that could no longer take
care of themselves.*

remain for me the ruler whose general outlook and attitude to the tasks of government are the most sympathetic in the world. You are the only one who sees the necessity of a profound change of methods and is attempting it without intolerance, tyranny or destruction. You are feeling your way by trial and error, and are felt to be, as you should be, entirely uncommitted in your own person to the details of a particular technique. In my country, as in your own, your position remains singularly untouched by criticism of this or the other detail. Our hope and our faith are based on broader considerations. . . .

The United States is ready to roll toward prosperity, if a good hard shove can be given in the next six months. Could not the energy and enthusiasm which launched the NRA in its early days be put behind a campaign for accelerating capital expenditures, as wisely chosen as the pressure of circumstances permits? You can at least feel sure that the country will be better enriched by such projects than by the involuntary idleness of millions. . . .

With these adaptations or enlargements of your existing policies, I should expect a successful outcome with great confidence. How much that would mean, not only to the material prosperity of the United States and the whole world, but in comfort to men's minds through a restoration of their faith in the wisdom and the power of the government!

With great respect,
Your obedient servant,
J. M. KEYNES.

The Social Security Act

The Social Security Act has been seen by most Americans as the crown jewel of the New Deal. In the following 1935 radio address, Secretary of Labor Frances Perkins, the first woman ever to hold a cabinet position and a longtime advocate of government-sponsored unemployment insurance and old-age pensions, explains the newly enacted system.

People who work for a living in the United States of America can join with all other good citizens on this forty-eighth anniversary of Labor Day in satisfaction that the Congress has passed the Social Security Act. This act establishes unemployment insurance as a substitute for haphazard methods of assistance in periods when men and women willing and able to work are without jobs.

It provides for old-age pensions which mark great progress over the measures upon which we have hitherto depended in caring for those who have been unable to provide for the years when they no longer can work. It also provides security for dependent and crippled children, mothers, the indigent disabled and the blind. . . .

Old-age benefits in the form of monthly payments are to be paid to individuals who have worked and contributed to the insurance fund in direct proportion to the total wages earned by such individuals in the course of their employment subsequent to 1936. The minimum monthly payment is to be $10, the maximum $85. These payments will begin in the year 1942 and will be to those who have worked and contributed.

Because of difficulty of administration not all employments are covered in this plan at this time so that the law is not entirely complete in coverage, but it is sufficiently broad to cover all normally employed industrial workers . . . .

This vast system of old-age benefits requires contributions both by employer and employee, each to contribute 3 percent of the total wage paid to the employee. This tax, collected by the Bureau of Internal Revenue, will be graduated, ranging from 1 percent in 1937 to the maximum 3 percent in 1939 and thereafter. That is, on this man's average income of $100 a month he will pay to the usual fund $3 a month and his employer will also pay the same amount over his working years.

In conjunction with the system of old-age benefits, the Act recognizes that unemployment insurance is an integral part of any plan for the economic security of millions of gainfully employed workers. It provides for a plan of cooperative Federal-State action by which a State may enact an insurance system, compatible with Federal requirements and best suited to its individual needs.

. . . It has been necessary, at the present time, to eliminate essentially the same groups from participation under the unemployment insurance plan as in the old-age benefit plan, though it is possible that at some future time a more complete coverage will be formulated. . . .

While it is not anticipated as a complete remedy for the abnormal conditions confronting us at the present time, it is designed to afford protection for the individual against future major economic vicissitudes. It is a sound and reasonable plan and framed with due regard for the present state of economic recovery. It does not represent a complete solution of the problems of economic security, but it does represent a substantial, necessary beginning. It has been developed after careful and intelligent consideration of

The average Mississippian can't imagine himself chipping in to pay pensions for able-bodied Negroes to sit around in idleness on front galleries, supporting all their kinfolks on pensions, while cotton and corn crops are crying for workers to get them out of the grass.

—*Jackson Daily News*, June 20, 1935

Among the programs included in the Social Security Act, along with old-age pensions, was a system of insurance to provide temporary payments to those who lost their jobs. These men are filing claims for unemployment compensation under the new system.

Neither Franklin Roosevelt nor his relief administrator, Harry Hopkins, liked direct relief payments to people. Both feared that putting people on "the dole" would destroy their initiative and self-respect. "Give a man a dole and you save his body and destroy his spirit," Hopkins said. "Give him a job and you save both body and spirit." The WPA was the New Deal's major attempt to achieve this goal.

all the facts and all of the programs that have been suggested or applied anywhere. . . .

This is truly legislation in the interest of the national welfare. We must recognize that if we are to maintain a healthy economy and thriving production, we need to maintain the standard of living of the lower income groups of our population who constitute 90 percent of our purchasing power. The President's Committee on Economic Security, of which I had the honor to be chairman, in drawing up the plan, was convinced that its enactment into law would not only carry us a long way toward the goal of economic security for the individual, but also a long way toward the promotion and stabilization of mass purchasing power without which the present economic system cannot endure. . . .

Our social security program will be a vital force working against the recurrence of severe depressions in the future. We can, as the principle of sustained purchasing power in hard times makes itself felt in every shop, store and mill, grow old without being haunted by the spectre of a poverty ridden old age or of being a burden on our children. . . .

The passage of this act with so few dissenting votes and with so much intelligent public support is deeply significant of the progress which the American people have made in thought in the social field and awareness of methods of using cooperation through government to overcome social hazards against which the individual alone is inadequate.

"W. P. A."

The Works Progress Administration (WPA), launched as part of the Second New Deal in 1935, came to symbolize the New Deal's efforts at providing work relief. Although WPA workers produced numerous projects of lasting value to the nation, critics lashed out at the agency from its inception. In the following song, popular stereotypes of WPA workers as "shovel-leaners" who did little work is given musical voice. It was written in 1938 by Jesse Stone and recorded in 1940 by Louis Armstrong and the Mills Brothers.

Now, wake up boys, get out on the rock.
It ain't daybreak, but it's four o'clock.

Oh, no, no, no, Pops, you know that ain't the play!
What you talking about? It's the W.P.A.

Oh, oh, the W.P.A.
Now, I said that!
The W.P.A.
Sleep while you work, while you rest, while you play.
Lean on your shovel, to pass the time away.
'Tain't what you do, you can jive for your pay.
Where is that?
The W.P.A., the W.P.A., the W.P.A.
Now, don't be a fool, workin' hard is passé,
You'll stand from five to six hours a day.
Sit down and joke,
While you smoke.
It's O.K.
The W.P.A.

Chorus: I'm so tired, I don't know what to do,
Can't get fired, so I take my rest, until my work is through.
The W.P.A., the W.P.A..
Don't mind the boss, if he's cross when you're gay,
He'll get a pink slip next month anyway.
Three little letters that make life O.K.:
W.P.A.!

By 1935 the New Deal had abandoned its attempts to build consensus among all classes and had cast its lot with the working class. One reflection of the new-found esteem for working people was the depiction of workers in heroic terms, as in this mural by Philip Guston, Work—The American Way, for the WPA Building at the 1939 New York World's Fair.

Chapter Four

"And I Welcome Their Hatred"

Business and the New Deal

When Franklin Roosevelt took office in 1933, the economic crisis was so great that many business leaders, who under ordinary circumstances would have been likely to oppose many of the New Deal measures, went along with the new President's program. As things began to look a little brighter, however, a substantial portion of the business community turned against Roosevelt and his policies. Many called the President—a descendant of two wealthy and long-established New York families—a "traitor to his class." For his part, Roosevelt never considered himself to be part of the business class. He had earned his money the old-fashioned way: he inherited it.

The bitterness so many businessmen showed toward Roosevelt upset the President, who thought that his programs were saving their necks—and the capitalist system.

The American Liberty League

Business and conservative opponents of the New Deal came together in 1934 to form the American Liberty League, an organization intended "to combat radicalism, preserve property rights, [and] uphold and preserve the Constitution." The leaders of the organization were conservative Democrats, most of whom had been prominent backers of Al Smith, one of Roosevelt's rivals for the Democratic nomination in 1932. Although the group's leaders insisted at the outset that it had not been formed to oppose

Although President Roosevelt would come to accept the fact that a majority of people in the world of big business were hostile to him and his programs, his early efforts at recovery helped to bring happier faces along Wall Street. This panel, entitled Wall Street, *from* Kindred McLeary's Scenes of New York, *1937–39, shows a more relaxed outlook from that in the same location in late 1929.*

Roosevelt's policies, the Liberty League became the most prominent conservative organization battling the New Deal. In the following selection from 1934, Jouett Shouse, the chairman of the Liberty League and former chairman of the Democratic Executive Committee, explains the purposes of the new association.

The American Liberty League . . . is a non-partisan organization formed, as stated in its charter, "to defend and uphold the Constitution of the United States, and to gather and disseminate information that

(1) will teach the necessity of respect for the rights of persons and property as fundamental to every successful form of government, and

(2) will teach the duty of government to encourage and protect individual and group initiative and enterprise, to foster the right to work, earn, save and acquire property, and to preserve the ownership and lawful use of property when acquired. . . . " As prescribed by its charter, the league is to be absolutely non-partisan in character. The question of party affiliation will not enter into consideration in the matter of membership.

All who believe in its aims will be invited to join. It has no covert purposes. There is no object sought to be attained beyond the simple statement contained in the charter and quoted above. It will unite several millions of people from all walks of life who are now without organized influence in legislative matters, and thus enable these people to have a consequential voice in securing constructive legislation and in preventing any measures designed to destroy the principles upon which our government was formulated and under which we have prospered as has no other nation in the history of the world.

Defending the New Deal

Though a majority of business leaders came to see Franklin Roosevelt and his New Deal as mortal enemies, this attitude was far from universal among leading businessmen. Some, especially in newer industries such as filmmaking and business machines, viewed the New Deal much as FDR did: a series of progressive measures that constituted the salvation, rather than the damnation, of capitalism. In 1934 one of the leading defenders of the New Deal among businessmen, Boston department store owner Edward A. Filene, expressed

the other side of the relationship between business and the New Deal.

When the so-called New Deal flashed into our nation's thinking, it seemed to be mistaken generally for a new theory of society. Many upheld it as a better social theory than any proposed before, while many viewed it with alarm, calling it a violation of our ancient liberties and a regimentation of life under a political bureaucracy. Still others waited to see what the New Dealers would propose; and the New Dealers proposed a number of measures which these critics did not believe to be economically sound.

It seems to me that the New Deal can never be comprehended from any such approach. The New Deal is not a new solution for old problems. It is a solution for a new problem—a problem arising from the evolution of machine industry and the evolution of American society from an agrarian to an industrial civilization. Nor is the New Deal to be confused with any one of the experimental measures adopted by the Administration in its efforts to get the New Deal going. The New Deal, as I see it, is a movement toward a nation-wide economic constitution, because the time had come when it was no longer possible for industry, agriculture, and trade to function in harmony with our American ideas unless we did evolve an economic constitution. If we want to go on with democracy, and I am sure we do, the New Deal points the way. It is, as I see it, the same way in principle as that by which our infant democracy was protected and nourished—by the nation-wide organization of democracy under an adequate code. I have, therefore, more than business reasons for supporting the New Deal. I have patriotic reasons, humanitarian reasons, even political reasons, for aside from the question of business profits, I loathe absolutism and dictatorship. As a business man, however, I prefer to keep the discussion within the realm of business. To business, the New Deal is imperative. It isn't a question of whether business shall or shall not be operated under a code. Business under any condition must have a code. It is merely a question of whether our big-community business can operate under the old, little community code, and it has been amply proved that it cannot.

The attitudes of anti-New Deal businessmen were not popular with a majority of the public and left such seeming ingrates and nay-sayers open to the ridicule of cartoonists. Here, in 1934, Rollin Kirby links Republicans, Wall Street, and the philosophy of the 20s as a trio with no solutions to offer.

. . . For whatever the details of such a code may be, its basic principle must be nation-wide planning to enable the masses to purchase the output of modern industry. Idealists may be content with a mere equitable distribution of wealth, but business, if it is to be prosperous, cannot stop at that. It must see that the masses have more and more buying power. There might be an equitable distribution of wealth which would still leave everybody poor, but business can achieve no lasting prosperity now unless the masses enjoy a standard of living which has scarcely yet been thought possible. Only such a standard of living can absorb the products of machine industry, and only such a standard, therefore, can keep the masses employed. . . .

Mr. Roosevelt himself admitted that he did not know what to do in this new era and promised to find out by fact-finding research and, where necessary, by experiment. The great thing about fact-finding as a method of procedure is that one may start out all wrong and still wind up all right; whereas, if we follow traditional practices instead of facts, we may start all right, but because of changing conditions we may nevertheless wind up all wrong. . . .

Nor did he try, as many would have liked, to scrap our existing business system and mold one nearer to our utopian ideals. He simply dug up the reasons that our mechanism of trade was not working successfully and proposed action in accordance with these reasons. Some economists, I know, claim that there can be no such nation-wide planning as is now necessary without the destruction of capitalism. But that is unimportant. Capitalism is just a name we give to describe a certain period in economic evolution. If it doesn't fit this new and necessary stage, I think we can find a word to describe the new set-up.

I am for the New Deal, then, because I am a business man. I am for the New Deal because I am an individualist, not a Socialist, and because the Old Deal unnecessarily restricted our individual liberties. I am for the New Deal because I believe in profits, and the New Deal opens up tremendously greater opportunities for legitimate and continuous profits, and opens them up to an incomparably greater number of people. . . .

Business in the old days had a certain fascination, but it lacked some of the elements of good, clean fun. It wasn't fun to hire little children until they were broken by disease or accident, and then bring on a new regiment of children to take their place. Employers, I am sure, didn't like to do that, but business, they were told, was business, and they had to do it because children were less expensive than adults. It wasn't fun to have to engage in misrepresentation. It wasn't fun to browbeat labor, or to corrupt government to secure those special favors which seemed so necessary. The great majority, I know, wanted to be decent, and only acted in ways like this because they did not feel free to act according to more humanitarian principles. In other words, business was regimented, and the meanest chiseler in the trade frequently did the regimenting. When he cut wages, they all cut. When he evolved some particularly sharp practice, others thought it necessary to follow suit.

I am for the New Deal because it liberates business from all that. Because it frees business from the dictatorship of the chiseler, and eliminates only those practices which are not socially helpful. . . . Business under the New Deal will be much more fun.

Schechter Poultry Corp. v. *U.S.*

Many business leaders and conservatives saw the Supreme Court, dominated throughout Roosevelt's first term by conservative Republican justices, as the last bulwark against what they believed to be the radical doctrines of the New Deal. The Court struck down a series of major New Deal laws in 1935 and 1936. The most sweeping of these decisions was the one that invalidated the National Recovery Administration, which had been a cornerstone of the early New Deal. These are excerpts from that decision, written by Chief Justice Charles Evans Hughes.

The Congress is not permitted to abdicate or to transfer to others the essential legislative functions with which it is thus vested. . . .

What is meant by "fair competition" as the term is used in the act? Does it refer to a category established in the law, and is the authority to make codes limited accordingly?

Or is it used as a convenient designation for whatever set of laws the formulators of a code for a particular trade or industry may propose and the President may himself prescribe, as being wise and beneficent provisions for the government of the trade or industry in order to accomplish the broad purposes of rehabilitation, correction and expansion [of the economy] which are stated in the first section of Title I?

The act does not define "fair competition." "Unfair competition" as known to common law is a limited concept . . . .

This 1936 cartoon by J. N. Darling represents a position on the New Deal and business opposite that of the preceding cartoon. This one, called "Halloween, 1936," suggests that Roosevelt and his followers are taking away the private rights of business and individuals.

"The Supreme Court says I must chuck you back again." This 1935 cartoon by Ernest H. Shepard addresses the Supreme Court's Schecter decision, taking the viewpoint that the Court was preventing FDR from saving the economy.

But it is evident that in its widest range "unfair competition," as it has been understood in the law, does not reach the objectives of the codes which are authorized by the National Industrial Recovery Act. The codes may, indeed, cover conduct which existing law condemns, but they are not limited to conduct of that sort. The government does not contend that the act contemplates such a limitation. It would be opposed both to the declared purposes of the act and to its administrative construction. . . .

The President is authorized to impose such conditions "for the protection of consumers, competitors, employes and others, and in furtherance of the public interest, and may provide such exemptions from the provisions of such codes as the President in his discretion deems necessary to effectuate the policy herein declared". . . .

The government urges that the code will "consist of rules of competition deemed fair for each industry by representative members of that industry, by the persons most vitally concerned and most familiar with its problems.". . .

But would it be seriously contended that Congress could delegate its legislative authority to trade or indus-trial associations or groups so as to empower them to enact the laws they deem to be wise and beneficent for the rehabilitation and expansion of their trade or industries? . . .

And could an effort of that sort be made valid by such a preface of generalities as to the permissible aims as we find in Section 1 of Title I? The answer is obvious. Such a delegation of legislative power is unknown to our law and is utterly inconsistent with the constitutional prerogatives and duties of Congress.

The question, then turns upon the authority which Section 3 of the Recovery Act vests in the President to approve or prescribe. If the codes have standing as penal statutes, this must be due to the effect of the executive action. But Congress cannot delegate legislative power to the President to exercise an unfettered discretion to make whatever laws he thinks may be needed or advisable for the rehabilitation and expansion of trade or industry. . . .

Instead of prescribing rules of conduct, it [the act] authorizes the making of codes to prescribe them. For that legislative undertaking, Section 3 sets up no standards . . . .

We think that the code-making authority thus conferred is an unconstitutional delegation of legislative power. . . .

If the commerce clause [Article 1, Section 8, Clause 3 of the U.S. Constitution: "The Congress shall have the power . . . To regulate commerce with foreign nations, and among the several States . . . ."] were construed to reach all enterprises and transactions which could be said to have an indirect effect upon interstate commerce, the Federal authority would embrace practically all the activities of the people and the authority of the State over its domestic concerns would exist only by sufferance of the Federal Government. . . . and for all practical purposes we would have a completely centralized government. . . .

It is not the province of the court to consider the economic advantages of such a centralized system. It is sufficient to say that the Federal Constitution does not provide for it. . . .

Stress is laid upon the great importance of maintaining wage distributions which would provide the necessary stimulus in starting "the cumulative forces making for expanding economic activity." Without in any way disparaging this motive, it is enough to say that the recuperative efforts of the Federal Government must be made in a manner consistent with the authority granted by the Constitution. . . .

On both the grounds we have discussed, the attempted delegation of legislative power and the attempted regulation of intrastate transactions which affect interstate commerce only indirectly, we hold the code provisions here in question to be invalid and that the judgment of conviction must be reversed.

Franklin D. Roosevelt Campaigns against Big Business

During the 1936 Presidential campaign, President Roosevelt gave up his attempts to win the backing of businessmen. He seemingly took an "if you can't join 'em, beat 'em" attitude. Given the low esteem in which many Americans held businessmen at this time, drawing a line between himself and business leaders was good politics for FDR. Never did he make that line any sharper than he did at New York's Madison Square Garden on October 31, in his last major speech before the election.

For 12 years this Nation was afflicted with hear-nothing, see-nothing, do-nothing Government. The Nation looked to Government but the Government looked away. Nine mocking years with the golden calf and three long years of the scourger! Nine crazy years at the ticker and three long years in the breadlines! Nine

Another Myth Exploded

FDR SAYS IT IS NOT AT ALL TRUE THAT HE "HAS GRILLED MILLIONAIRE FOR BREAKFAST;" THAT WHAT HE REALLY LIKES IS SCRAMBLED EGGS.

President Roosevelt was sometimes able to joke about the hatred so many businessmen had for him. This 1938 cartoon by Quincy Scott in the Portland Oregonian *captures some of that humor. One assumes that many millionaires were not so amused.*

mad years of mirage and three long years of despair! Powerful influences strive today to restore that kind of government with its doctrine that that Government is best which is most indifferent.

For nearly four years you have had an Administration which instead of twirling its thumbs has rolled up its sleeves. We will keep our sleeves rolled up.

We had to struggle with the old enemies of peace—business and financial monopoly, speculation, reckless banking, class antagonism, sectionalism, war profiteering.

They had begun to consider the Government of the United States as a mere appendage to their own affairs. We know now that Government by organized money is just as dangerous as Government by organized mob.

Never before in all our history have these forces been so united against one candidate as they stand today. They are unanimous in their hate for me—and I welcome their hatred.

I should like to have it said of my first Administration that in it the forces of selfishness and of lust for power met their match. I should like to have it said of my second Administration that in it these forces met their master.

The American people know from a four-year record that today there is only one entrance to the White House—by the front door.

Since March 4, 1933, there has been only one pass-key to the White House. I have carried that key in my pocket. It is there tonight. So long as I am President, it will remain in my pocket.

Those who used to have pass-keys are not happy. Some of them are desperate. . . .

Of course we will provide useful work for the needy unemployed; we prefer useful work to the pauperism of a dole.

Here and now I want to make myself clear about those who disparage their fellow citizens on the relief rolls. They say that those on relief are not merely jobless—that they are worthless. Their solution for the relief problem is to end relief—to purge the rolls by starvation. To use the language of the stock broker, our needy unemployed would be cared for when, as, and if some fairy godmother should happen on the scene.

You and I will continue to refuse to accept that estimate of our unemployed fellow Americans. Your Government is still on the same side of the street with the Good Samaritan and not with those who pass by on the other side.

Again—what of our objectives?

Of course we will continue our efforts for young men and women so that they may obtain an education and an opportunity to put it to use. Of course we will continue our help for the crippled, for the blind, for the mothers, our insurance for the unemployed, our security for the aged. Of course we will continue to protect the consumer against unnecessary price spreads, against the costs that are added by monopoly and speculation. We will continue our successful efforts to increase his purchasing power and to keep it constant.

For these things, too, and for a multitude of others like them, we have only just begun to fight.

Chapter Five

Which Side Are You On?

Labor Organizing in the Thirties

The initial effects of the depression on labor were devastating. Even during the boom times of the twenties, unions had failed to benefit from the general prosperity. Part of the reason for the decline in union membership during the twenties was that unemployment remained uncomfortably high even in the midst of general prosperity. This meant that workers did not feel secure enough in their jobs to risk organizing and striking. The depression made matters far worse. Hungry, unemployed people cannot afford to pay union dues. Unions have little leverage to improve workers' wages or working conditions while large numbers of jobless people are eager for almost any job under almost any conditions.

But the mid-1930s saw the greatest expansion of union membership and the greatest degree of labor militancy in American history. The depression convinced many workers that class divisions were real and that they needed to unite with fellow laborers if they were ever to receive fair treatment from employers. The New Deal helped to bring about a new spirit among workers. This was evident in a series of strikes in 1934, among which the general strike in San Francisco was the most significant. Organizing took off as never before in 1935, following the passage of the National Labor Relations Act, also known as the Wagner Act. The law provided government protection for workers who sought to unionize and authorized government-supervised elections to determine if workers wanted to be represented by a union. As these measures took effect, the newly formed Congress of Industrial Organizations (CIO) became the principal agency in the rapid expansion of union membership in such mass-production industries as steel, automobiles, and rubber.

The bitter labor conflict in the mining areas of eastern Kentucky, centered in Harlan County, inspired Florence Reece to write the following song, one of the most memorable of the labor movement.

Which Side Are You On?

1.Come all of you good workers,
Good news to you I'll tell,
Of how the good old union
Has come in here to dwell.
Chorus:Which side are you on?
Which side are you on?
Which side are you on?
Which side are you on?
2.My daddy was a miner
And I'm a miner's son,
And I'll stick with the union
Till every battle's won.
3.They say in Harlan County
There are no neutrals there;
You'll either be a union man
Or a thug for J. H. Blair
4.Oh, workers, can you stand it?
Oh, tell me how you can.
Will you be a lousy scab
Or will you be a union man?
5.Don't scab for the bosses,
Don't listen to their lies.
Us poor folks haven't got a chance
Unless we organize.

The National Labor Relations Act

The hopes of organized labor that Section 7(a) of the National Industrial Recovery Act would provide genuine protection for workers who wanted to join unions proved to be misplaced. Senator Robert Wagner of New York, one of organized labor's strongest advocates in Congress, pushed for genuine protection for union activities. President Roosevelt, who had never before been particularly friendly toward

National Industrial Recovery Act, Section 7(a) (1933)

Every code of fair competition, agreement, and license approved, prescribed, or issued under this title shall contain the following conditions:
(1) that employees shall have the right to organize and bargain collectively through representatives of their own choosing,
(2) that no employee and no one seeking employment shall be required as a condition of employment to join any organization or to refrain from joining a labor organization of his own choosing, and
(3) that employers shall comply with the maximum hours of labor, minimum rates of pay, and other working conditions approved or prescribed by the President.

unions, joined the campaign only when Wagner had gained enough support to assure passage of the bill, which took place in 1935.

An Act

To diminish the causes of labor disputes burdening or obstructing interstate and foreign commerce, to create a National Labor Relations Board, and for other purposes. . . .

Findings and Policy

Sec. 1. The denial by employers of the right of employees to organize and the refusal by employers to accept the procedure of collective bargaining lead to strikes and other forms of industrial strife or unrest, which have the intent or the necessary effect of burdening or obstructing commerce by (a) impairing the efficiency, safety, or operation of the instrumentalities of commerce; (b) occurring in the current of commerce; (c) materially affecting, restraining, or controlling the flow of raw materials or manufactured or processed goods from or into the channels of commerce; or the prices of such materials or goods in commerce; or (d) causing diminution of employment and wages in such volume as substantially to impair or disrupt the market for goods flowing from or into the channels of commerce.

The inequality of bargaining power between employees who do not possess full freedom of association or actual liberty of contract, and employers who are organized in the corporate or other forms of ownership association substantially burdens and affects the flow of commerce, and tends to aggravate recurrent business depressions, by depressing wage rates and the purchasing power of wage earners in industry and by preventing the stabilization of competitive wage rates and working conditions within and between industries.

Experience has proved that protection by law of the right of employees to organize and bargain collectively safeguards commerce from injury, impairment, or interruption, and promotes the flow of commerce by removing certain recognized sources of industrial strife and unrest, by encouraging practices fundamental to the friendly adjustment of industrial disputes arising out of differences as to wages, hours, or other working conditions, and by restoring equality of bargaining power between employers and employees. . . .

"Come on in out of the rain, boys!"

Labor unions turned to the techniques of advertising that business had perfected to advance their cause. Union advertisers may not have had the same level of professional skill that business advertisers had, but they got their message across. The union organizer is depicted here as being stronger and more "manly" than the workers who have not yet joined the cause.

Sec. 7. Employees shall have the right to self-organization, to form, join, or assist labor organizations, to bargain collectively through representatives of their own choosing, and to engage in concerted activities, for the purpose of collective bargaining or other mutual aid or protection.

Sec. 8. It shall be an unfair labor practice for an employer—

(1) To interfere with, restrain, or coerce employees in the exercise of the rights guaranteed in Section 7.

(2) To dominate or interfere with the formation or administration of any labor organization or contribute financial or other support to it. . . .

(3) By discrimination in regard to hire or tenure of employment or any term or condition of employment to encourage or discourage membership in any labor organization: Provided, That nothing in this Act . . . or in any other statute of the United States, shall preclude an employer from making an agreement with a labor organization (not established, maintained, or assisted by any action defined in this Act as an unfair labor practice) to require as a condition of employment membership therein, if such labor organization is the representative of the employees as provided in Section 9(a), in the appropriate collective bargaining unit covered by such agreement when made.

(4) To discharge or otherwise discriminate against an employee because he has filed charges or given testimony under this Act.

(5) To refuse to bargain collectively with the representatives of his employees, subject to the provisions of Section 9(a).

Representatives and Elections

Sec. 9. (a) Representatives designated or selected for the purposes of collective bargaining by the majority of the employees in a unit appropriate for such purposes, shall be the exclusive representatives of all the employees in such unit for the purposes of collective bargaining in respect to rates of pay, wages, hours of employment, or other conditions of employment: Provided, That any individual employee or a group of employees shall have the right at any time to present grievances to their employer. . . .

The warming of President Roosevelt's attitude towards organized labor allowed for a mutually advantageous relationship between the administration and unions, particularly the newly formed Congress of Industrial Organizations. The CIO's organizing tactics are evident in this poster's attempt to transfer the President's popularity to the union.

Limitations

Sec. 13. Nothing in this Act shall be construed so as to interfere with or impede or diminish in any way the right to strike.

A Call for Industrial Unionism

The Wagner Act did nothing to assure that workers would join unions. It merely made it possible for them to do so, without fear of retaliation from their employers. The man who moved most forcefully to take advantage of this opportunity in response to the demands for organization from the workers themselves) was John L. Lewis, president of the United Mine Workers. Lewis pushed for the American Federation of Labor (AFL) to organize workers in mass-production industries on an industry-wide basis. This approach, known as industrial unionism, represented a bold departure from the AFL's traditional practice of craft unionism, in which each craft within an industry had its own union.

At the 1935 convention of the AFL, Lewis urged the organization to commit itself to the "industrial organization of mass production workers." When the plan for which Lewis speaks in the following excerpt was rejected, he joined with like-minded union leaders to form a Committee for Industrial Organization (CIO) within the AFL. A year later, the CIO separated from the AFL, changing its name to the Congress of Industrial Organizations. Its success over the next several years may have been more important than any aspect of the New Deal in raising industrial workers into the middle class and thereby changing the social fabric of the nation.

John L. Lewis, shown here speaking in Detroit in 1940, became the symbol and chief spokesperson for the new industrial unionism that swept the nation's mass-production industries in the second half of the 1930s. The agreement of several formerly staunch anti-union companies, including General Motors and U.S. Steel, to contracts with CIO unions in 1937 marked a turning point in the history of American labor relations. Progress by the unions slowed markedly when the economy took another downturn later that year and agreement with other major industrial employers would not come until the United States was about to enter World War II in 1941.

Those of us who have had experience in these mass production industries are ready to state our professional judgment for what it may be worth and say that it is an absolute fact that America's great modern industries cannot be successfully organized and those organizations maintained against the power of the adversaries of labor in this country under the policy which has been followed for the last quarter of a century in dealing with that subject.

There has been a change in industry, a constant daily change in its processes, a constant change in its employment conditions, a great concentration of opposition to the extension and the logical expansion of the trade union movement. Great combinations

The "sit-down strike" against General Motors, which had begun spontaneously in Atlanta late in 1936, closed down the company's main plants in Flint, Michigan, by the beginning of 1937. The tactic, which can be seen here in Fisher Body Plant No. 3 in Flint, was simple: rather than leaving a factory and picketing outside, workers occupied the production area, making it impossible for the company to bring in strike-breakers. The sit-down strike was highly effective, but the Supreme Court outlawed the tactic in 1939.

Sit Down

When they tie the can
To a union man,
Sit down! Sit down!
When they give him the sack,
They'll take him back.
Sit down! Sit down!

Chorus
Sit down, just take a seat,
Sit down, and rest your feet.
Sit down, you've got 'em beat.
Sit down! Sit down!

When they smile and say, "No raise
  in pay,"
Sit down! Sit down!
When you want the boss to come across,
Sit down! Sit down!

When the speed-up comes, just
  twiddle your thumbs,
Sit down! Sit down!
When you want 'em to know, they'd
  better go slow,
Sit down! Sit down!

When the boss won't talk, don't
  take a walk,
Sit down! Sit down!
When the boss sees that, he'll want
  a little chat,
Sit down! Sit down!

—Maurice Sugarman

of capital have assembled great industrial plants, and they are strung across the borders of our several states from the north to the south and from the east to the west in such a manner that they have assembled to themselves tremendous power and influence, and they are almost 100 per cent effective in opposing organization of the workers under the policies of the American Federation of Labor.

What are we going to do about it? There are some of us who say, let us take council, one with the other, let us put into effect a policy in these certain specified mass production industries that will enable the workers to stand together as a unit against these great commercial units that are exploiting industry at the present time. And the great voice of the workers in those industries, as articulate as their own circumstances will permit, comes to the American Federation of Labor in the form of messages and communications and resolutions to this convention and articles in the press, and in the liberal press, encouraging attention to that subject. Why do we hesitate? . . .

There are great influences abroad in the land, and the minds of men in all walks of life are disturbed. We are all disturbed by reason of the changes and the hazards in our economic situation and as regards our own political security. There are forces at work in this country that would wipe out, if they could, the labor movement of America, just as it was wiped out in Germany or just as it was wiped out in Italy.

There are those of us who believe that the best security against that menace and against that trend and against that tendency is a more comprehensive and more powerful labor movement. We believe that the way should be paved so that those millions of workers who are clamoring for admission into our councils might be made welcome upon a basis that they understand and that they believe is suited to their requirements. . . .

The average worker, however circumscribed, does not need to be told that a trade union or labor organization is of advantage to him if he is given the privilege of being a member of it under circumstances that he can accept. The average man who does not belong to a union but who works for a corporation in this country understands the contribution that the American labor movement makes toward the improvement of his standards and the well-being of his dear ones, and down in the recesses of his heart, no matter how much he may be compelled by circumstances to conceal it, there burns the feeling of warm appreciation for those forward souls, for those daring spirits who comprise the membership of organized labor in this country and who stand upon their feet four square to the world, asking for their rights as men and asking for the rights of all men. . . .

And, whereas, today the craft unions of this country may be able to stand upon their own feet and like mighty oaks stand before the gale, defy the lightning, yet the day may come when this changed scheme of things—and things are changing rapidly now —the day may come when those organizations will not be able to withstand the lightning and the gale. Now, prepare yourselves by making a contribution to your less fortunate brethren, heed this cry from Macedonia that comes from the hearts of men. Organize the unorganized and in so doing you make the American Federation of Labor the greatest instrumentality that has ever been forged in the history of modern civilization to befriend the cause of humanity and champion human rights. . . .

Finding Common Ground

One of the obstacles to organizing American workers had long been the ethnic diversity of the American workforce. Employers frequently used racial and ethnic hostilities to divide their workers. Among the accomplishments of some unions during the depression was to bring together workers

For all the emphasis by labor organizers on persuading workers that joining a union was a "manly" thing to do— a way to "stand up like men" to their bosses—many leaders of CIO unions understood the necessity of organizing all workers, including women. This FSA photo by Russell Lee shows a mother and her children attending an agricultural workers' union meeting in Taber, Oklahoma, in 1940.

Union Maid

There once was a union maid,
Who never was afraid
of goons and ginks and company finks
and deputy sheriffs who made the raids;
She went to the union hall
when a meeting it was called,
And when the company boys came 'round
Always stood her ground.

Chorus:
Oh, you can't scare me, I'm sticking
   to the union,
I'm sticking to the union, I'm sticking to
   the union,
Oh, you can't scare me, I'm sticking
   to the union,
I'm sticking to the union till the day
   I die.

This union maid was wise
to the tricks of company spies;
She never got fooled by company stool;
She'd always organize the guys;
She always got her way
when she struck for higher pay;
She'd show her card to the company Guard
And this is what she'd say:
[Repeat chorus]

You gals who want to be free,
just take a little tip from me;
Get you a man who's a union man
and join the Ladies' Auxiliary;
Married life ain't hard
when you've got a union card,
A union man has a happy life
when he's got a union wife.
[Repeat chorus]

—Woody Guthrie and the
Almanac Singers (1940)

of various nationalities. Another important feature of the 1930s union movement, particularly CIO unions, was the growing trend toward organizing women workers. The following account of a union meeting of women walnut-shellers in California, written by Carey McWilliams—who was researching a book on California farm practices, *Factories in the Field*—to labor writer Louis Adamic, exemplifies both of these features of depression-era labor. The letter is dated October 3, 1937.

A few nights ago I spoke to 1,500 women—women who work picking walnuts out of shells. It was one of the most amazing meetings I've ever attended. The remarks of the speakers were translated into five different languages. There were Russians, Armenians, Slavs, Mexicans, etc. All ages of women, from young girls to old women. A whole row of old Russian women who couldn't speak a word of English, dressed in their shawls and scarfs. The meeting was presided over by a young slip of a girl—president of the union—she was about 19. This was the first meeting these people had ever attended—that is, their first union meeting. You should have been there to feel the thing: the excitement, the tension. And you should have watched some of these women as they got up to their feet and tried to tell about their experiences. They had to struggle with themselves to get a word or words. But the profound meaning that they conveyed! I felt, honestly, very weak, meaningless, and ineffectual. They were kind and listened to what I had to say about the National Labor Relations Act. But they wanted to hear their own leaders—Mary and Vera, and the others. The employers recently took their hammers away from them—they were making "too much money." For the last two months, in their work, they have been cracking walnuts with their fists. Hundreds of them held up their fists to prove it—the lower portion of the fist being calloused, bruised, swollen. They told of the hatred they feel for the miserable stooges who spy upon them, speed up their work, nose into their affairs. They were really wonderful people. You had the feeling that here, unmistakably, was a section of the American people. And you felt stirred, profoundly stirred, by their wonderful good sense, the warmth and excitement in their faces, their kindliness, their sense of humor. Someone complained of working conditions, etc., the fact that the floors were not swept and that they were constantly falling on shells. One woman jumped up, tossed back her skirts, and laughingly exhibited a huge bruise well above the knee, and in the general vicinity of her ass. The others howled and poor Mary, the president, had to pound with her hammer to get them back into any kind of order. It was a warm evening, sticky hot. They packed the hall, stood on benches, crowded the doorways. I've never seen so many women at one time in my life! And such extraordinary faces—particularly the old women. . . .

"Dis What de Union Done"

The following song, composed in 1940 by "Uncle" George Jones, an aged, severely disabled African-American coal miner and unionist from Alabama, summarizes what many American workers believed the success of the union movement in the thirties meant for them.

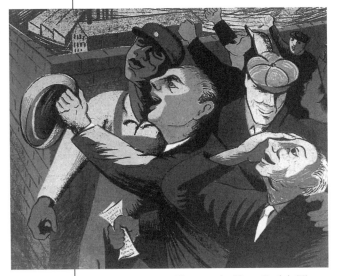

This poster by Harry Gottlieb, The Strike is Won, *was created under the WPA Art Project. It captures the feeling of joy and new-found power that many long-oppressed workers felt when their unions achieved victory for them, reflecting one of the most important legacies of the depression decade.*

In nineteen hundred an' thirty-two
We wus sometimes sad an' blue,
Travelin' roun' from place to place
Tryin' to find some work to do.
If we's successful to find a job,
De wages wus so small,
We could scarcely live in de summertime—
Almost starved in de fall.
Befo' we got our union back,
It's very sad to say,
Ole blue shirts an' overalls
Wus de topic of de day.
Dey wus so full of patches
And so badly to'n,
Our wives had to sew for 'bout a hour
Befo' dey could be wo'n.
Now when our union men walks out,
Got de good clothes on deir backs,
Crepe de chine and fine silk shirts,
Bran' new Miller block hats;
Fine silk socks an' Florsheim shoes,
Dey're glitterin' against de sun,
Got dollars in deir pockets, smokin' good cigars—
Boys, dis what de union done.

Chapter Six

Production for Use, Not Profit

The Left

The Left, including Socialists, Communists, and other groups seeking alternatives to an economic system based solely on the pursuit of profit, enjoyed greater success and more respectability during the depression than at any other time in U.S. history. (The electoral strength of the Socialist Party had peaked in the second decade of the 20th century, but during the depression leftist ideas went far beyond the Socialist and Communist parties.) The depression's apparent discrediting of the capitalist system provided leftists of various persuasions with an opening. Far more Americans were willing to give a serious hearing to left-wing critiques of capitalism and claims for the prospective benefits offered by a socialist system.

"Whither the American Writer?"

The Great Depression cast doubt upon the capitalist system in the eyes of many observers. Some of them turned to Marxism, which predicted the collapse of capitalism and promised the creation of a utopian society to replace it. The Communist Party of the United States increased its following substantially in the early years of the depression. (Communist leaders secretly took their orders directly from the Soviet Union, but many members set their own agendas.) The party made some inroads among the working class it claimed to represent and had more success among minorities

Like other groups on the Left, the Communists had their greatest success in the United States during the depression. As this photo of the 1936 May Day Parade in Union Square in New York City indicates, Communists gained support by opposing racism, fascism, and war, as well as capitalism.

by taking a forthright stance in favor of racial equality (to the point of naming an African American, James Ford, as its Vice Presidential candidate in 1932). But the Communists' greatest appeal in the early thirties was to intellectuals. In 1932, a group of 53 writers and intellectuals ("brain workers" was the term they used) issued a manifesto, "Culture and Crisis," in which they declared their allegiance to the Communist Party.

Among the signers of the manifesto were many of the leading names in American literature, including Theodore Dreiser, John Dos Passos, Edmund Wilson, Langston Hughes, Lincoln Steffens, Sherwood Anderson, and Malcolm Cowley. In the following selections from responses by some of these writers to a 1932 questionnaire formulated by the independent leftist periodical *The Modern Quarterly*, intellectuals' attitudes toward capitalism, the depression, communism, and the role of culture in politics and society are evident.

1.—Do you believe that American capitalism is doomed to inevitable failure and collapse?

If not, what reasons do you entertain as to why it will not collapse in the next decade?

2.—What position should the American writer take in the social crisis that confronts him?

a. Should he keep out of it?

If so why?

b. Should he participate in it?

If so why?

c. Should he dedicate his art to its interpretation?

If not, why not?

3.—What should be the relationship between a writer's work and the (radical) political party?

(1) Should he strive to conjoin Art and Conscious propaganda?

(2) Should he write what he feels regardless of the party's philosophy?

4.—Do you believe that becoming a communist deepens an artist's work?

a. If so how?

b. If not, why not?

c. Would not becoming a socialist have the same effect?

d. If not, why not?. . .

6.—Do you believe in the near possibility of a proletarian literature in America?

a. If not, why not?

b. Of what, in your opinion should proletarian literature consist?

John Dos Passos

1.—Sure, but the question is when. We've got the failure, at least from my point of view. What I don't see is the collapse. . . .

b. It might change pretty radically, and is changing into a centralized plutocracy like that of ancient Rome. Ten years seems a pretty short time for that to ripen and drop off the tree in. Of course if enough guys shake the tree. . . .

2.—a. How the hell can he?

b. It will participate in him, right in the neck. As a producer and worker, any writer who's not a paid propagandist for the exploiting group (and most of them will be) will naturally find his lot with the producers.

c. The writer's business is to justify God's ways to man as Milton said. For God read society, or history.

3.—(1) Art is an adjective not a noun.

(2) It's his own goddam business. Some people are natural party men and others are natural scavengers and campfollowers. Matter of temperament. I personally belong to the scavenger and campfollower section.

4.—a. I don't see how a novelist or historian could be a party member under present conditions. The communist party ought to produce some good pamphleteers or poets. By the way, where are they? . . .

c. I personally think the socialists, and all other radicals have their usefulness, but I should think that becoming a socialist right now would have just about the same effect on anybody as drinking a bottle of near-beer. . . .

6.—Theodore Dreiser is, and has been for many years, a great American proletarian writer. He has the world picture, the limitations, and the soundness of the average American worker, and expresses them darn well. Sherwood Anderson does too. So did Jack London. We have had a proletarian literature for years, and are about the only country that has. It hasn't been a revolutionary literature, exactly, though it seems to me that Walt Whitman's a hell of a lot more revolutionary than any Russian poet I've ever heard of.

a. It seems to me that Marxians who attempt to junk the American tradition, that I admit is full of dryrot as well as sap, like any tradition, are just cutting themselves off from the continent. Somebody's got to have the size to Marxianize the American tra-

"Culture and Crisis"

In this excerpt from "Culture and Crisis" (1932), a manifesto issued in the depths of the depression by 53 writers and intellectuals, the signers indicate their reasons for aligning with the Communist Party.

"Very well, we strike hands with our true comrades. We claim our own and we reject the disorder, the lunacy spawned by grabbers, advertisers, traders, speculators, salesmen, the much-adulated immensely stupid and irresponsible 'business men.' We claim the right to live and function. It is our business to think and we shall not permit business men to teach us our business. It is also, in the end, our business to act.

"We have acted. As responsible intellectual workers we have aligned ourselves with the frankly revolutionary Communist Party, the party of the workers. In this letter, we speak to you of our own class—to the writers, artists, scientists, teachers, engineers, to all honest professional workers—telling you as best we can why we have made this decision and why we think that you too should support the Communist Party in the political campaign now under way."

dition before you can sell the American worker on the social revolution. Or else Americanize Marx.

b. Stalin's phrase, "national in form, proletarian in content," is damn good, I think. The trouble is that "proletarian" is a word that means a band playing the Internationale, everything or nothing. Good writing was good writing under Moses and the Pharaohs and will be good writing under a soviet republic or a money oligarchy, and until the human race stops making speech permanent in print.

Sherwood Anderson

1.—It seems inevitable, but how is a man to say? There seems a surprising life in it.

2.—a. No.

b. Yes. Because the whole thing, drama and life, is wrapped up in it.

c. It seems to me that he should be trying to do that now. . . .

6.—I hope rather than believe.

b. Anything that will make us see that the desire for money and position poisons all life. . . that the common man and woman defeated by life had in him all the possibilities of life. To help make people quit believing in lies. . . .

Malcolm Cowley

1.—Inevitable, but not immediately so.

a. Simply because we may come out of this depression as we came out of others, by the discovery of new markets. But it's likely that we shall turn Fascist before the recovery.

2.—a. No.

b. Yes, because it's his job to participate in every important struggle—at the cost, if he refrains, of finding that his talent has shriveled away. . . .

4.—The questions under (4) impress me as being stupid ones. An understanding of the class struggle ought to deepen a writer's understanding of the world, and thereby deepen his work—if his work depends on understanding the world.

The philosophy of the Communists, being more active, is more of a stimulus to the imagination than that of the Socialists. But at the present moment, actually joining the Communist party and doing party work might make it physically impossible for an author to "deepen"—he wouldn't have time. . . .

The Communist Party was successful in mobilizing mass protests against various injustices during the depression decade. In March 1932, after a march on the Ford Motor Company's River Rouge plant in Dearborn, Michigan, ended with the police killing four demonstrators, the communists organized a huge funeral march to honor the victims and condemn the Ford Company. Approximately 40,000 people participated in the funeral march.

6.—No. You would have to have a proletarian subconsciousness as well as a proletarian consciousness to create an art—and it takes a whole generation to create such a subconsciousness. There could be, however, a revolutionary literature in America. . . .

Granville Hicks

1.—Yes. I am not absolutely sure it will collapse in the next decade. In fact, I would make no predictions about the date. But I am sure it will collapse, and I see no good reason for doubting that the collapse will come relatively soon.

2.—b. Of course he must participate in it. To ask the question is to answer it; it is like asking a man in a lake if he ought to get wet. Even sinking to the bottom is a form of participation. So running away to Tahiti is a form of participation in the social crisis. But I would say definitely that the writer should consciously and intelligently and actively participate in it. To do otherwise is death for a writer—as plenty of cases show.

c. And for the writer as writer participation, whatever else it may mean, means dedicating his art to the portrayal of the greatest reality of our time—i.e., the class struggle in its present acute form. That course is indicated on both social and literary grounds; on literary grounds I would say that it is the only course that promises literary growth.

3.—(1) In the long run and for mature artists the best art should be the best propaganda. But of course we have as yet no mature artists in that sense, and therefore the question raises itself for every author. . . .

"I Have Seen Black Hands"

A member of two groups attracted to communism during the depression—African Americans and writers—Richard Wright joined the Communist Party in the early thirties. Born in Mississippi, Wright had moved to Chicago in 1927. He wrote for Communist journals, such as *New Masses,* in the mid-thirties, but finally broke with the party after the 1940 publication of his masterpiece, *Native Son,* which did not sufficiently follow party directives on writing to satisfy the Stalinist leaders. By that time, most of the U.S. writers and intellectuals who had been attracted to the Communists early in the depression had also broken with the party. He wrote the following poem in 1934.

This photograph, To Play Dolls, was taken in Richard Wright's home state of Mississippi by Eudora Welty, who would later become a world-famous writer.

I am black and I have seen black hands, millions and millions
  of them—
Out of millions of bundles of wool and flannel tiny black fingers have reached restlessly and hungrily for life.
Reached out for the black nipples at the black breasts of black
  mothers,
And they've held red, green, blue, yellow, orange, white, and
  purple toys in the childish grips of possession,
And chocolate drops, peppermint sticks, lollypops, wineballs,
  ice cream cones, and sugared cookies in fingers sticky and
  gummy,
And they've held balls and bats and gloves and marbles and
  jack-knives and sling-shots and spinning tops in the thrill of
  sport and play,
And pennies and nickels and dimes and quarters and sometimes
  on New Year's, Easter, Lincoln's Birthday, May Day, a brand
  new green dollar bill,
They've held pens and rulers and maps and tablets and books
  in palms spotted and smeared with ink,
And they've held dice and cards and half-pint flasks and cue
  sticks and cigars and cigarettes in the pride of new
  maturity. . .

II

I am black and I have seen black hands, millions and
  millions of them—
They were tired and awkward and calloused and grimy
  and covered with hangnails,
And they were caught in the fast-moving belts of
  machines and snagged and smashed and crushed,
And they jerked up and down at the throbbing machines
  massing taller and taller the heaps of gold in the banks
  of bosses,
And they piled higher and higher the steel, iron, the
  lumber, wheat, rye, the oats, corn, the cotton, the
  wool, the oil, the coal, the meat, the fruit, the glass,
  and the stone until there was too much to be used,
And they grabbed guns and slung them on their shoulders
  and marched and groped in trenches and fought
  and killed and conquered nations who were customers for
  what the goods black hands had made,
And again black hands stacked goods higher and higher until
  there was too much to be used,

And then the black hands held trembling at the factory gates
the dreaded lay-off slip,
And the black hands hung idle and swung empty and grew soft
and got weak and bony from unemployment and starvation,
And they grew nervous and sweaty, and opened and shut in
anguish and doubt and hesitation and irresolution. . . .

III

I am black and I have seen black hands, millions and millions
of them—
Reaching hesitantly out of days of slow death for the goods
they had made, but the bosses warned that the goods were
private and did not belong to them,
And the black hands struck desperately out in defense of life
and there was blood, but the enraged bosses decreed that
this too was wrong,
And the black hands felt the cold steel bars of the prison they
had made, in despair tested their strength and found that
they could neither bend nor break them,
And the black hands fought and scratched and held back but a
thousand white hands took them and tied them,
And the black hands, lifted palms in mute and futile supplica-
tion to the sodden faces of mobs wild in the revelries of
sadism,
And the black hands strained and clawed and struggled in vain
at the noose that tightened about the black throat,
And the black hands waved and beat fearfully at the tall flames
that cooked and charred the black flesh . . .

IV

I am black and I have seen black hands
Raised in fists of revolt, side by side with the white fists of
white workers,
And some day—and it is only this which sustains me—
Some day there shall be millions and millions of them,
On some red day in a burst of fists on a new horizon!

"End Poverty in Civilization"

**Novelist Upton Sinclair, best known as the author of *The Jun-
gle* (1906), had been a socialist most of his adult life. Believing
that the depression made the problems of capitalism apparent
and so provided an unprecedented opportunity to move away**

from a profit-based economy, Sinclair registered as a Democrat and sought that party's gubernatorial nomination in 1934.

Sinclair turned his campaign into a crusade, which he named End Poverty in California (EPIC). Calling for an economy based on production for use, the writer swept to a startling victory in the primary and appeared headed toward election in November. This prospect so frightened many prominent Californians that they organized a massive propaganda campaign that used faked newsreels to propagate charges of communism and atheism against Sinclair. (In fact, Sinclair's socialism was rooted in his Christianity, and he and the Communists bitterly opposed each other.) Sinclair's opponents succeeded both in defeating him and in setting a precedent for modern campaigns that use the media for character assassination.

In the selection that follows, written in 1934 after Sinclair's victory in the primary, he outlines his ideas for "ending poverty in California"—and elsewhere.

Los Angeles, September 12

It is a movement of the whole people, and the people are doing the work. I have explained to them everywhere that I am not hankering for the job of being governor of a State; but we are confronting a crisis, and it just so happens that I have been giving my whole lifetime to the study of that crisis and the remedies and efforts at remedies which men all over the world have worked out and presented. We have a plan, a perfectly definite and concrete plan; we have put it before the people; and 450,000 voters have gone to the polls and said that they were for it.

It is an American plan. It has been especially worked out from that point of view. It is in line with our traditions of self-help and self-reliance. It makes use of no long foreign words and it says nothing about class struggle. It takes note of the fact that almost everybody in California is middle-class; even those who belong to the working class don't know it or won't admit it.

Many people question whether the plan will work. We who are promoting it intend to make it work. Thirty years ago I wrote, "Socialism is not a theory but an act of will." And we of the "End Poverty in California" movement know that we can do it, because we know ourselves and we know the people of our State. All through these dreadful five years of depression the people have been organizing and helping themselves. They have formed barter groups, and have managed to produce a little bit of this and that; they have overcome all the obstacles which businessmen and politicians have been able to put in their way. Now we are going to put the credit power of the State of California behind them, and they are going to expand into a giant cooperative in which 1,250,000 persons will take care of themselves.

We know something about the preparations our enemies are making to try to frighten the people. A confi-

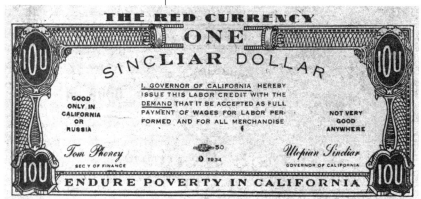

dential friend of ours has been inside the two rooms where they have prepared hundreds of forged photographs, showing, for example, such things as "Upton Sinclair trampling on the American flag at San Pedro." During the primary campaign it was charged that I was in agent of Moscow, and I have no doubt that before long they will produce plenty of letters to prove that I am directly in the pay of Stalin. They have charged that I am an atheist—and does it make any difference that several years ago I wrote the sentence, "An atheist is as dogmatic as any theologian"? They have been saying that I am a millionaire, and they will go on saying it despite the fact that I was afraid to write a small check in New York, not being sure that I had the money in the bank at home. They have accused me of the dreadful offense of being a vegetarian—despite the fact that I abandoned this evil practice twenty-five years ago. I suppose I ought to be happy over the fact that the only true charge they have been able to bring against me so far is that I am a "believer in telepathy."

How much all this will frighten the people, who can say? To win the general election on November 6 we shall have to get about twice as many votes as we got at the primaries. We shall get a good many of the votes which went to our Democratic rivals, but three of the old-time Democratic politicians have already gone over to the enemy, and each will take a few of his followers with him. To make up for this we shall have to get the votes of the progressive Republicans; and of course we shall get many votes from persons who believe in our program but who didn't trouble to vote in the primary. Only 55 per cent of the registered voters voted in the primary, but in the general election the number ought to run to 75 per cent. . . .

We need money desperately, for it always has to be spent before we get it. Nobody in any of our headquarters gets any pay, but there are rent and telephone bills and postage and printing,

This "Sincliar Dollar" is one example of the propaganda techniques employed by Upton Sinclair's opponents to discredit him before the 1934 general election. The tactics developed in this campaign by Republicans and others who feared Sinclair set an example that would be followed all too often in later American politics.

Support for Strong Government

March 1933

MY DEAR MR. PRESIDENT:
. . . It is time that we scrap our industrial and financial leaders. No salvation to the country can come from them. . . . If the so-called "depression" deepens, I strongly recommend to you, Mr. President, that the Government take over and operate the key industries to this country. Put the people back to work. If necessary to relieve public suffering, the Government should not hesitate to go as far as to conscript wealth. The welfare of the public is paramount to all considerations.

Sincerely,
Floyd B. Olson,
Governor of Minnesota

and, above all, radio time. Our opponents have hired most of it, but there is still a little left—if we are quick. In order to engage time we have to pay cash in advance—no favors are granted to disturbers of the social order. The radio is the most powerful of all campaign weapons. The newspapers don't mention our Epic programs, but we get word to our clubs all over the State and they get busy on the telephone and so we have large audiences. What we need is to have a regular quarter-hour period every evening on a certain station; then gradually we can teach the whole State to listen in at that hour. . . . Our name Epic means "End Poverty in California," but there is no reason why the slogan cannot be changed to read "End Poverty in Civilization."

"Ballad of Roosevelt"

Although FDR and the New Deal were so popular in 1934 that Democrats increased their majorities in the House and Senate, there was a widespread feeling that the New Deal had not gone far enough. In those states—such as California and Minnesota—where alternatives to the left of the New Deal were offered, voters flocked to them.

In the following 1934 poem, Langston Hughes, one of the leading figures of the Harlem Renaissance—the flowering of black literature and art in the 1920s and 1930s—gives voice to the belief that Roosevelt was not doing enough.

The pot was empty,
The cupboard was bare.
I said, Papa,
What's the matter here?
I'm waitin' on Roosevelt, son,
Roosevelt, Roosevelt,
Waitin' on Roosevelt, son.
The rent was due,
And the lights was out.
I said, Tell me, Mama,
What's it all about?
We're waitin' on Roosevelt, son,
Roosevelt, Roosevelt,
Just waitin' on Roosevelt.

Sister got sick
And the doctor wouldn't come

Cause we couldn't pay him
The proper sum —
A-waitin' on Roosevelt,
Roosevelt, Roosevelt,
A-waitin' on Roosevelt.

Then one day
They put us out o' the house.
Ma and Pa was
Meek as a mouse
Still waitin' on Roosevelt,
Roosevelt, Roosevelt.

But when they felt those
Cold winds blow
And didn't have no
Place to go
Pa said, I'm tired
O' waitin' on Roosevelt,
Roosevelt, Roosevelt.
Damn tired o' waitin' on Roosevelt.

I can't git a job
And I can't git no grub
Backbone and navel's
Doin' the belly-rub —
A-waitin' on Roosevelt,
Roosevelt, Roosevelt.

And a lot o' other folks
What's hungry and cold
Done stopped believin'
What they been told
By Roosevelt
Roosevelt, Roosevelt —

Cause the pot's still empty,
And the cupboard's still bare
And you can't build a bungalow
Out o'air —
Mr. Roosevelt, listen!
What's the matter here?

Now I am frank to say that I am not a liberal. I enjoy working on a common basis with liberals for their platforms, etc., but I am not a liberal. I am what I want to be—I am a radical. I am a radical in the sense that I want a definite change in the system. I am not satisfied with tinkering, I am not satisfied with patching, I am not satisfied with hanging a laurel wreath upon burglars and thieves and pirates and calling them code authorities or something else.

—Floyd B. Olson, keynote address to Convention of Minnesota Farmer-Labor Party, March 1934

The Townsend Plan
»»»in Brief

Have the National Government enact legislation to the effect that every citizen of the United States, man or woman—over the age of 60 years may retire on a pension of $200 per month on the following conditions:

1. That they engage in no further labor, business or profession for gain.

2. That their past life is free from habitual criminality.

3. That they take oath to, and actually do spend, within the confines of the United States, the entire amount of their pension within thirty days after receiving same.

Have the National Government create the revolving fund by levying a national transaction-sales tax; have the rate just high enough to produce the amount necessary to keep the Old Age Revolving Pensions Fund adequate to pay the monthly pensions.

Have the act so drawn that such transaction-sales tax can only be used for the Old Age Revolving Pensions Fund.

OLD AGE REVOLVING PENSIONS, LTD.

ARCADE BUILDING   LOS ANGELES, CALIF.

Chapter Seven

The Quick Fix

Panaceas

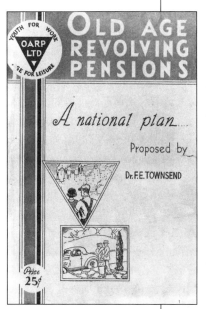

The Townsend Plan was a prime example of a variety of schemes that caught on during the 1930s for quickly and easily curing the ills of the depression. Simple answers to complex problems often have a strong appeal, particularly in times when people are desperate. This brief statement of the Townsend Plan is simplicity itself.

I n addition to stimulating the revival of the more formal Left, the Great Depression also opened the way for a host of political upstarts who preached a variety of simple solutions to the economic disaster. Among these the most important were Dr. Francis Townsend of California, Father Charles Coughlin of Michigan, and Senator Huey Long of Louisiana. Although some observers dismissed these men and their followers as the "lunatic fringe," they gained enormous support in the mid-thirties. The "thunder on the left" during the depression reached a very high decibel level. Its sound came in different voices, reflecting the diversity of the United States. Dr. Townsend spoke more for (and to) California and the elderly; Father Coughlin, mainly to Catholics and urban residents, especially in the Northeast and Midwest; Huey Long, most forcefully to those in the South and rural areas. Their schemes differed, but each appealed to the very great dissatisfaction with the existing economic system.

"Cure for Depressions"

Dr. Francis Everett Townsend, a retired physician who had recently moved to California, began one of the largest mass movements in American history when he wrote a letter to the editor of the *Long Beach Press-Telegram*, which published the communication on September 30, 1933. That letter, reprinted below, outlined Townsend's "Cure for Depressions." It produced an immense response. A few weeks later a full page of letters discussing the so-called Townsend Plan appeared in the paper each day. By the beginning of 1934, Dr. Townsend had established a national organization, Old Age Revolving Pensions, Ltd. (OARP) to promote his idea. Eventually, Townsend's followers collected more than 20 million signatures on petitions endorsing the plan.

Dr. Francis E. Townsend was thrust into nationwide fame and became the head of a huge movement favoring the establishment of old age pensions. He appears to have sincerely believed that his plan would work, but his organization was soon transformed into a money-making scheme that its promoter and Townsend's former employer, Robert E. Clements, privately called "the racket."

If the human race is not to retrogress, two facts of essential importance must be recognized; the stimulus to individual effort must be maintained by the certainty of adequate monetary reward.

If business is good at all times, we need not worry about the reward of individual effort; and if money is plentiful we need have no fears that business will become bad.

Of late years it has become an accepted fact that because of man's inventiveness less and less productive effort is going to be required to supply the needs of the race. This being the case, it is just as necessary to make some disposal of our surplus workers, as it is to dispose of our surplus wheat or corn or cotton. But we cannot kill off the surplus workers as we are doing with our hogs; nor sell them to the Chinese on time [that is, on the installment plan] as we do our cotton. We must retire them from business activities and eliminate them from the field of competitive effort.

What class should we eliminate, and how should it be done: Wars have served in the past to hold down surplus population, but the last big war, in spite of the unprecedented slaughter, served only to increase production, while reducing the number of consumers.

It is estimated that the population of the age of 60 and above in the United States is somewhere between nine and twelve millions. I suggest that the national government retire all who reach that age on a monthly pension of $200 a month or more, on condition that they spend the money as they get it. This will insure an even distribution throughout the nation of two or three billions of fresh money each month. Thereby assuring a healthy and brisk state of business, comparable to that we enjoyed during war times.

"Where is the money to come from? More taxes?" Certainly. We have nothing in this world we do not pay taxes to enjoy. But do not overlook the fact that we are already paying a large proportion of the amount required for these pensions in the form of life insurance policies, poor farms, aid societies, insane asylums and prisons. The inmates of the last two mentioned institutions would undoubtedly be greatly lessened when it once became assured that old age meant security from want and care. A sales tax sufficiently high to insure the pensions at a figure adequate to maintain the business of the country in a healthy condition, would be the easiest tax in the world to collect, for all would realize that the tax was a provision for their own future, as well as the assurance of good business now.

Would not a sales tax of sufficient size to maintain a pension system of such magnitude exhaust our taxability from other sources?, I am asked. By no means—income and inheritance taxes would still remain to us, and would prove far more fertile sources of Government income than they are today. Property taxes could be greatly reduced and would not constitute a penalty upon industry and enterprise.

Our attitude toward Government is wrong. We look upon Government as something entirely foreign to ourselves; as something over which we have no control, and which we cannot expect to do us a great deal of good. We do not realize that it can do us infinite harm, except when we pay our taxes. But the fact is, we must learn to expect and demand that the central Government assume the duty of regulating business activity. When business begins to slow down and capital shows signs of timidity, stimulus must be provided by the National Government in the form of additional capital. When times are good and begin to show signs of a speculative debauch such as we saw in 1929, the brakes must be applied through a reduction of the circulation medium. This function of the Government could be easily established and maintained through the pension system for the aged.

Dr. Francis E. Townsend

Lecture on Social Justice

Father Charles Coughlin was well known to Americans of all faiths during the depression years as the Radio Priest. His broadcasts, which began to reach a wide audience when he signed a contract with CBS in 1930, soon came to be among the most popular programs on radio. Estimates of Coughlin's audience ranged from 30 to 45 million. In attacking both capitalism and communism, Coughlin used a technique similar to that employed by Adolf Hitler in Germany: both men appealed to a wide spectrum of discontented people by combining all enemies into one. In the second half of the decade, Coughlin's anti-Semitism and fascism would become apparent and would lead to his being silenced by the Roman Catholic hierarchy. But at the height of his popularity in the mid-thirties, he seemed to be preaching (as in the broadcast below) a non-Communist brand of socialism, not fascism.

Coughlin long vacillated between praise for and condemnation of FDR and the New Deal. Here, speaking just after the enormous Democratic victory in the congressional elections of 1934, he is careful not to be too harsh on the New Deal. Yet he makes it plain that he does not think Roosevelt has gone nearly far enough. In this speech Coughlin

Concern for the Old Folks

July-16-1937

Dear Mrs Roosevelt.
Washington D. C.

I hope you will take the time to read my letter. When I see so much suffering and crime, I am wondering if you or the President realy cared what happens. I have been reading about your son Franklin's wedding. Did you ever stop to think that there are thousands of young men that would like to get married and have a home if they could get a job, and earn enough to support a wife. . . .

Just where was the Presidents mind when he wanted to pension off the Justices of the Supreme Court on over $400 a week. when every one are wealthy and he thout 15 a month pension for the old folks was plenty. What does he think the old folks live on. None has ever lived on that small sum or they wouldn't be alive at 65 now. Ever few weeks a high salaried man calls to see what you have spent the $15 for and if you can't get along on less. What do you think the old folks thinks about the President in this matter.

The answer to all, is the Townsend Plan Why not investigate it. The old folks who have paid taxes all their lives and built this country up will live in comfort. (so many need glasses, new teeth and doctors care) It will banish crime, give the young a chance to work, pay off the national debt which is mounting every day. So please investigate it, and you will have as many friends as our good Dr Townsend.

Yours Truly
Mrs. E. E. H.
Brainerd Minn

proposes to found a new organization, the National Union for Social Justice, that will offer an alternative not only to capitalism and communism but also, potentially, to the Democratic and Republican parties.

Truly, democracy itself is on trial. It has been given the final mandate to face the real causes of this depression and to end them instead of temporizing with useless efforts for the preservation of a system, both economic and political, which once before watered the fields of Europe with blood and the highways of America with tears. . . .

Now let me speak about this problem of distribution which we must solve within the next two years or else witness a new form of government that will face it and attempt to solve it by some communistic means.

As far as production is concerned, we have more acreage under cultivation, more factories equipped with the finest machinery, more educated scientists and skilled mechanics than any other nation in all history. Our struggle against the blind forces of destructive nature, as well as against the ignorance of the past, has been successful. The Great War [World War I, 1914–18] has driven in and riveted down this nail of progress so firmly that no longer shall there be want in the midst of need. Today there is want in the midst of plenty. . . .

Now, my friends, let no one deceive you with the economic lie that there is over-production when millions are hungry, when millions more are in the bread line and when 16-million homes in America are deprived of the ordinary conveniences of life—running water, modern plumbing, electricity and modern heat.

There is simply a lack of distribution. . . .

If there is plenty for all in this country—plenty of fields of wheat and of cotton, plenty of factories, mechanics and scientists—the only reason why this plentitude of God's blessing is not shared by all is because our Government has not, as yet, faced the problem of distribution. In other words, it may boast that it has driven the money changers from the temple but it permits industry to cling tenaciously to the cast-off philosophy of the money changers. Our Government still upholds one of the worst evils of decadent capitalism, namely, that production must be only at a profit for the owners, for the capitalist, and not for the laborer. . . .

There are 21-million boys and girls in our public school system. Approximately 1-million in our colleges and universities soon will be knocking at your doors for employment. For the older ones you will try to re-write the natural law of God as you preach to them the reasonableness of birth control when you really mean the godlessness of wealth control.

"Increase and multiply" was the command of God—a command that has been sterilized in the heart of every thinking young man who dares not marry because he dares not inflict poverty upon his children. . . .

Oh! how this Sacred Scripture has become perverted as, in the midst of plenty, we struggle to create want—we struggle to create profits—all for the purpose of perpetuating a slavery which has been so often described as the concentration of wealth in the hands of a few!

My friends, the outworn creed of capitalism is done for. The clarion call of communism has been sounded. I can support one as easily as the other. They are both rotten! But it is not necessary to suffer any longer the slings and arrows of modern capitalism any more than it is to surrender our rights to life, to liberty and to the cherished bonds of family to communism.

The high priests of capitalism bid us beware of the radical and call upon us to expel him from our midst. There will be no expulsion of radicals until the causes which breed radicals will first by destroyed! . . .

My friends, I have spent many hours during these past two weeks—hours, far into the night, reading thousands of letters which have come to my office from the young folks and the old folks of this nation. I believe that in them I possess the greatest human document written within our times.

I am not boasting when I say to you that I know the pulse of the people. I know it better than all your newspaper men. I know it better than do all your industrialists with your paid-for advice. I am not exaggerating when I tell you of their demand for social justice which, like a tidal wave, is sweeping over this nation. . . .

But, happy or unhappy as I am in my position, I accept the challenge to organize for obtaining, for securing and for protecting the principles of social justice.

To organize for action, if you will! To organize for social united action which will be founded on God-given social truths which belong to Catholic and Protestant, to Jew and Gentile, to black and white, to rich and poor, to industrialist and to laborer. . . .

. . . [T]hese shall be the principles of social justice towards the realization of which we must strive: . . .

2. I believe that every citizen willing to work and capable of

Father Charles Coughlin was an extraordinarily effective radio orator who knew how to do what a later generation of political operatives would call "touching people's hot buttons," that is, speaking to their fears and hates. His rousing speaking style is evident in this photo of him addressing a rally in April 1935.

"Golden Hour of The Little Flower"

Beginning Sunday, Oct. 5th
7-8 P. M. Eastern Standard Time

Radio League of the Little Flower

Woodward at 12 Mile Rd.
Detroit (Royal Oak), Mich.
Columbia Broadcasting System

To Inform You:

Catholics, Protestants and Jews are invited to join in this movement for truth, charity and patriotism.

You may enroll your dear departed loved ones as a token of fond remembrance. Have their membership card sent to your address.

Membership holds good for one year. The fee for each person is one dollar. This money will be spent in maintaining the Golden Hour of the Little Flower.

In return, you will be remembered every day in the masses said at Calvary and at the Shrine, as well as in all the special prayers and novenas throughout the year.

If you care to join the Radio League in defending the principles of Christianity and Patriotism against the modern heresy of Communism; if you care to assist in bringing back to the fold those who have fallen away, you are most welcome in our midst.

Please feel free to write in for a sermon.

Cordially yours,

Rev. Chas. E. Coughlin.

Coughlin's first vehicle for organizing his followers was the Radio League of the Little Flower, but his appeal reached well beyond the ranks of Catholics. In 1935 he launched an organization called the National Union for Social Justice.

working shall receive a just, living, annual wage which will enable him both to maintain and educate his family according to the standards of American decency.

3. I believe in nationalizing those public resources which by their very nature are too important to be held in the control of private individuals.

4. I believe in private ownership of all other property.

5. I believe in upholding the right to private property but in controlling it for the public good. . . .

10. I believe not only in the right of the laboring man to organize in unions but also in the duty of the Government, which that laboring man supports, to protect these organizations against the vested interests of wealth and of intellect. . . .

15. I believe that, in the event of a war for the defense of our nation and its liberties, there shall be a conscription of wealth as well as a conscription of men.

16. I believe in preferring the sanctity of human rights to the sanctity of property rights; for the chief concern of government shall be for the poor because, as it is witnessed, the rich have ample means of their own to care for themselves.

These are my beliefs. These are the fundamentals of the organization which I present to you under the name of the NATIONAL UNION FOR SOCIAL JUSTICE. It is your privilege to reject or to accept my beliefs; to follow me or to repudiate me.

Hitherto you have been merely an audience. Today, in accepting the challenge of your letters, I call upon everyone of you who is weary of drinking the bitter vinegar of sordid capitalism and upon everyone who is fearsome of being nailed to the cross of communism to join this Union which, if it is to succeed, must rise above the concept of an audience and become a living, vibrant, united, active organization, superior to politics and politicians in principle, and independent of them in power. . . .

This is the new call to arms—not to become cannon fodder for the greedy system of an outworn capitalism nor factory fodder for the slave whip of communism.

This is the new call to arms for the establishment of social justice! God wills it! Do you?

Share Our Wealth

Governor/Senator Huey P. Long (for a brief time he held both offices simultaneously) of Louisiana was the closest thing to a dictator that any American state has ever experienced. Long was, though, a generally benevolent dictator who did much to advance the interests of the poor in his state. He also differed from other southern populists of the first two-thirds of the 20th century by his refusal to stoop to making racist appeals. His call for a redistribution of wealth and income brought Long great national attention and popularity.

An influential backer of Roosevelt in 1932, Long soon broke with the new President. In 1934 he launched the Share Our Wealth Society. By the following year he claimed to have organized over 27,000 Share Our Wealth clubs with a membership of 4,684,000 and a mailing list of 7,500,000. He was popular enough to represent a serious threat to FDR's reelection if he chose to run as a third-party candidate in 1936. Long was not at all likely to win, but Democrats feared that he might well siphon off enough votes from the President to throw the election to the Republicans. That possibility ended in September 1935 when a disgruntled constituent shot Long to death in the State Capitol in Baton Rouge. (Note: The figures Long gives on income and wealth distribution are not correct.)

Huey Long became perhaps the most skilled populist demagogue the United States has ever seen. His calls to "share our wealth" reflected the popular values that were resurgent during the depression decade. His ability to speak over the radio and sway listeners rivaled that of President Roosevelt and Father Coughlin.

To Members and Well-Wishers of the Share Our Wealth Society: It is not out of place for me to say that the support which I brought to Mr. Roosevelt to secure his nomination and election as President—and without which it was hardly probable he would ever have been nominated—was on the assurances which I had that he would take the proper stand for the redistribution of wealth in the campaign. He did that much in the campaign; but after his election, what then? I need not tell you the story. We have not time to cry over our disappointments, over promises, which others did not keep, and over pledges which were broken

We have not a moment to lose.

It was after my disappointment over the Roosevelt policy, after he became President, that I saw the light. I soon began to understand that, regardless of what we had been promised, our only chance of securing the fulfillment of such pledges was to organize the men and the women of the United States so that they were

As this 1934 Washington Star cartoon by C.K. Berryman suggests, the popularity of Senator Long's calls to "soak the rich" and redistribute wealth put heavy pressure on President Roosevelt to move to the Left. In the spring of 1935, Roosevelt told one of his advisers that he must do something "to steal Long's thunder." When, in June of that year, the President sent a message to Congress calling for heavy new taxes on the wealthy, Long rightly pointed to himself as the cause of Roosevelt's seeming conversion on the issue.

THE PIED PIPER IS WILLING TO PASS OVER HIS PIPES.

a force capable of action, and capable of requiring such a policy from the lawmakers and from the President after they took office. That was the beginning of the Share Our Wealth Society movement. . . .

It is impossible for the United States to preserve itself as a republic or as a democracy when 600 families own more of this Nation's wealth—in fact, twice as much—as all the balance of the people put together. Ninety-six percent of our people live below the poverty line, while 4 percent own 87 percent of the wealth. America can have enough for all to live in comfort and still permit millionaires to own more than they can ever spend and to have more than they can ever use; but America cannot allow the multimillionaires and the billionaires, a mere handful of them, to own everything unless we are willing to inflict starvation upon 125,000,000 people. . . .

Here is the whole sum and substance of the share-our-wealth movement:

1. Every family to be furnished by the Government a homestead allowance, free of debt, of not less than one-third the average family wealth of the country, which means, at the lowest, that every family shall have the reasonable comforts of life up to a value of from $5,000 to $6,000. No person to have a fortune of more than 100 to 300 times the average family fortune, which means that the limit to fortunes is between $1,500,000 and $5,000,000, with annual capital levy taxes imposed on all above $1,000,000.

2. The yearly income of every family shall be not less than one-third of the average family income, which means that, according to the estimates of the statisticians of the United States Government and Wall Street, no family's annual income would be less than from $2,000 to $2,500. No yearly income shall be allowed to any person larger than from 100 to 300 times the size of the average family income, which means that no person would be allowed to earn in any year more than from $600,000 to $1,800,000, all to be subject to present income-tax laws.

3. To limit or regulate the hours of work to such an extent as to prevent overproduction; the most modern and efficient machinery would be encouraged, so that as much would be produced as possible so as to satisfy all demands of the people, but to also allow the maximum time to the workers for recreation, convenience, education, and luxuries of life.

4. An old-age pension to the persons of 60. . . .

8. The raising of revenue and taxes for the support of this program to come from the reduction of swollen fortunes from the top, as well as for the support of public works to give employment whenever there may be any slackening necessary in private enterprise.

I now ask those who read this circular to help us at once in this work of giving life and happiness to our people—not a starvation dole upon which someone may live in misery from week to week. Before this miserable system of wreckage has destroyed the life germ of respect and culture in our American people let us save what was here, merely by having none too poor and none too rich. The theory of the Share Our Wealth Society is to have enough for all, but not to have one with so much that less than enough remains for the balance of the people. . . .

Yours sincerely,
HUEY P. LONG,
United States Senator, Washington, D.C.

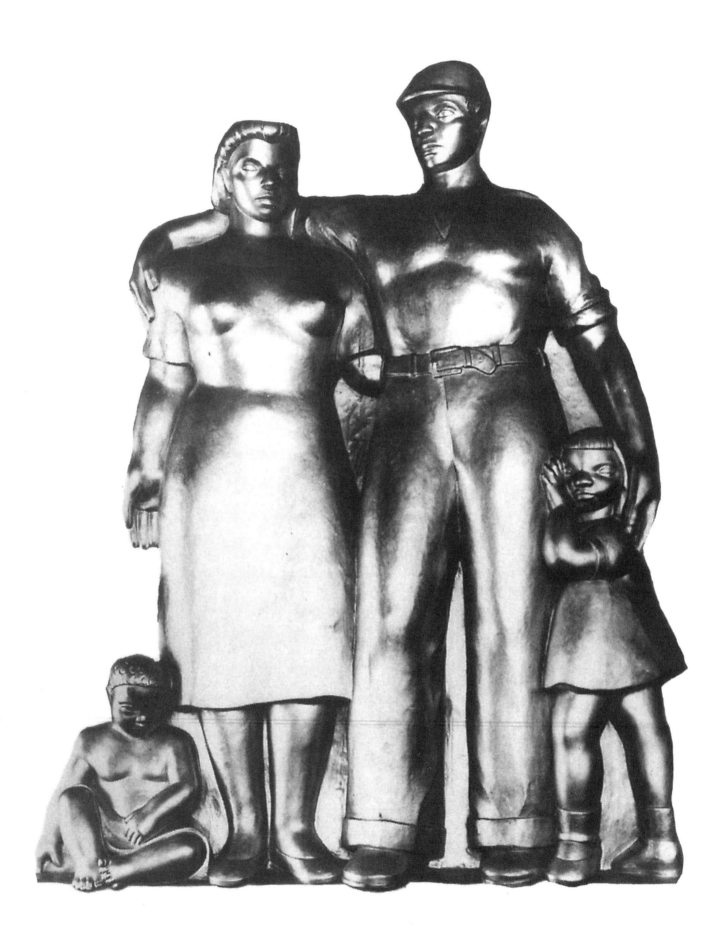

Chapter Eight

"Woman Can Change Better'n a Man"

Women, Men, and Children in the Depression

The depression's effects on women, men, and children varied greatly. Yet it is possible to make some generalizations that are valid in a large number of cases. The ordeal of joblessness and the lack of money to provide for children could not help but cause strains within families. The anxiety of parents was often contagious within the close quarters of the household. Some children blamed themselves for being a burden on their hard-pressed parents, but on the whole self-blame seems to have been much less common among children than adults. Roles were frequently reversed during the depression. Children found themselves comforting parents. Often children could find small jobs to help the family survive, even though their parents could not find work, especially at wages that would support their families.

As the depression affected children differently than it did adults, so its impact on women was different from that on men. When the traditional male role of provider became difficult for men to fulfill under depression conditions, women holding jobs came under greater scrutiny. Many people demanded that women, especially married women, be fired to make way for unemployed men. The fallacy of this argument is shown in the article by Norman Cousins in this chapter.

The theme of restoring working men to their traditional roles as the providers and protectors of women and children was one that was seen repeatedly during the depression. Although the wife looks like she would be capable of caring for herself, the idea of the family under the leadership of a male provider/protector is well represented in this sculpture by Mildred Jerome, Steelworker and Family.

Actually, men did not want most of the jobs women held. If women lost fewer jobs than men did during the depression, it was because women had traditionally been excluded from the types of jobs, such as those in heavy industry, that were hardest hit by the depression.

The depression threatened traditional female roles less than it did the image of male-as-provider. The comforting traditionally expected from women was more needed than ever during the economic crisis. Indeed, the government itself took on a "maternal" role with many of the New Deal programs.

The loss of self-esteem that many men experienced affected them in various areas of their lives, as some of the documents in this chapter illustrate.

Birth Rates

In July 1933, Lorena Hickok, a close friend of Eleanor Roosevelt, was asked by Harry Hopkins, the head of the Federal Emergency Relief Administration, "to go out around this country and look this thing over. I don't want statistics from you. I don't want the social-worker angle. I just want your own reaction, as an ordinary citizen." Her reports, along with those of writer Martha Gellhorn, constitute a revealing glimpse into the lives and thinking of "ordinary" Americans in the mid-thirties. In the following report, Hickok speaks of some of the less-talked-about but extremely important effects the depression had on women.

Salt Lake City, September 1, 1934
Dear Mr. Hopkins:

. . . While we're on this subject of birth rates, I'll tell you another story. Yesterday, going through one of those big bundles of stuff the office sends out, I came upon "Confidential Research Bulletin" (Not for Release) No. 3046,11 put out by the research section of the Division of Research and Statistics. It was carefully encased in a yellow cover, was dated August 13, and was entitled "Fertility of Relief and Non-Relief Families." It was based on a study made by Dr. S. A. Stouffer of the University of Wisconsin of 5,520 families in Milwaukee. The study indicated that between October 1, 1930, and December 31, 1933, there were 35 percent more confinements in the relief group than in the non-relief group.

Now this may not be the whole answer, but I think it deserves consideration.

Many artists and photographers in the 1930s shared the leftist sentiments of many intellectuals (and a substantial portion of the general populace). One of the ways in which they attempted to shape more favorable perceptions of poor and working-class people was by portraying them in poses traditionally reserved for figures held in reverence. One of the most often used of these familiar poses was that of the Madonna and child, as in this 1937 Russell Lee photo of a rural refugee mother and infant in Missouri.

A couple of weeks ago, while I was down in the San Joaquin Valley, California, several clients and former clients were brought in to tell me about working conditions in the cotton and fruit industry. Among them was a woman, rather above the average, who had gone out with her husband last year into the cotton fields. They didn't make enough even to support themselves while they were working, but that has nothing to do with this story.

The next morning the case worker who used to visit that family—the woman's husband is back at work now, temporarily at least, and they are off relief—called me up and said the woman wanted to see me, alone. So I went to see her.

Falteringly, terribly ill at ease at first, she told me she wanted to talk to me about something that had nearly driven her crazy when she and her husband were on relief and that she knew was one of the worst problems of women whose husbands were out of work.

"It's this thing of having babies," she said. "You've got no protection at all. And here you are, surrounded by young ones you can't support and never knowing when there's going to be another.

"You don't have any money, you see, to buy anything at the drugstore. All you have is a grocery order. I've known women to try to sell some of their groceries to get a little money to buy the things needed. But if they catch you at it, they'll take you off relief. Maybe they wouldn't really, but there's always that fear.

"Maybe you could tell your case worker, but lots of women don't like to talk about those things to outsiders. You understand, I'm not asking any help for myself. My husband's working now, and it's alright with us."

She looked at me timidly.

"I suppose you can say the easiest way would be not to do it. But it wouldn't be. You don't know what it's like when your husband's out of work. He's gloomy and unhappy all the time. Life is terrible. You must try all the time to keep him from going crazy. And many times—that's the only way."

Waiting for me in a car outside while I was talking with her was Stanley Abel, one of the best county commissioners I ever met. He is welfare commissioner, and they tell me he has nearly been run out of the county several times because he set up a rule that no pregnant woman, no matter where she came from, whether she was a resident of the county or not, can be turned away from the county hospital of which he is in charge.

Mr. Abel's county hospital operates a free prenatal clinic, too, but when I asked him if the clinic gave any birth control assistance, he looked terribly shocked and shook his head.

The problems of women during the depression were not confined to any particular race or ethnic group. Many of the difficulties that were new to the experiences of formerly middle-class white women had been the steady lot in life for minority women, such as this Mississippi Woman, photographed by Eudora Welty.

I did what I had to do. I seemed to always find a way to make things work. I think hard times is harder on a man, 'cause a woman will do something. Women just seem to know where they can save or where they can help, more than a man. It's just a worry for him, and he feels so terrible when he can't take care of his family.

My husband got very despondent, you know. Oh, he'd say you can't have this and you're not getting that, and I don't want to hear about this; just fighting against it all the time. A woman, like I said, can take more. I always said that she can stand more pain. Take, for instance, when a man gets sick; why everybody within yelling distance has to wait on him. But a woman, now, will go along with pain and never say anything. Least that's how it seems to me.

—Erma Gage

Men Are Alike

ANNOUNCER: Ladies, here's a story for you about men.

WOMAN: Pardon me, young man. You can't tell us about men. They're all alike.

ANNOUNCER: I know, I know. That's almost what I was going to say. In one way men are all alike. For instance, when they're very young, they go running to Mother with . . .

CHILD [crying]: Mommee . . . Mommee . . . I fell down and scratched my knee.

ANNOUNCER: Then, when they're older, they come to wifey with . . .

MAN: Oh, Mary, I got a blister on my hand from that darned hoe.

ANNOUNCER: Yes, sir. At all ages, men are alike. And it's to you, the woman of the house, that they come with their troubles. And you know what to do, because you know that Johnson & Johnson adhesive tape and Johnson & Johnson sterile gauze bandage and absorbent cotton help you care for those little nicks and cuts before they cause real trouble. So, remember the name Johnson & Johnson, first name in first aid.

—Radio commercial for Johnson & Johnson

Maternalism

The depression played havoc with the traditional roles of men and women. Men, traditionally seen as providers, were frequently left with feelings of bewilderment and inadequacy when they could no longer provide for their families. Women often took on different, more prominent roles within the family.

Traditional female roles also came into prominence in the thirties in a different, larger way. For all the talk of the supposed "paternalism" of the New Deal, the cooperative, nurturing values that grew during the depression era were those more often associated with women and might more accurately be termed maternalism.

Both of these effects of the depression are evident in John Steinbeck's 1939 novel, *The Grapes of Wrath*, about migrant "Okies" who, having been forced out of their homes in Oklahoma by drought and absentee owners, migrated to California in search of what they fervently hoped would be the pot of gold at the end of the rainbow.

In both of the selections that follow, the men of the Joad family are baffled, but the women—the mothers, the nurturers—come into prominence and seem to know what to do.

Ma sighed. "I foun' Tom," she said softly. "I—sent 'im away. Far off."

Pa nodded slowly. Uncle John dropped his chin on his chest. "Couldn't do nothin' else," Pa said. "Think he could, John?"

Uncle John looked up. I can't think nothin' out," he said. "Don' seem like I'm hardly awake no more."

"Tom's a good boy," Ma said; and then she apologized, "I didn't mean no harm a-sayin' I'd talk to Al."

"I know," Pa said quietly. "I ain't no good any more. Spen' all my time a-thinkin' how it use' ta be. Spend all my time thinkin' of home, an' I ain't never gonna see it no more."

"This here's purtier—better lan'," said Ma.

"I know. I never even see it, thinkin' how the willow's los' its leaves now. Sometimes figgerin' to mend that hole in the south fence. Funny! Woman takin' over the fambly. Woman sayin' we'll do this here, an' we'll go there. An' I don't even care."

"Woman can change better'n a man," Ma said soothingly. Woman got all her life in her arms. Man got it all in his head. Don' you mind. Maybe—well, maybe nex' year we can get a place."

"We got nothin', now," Pa said. Comin' a long time—no work, no crops. What we gonna do then? How we gonna git stuff to eat? An' I tell you Rosasharn ain't so far from due. Git so I hate to think. Go diggin' back to a ol' time to keep from thinkin'. Seems like our life's over an' done."

"No, it ain't," Ma smiled. "It ain't, Pa. An' that's one more thing a woman knows. I noticed that. Man, he lives in jerks—baby born an' a man dies, and that's a jerk—gets a farm an' loses his farm, an' that's a jerk. Woman, it's all one flow, like a stream, like eddies, little waterfalls, but the river, it goes right on. Woman looks at it like that. We ain't gonna die out. People is goin' on—changin' a little, maybe, but goin' right on."

"How can you tell?" Uncle John demanded. "What's to keep ever'thing from stoppin'; all the folks from jus' gettin' tired an' layin' down?"

Ma considered. She rubbed the shiny back of one hand with the other, pushed the fingers of her right hand between the fingers of her left. "Hard to say," she said. "Ever'thing we do—seems to me is aimed right at goin' on. Seems that way to me. Even gettin' hungry—even bein' sick; some die, but the rest is tougher. Jus' try to live the day, jus' the day."

Uncle John said, "If on'y she didn' die that time—"

"Jus' live the day," Ma said. "Don' worry yaself."

Nowhere is the message of the need for maternalism more pointed than in the unforgettable closing passage of _The Grapes of Wrath_. Shortly before this scene, Rose of Sharon, one of Ma and Pa Joad's daughters, has given birth to a stillborn baby and then gotten soaked in a terrible rainstorm. Seeking shelter, the Joads enter an old barn.

Ma looked. There were two figures in the gloom; a man who lay on his back, and a boy sitting beside him, his eyes wide, staring at the newcomers. As she looked, the boy got slowly to his feet and came toward her. His voice croaked. "You own this here?"

"No," Ma said. "Jus' come in outa the wet. We got a sick girl. You got a dry blanket we could use an' get her wet clothes off?"

The boy went back to the corner and brought a dirty comfort and held it out to Ma.

"Thank ya," she said. "What's the matter'th that fella?"

Migrant Mother, taken by Dorothea Lange in Nipomo, California, in 1936, is the most famous photograph from the depression era. Roy Stryker, the head of the Farm Security Administration photographic project, called this picture "the ultimate. . . . She has all the suffering of mankind in her, but all the perseverance too." Lange often presented images of women depression victims as noble and determined.

CHICAGO'S UNDERNOURISHED SCHOOL CHILDREN

CHICAGO, April 8.—A group of University of Chicago faculty members warns against the ravages of undernourishment among children in the public schools. It appears that principals and teachers in many schools have for several months been contributing from their salaries in order to provide free lunches for hungry children. Allowances have been made to the schools from the fund raised by the Governor's Commission on Unemployment, but the money has been insufficient to meet the need.

—*New York Times*, April 12, 1936.

The boy spoke in croaking monotone. "Fust he was sick—but now he's starvin'."

"What?"

"Starvin'. Got sick in the cotton. He ain't et for six days."

Ma walked to the corner and looked down at the man. He was about fifty, his whiskery face gaunt, and his open eyes were vague and staring. The boy stood beside her. "Your pa?" Ma asked.

"Yeah! Says he wasn' hungry, or he jus' et. Give me the food. Now he's too weak. Can't hardly move."

The pounding of the rain decreased to a soothing swish on the roof. The gaunt man moved his lips. Ma knelt beside him and put her ear close. His lips moved again.

"Sure," Ma said. "You jus' be easy. He'll be awright. You jus' wait'll I get them wet clo'es off'n my girl."

Ma went back to the girl. "Now slip 'em off," she said. She held the comfort up to screen her from view. And when she was naked, Ma folded the comfort about her.

The boy was at her side again, explaining, "I didn' know. He said he et, or he wasn' hungry. Las' night I went an' bust a winda an' stoled some bread. Made 'im chew 'er down. But he puked it all up, an' then he was weaker. Got to have soup or milk. You folks got money for milk?"

Ma said, "Hush. Don' worry. We'll figger somepin out."

Suddenly the boy cried, "He's dyin', I tell you! He's starvin' to death, I tell you."

"Hush," said Ma. She looked at Pa and Uncle John standing helplessly gazing at the sick man. She looked at Rose of Sharon huddled in the comfort. Ma's eyes passed Rose of Sharon's eyes, and then came back to them. And the two women looked deep into each other. The girl's breath came short and gasping.

She said "Yes."

Ma smiled. "I knowed you would. I knowed!" She looked down at her hands, tight-locked in her lap.

Rose of Sharon whispered, "Will—will you all—go out?" The rain whisked lightly on the roof.

Ma leaned forward and with her palm she brushed the tousled hair back from her daughter's forehead, and she kissed her on the forehead. Ma got up quickly. "Come on, you fellas," she called. "You come out in the tool shed."

Ruthie opened her mouth to speak. "Hush," Ma said. "Hush and git." She herded them through the door, drew the boy with her; and she closed the squeaking door.

For a minute Rose of Sharon sat still in the whispering barn. Then she hoisted her tired body up and drew the comfort about her. She moved slowly to the corner and stood looking down at the wasted face, into the wide, frightened eyes. Then slowly she lay down beside him. He shook his head slowly from side to side. Rose of Sharon loosened one side of the blanket and bared her breast. "You got to," she said. She squirmed closer and pulled his head close. "There!" she said. "There." Her hand moved behind his head and supported it. Her fingers moved gently in his hair. She looked up and across the barn, and her lips came together and smiled mysteriously.

"Boy and Girl Tramps of America"

Thomas Minehan, a graduate student at the University of Minnesota, posed as a tramp and traveled around the country to collect information for his thesis. The following excerpt from the book that resulted, published in 1934, provides a glimpse into life "on the road" for young people during the depression.

The American young tramps, if one may judge by appearances, are not hungry. To a casual observer, they seem in good health and not bad spirits. When you talk to them, however, or listen to their talk, you realize the important part food plays in their lives. Almost one-fourth of all their conversation concerns food. When you live with them, eating at the missions or in the jungles, you understand almost too well why they are so concerned with food.

The young tramps, I repeat, are not starving. But for growing, healthy boys engaged in strenuous outdoor life, the food they eat is shamefully inadequate. Many relief stations serve but two meals a day, others three, and some only one. No station ever serves second helpings and the Oliver who asks for more [a reference to a famous incident in Charles Dickens's novel *Oliver Twist*] is expelled before breakfast. Jungle food is better in quality and, if the pickings are good, more generous in quantity, but meals are uncertain. ["Hobo jungle" was a term used to refer to the places where transients gathered to eat and sleep.] One day the boys may gorge themselves. The next there may not be a slice of bread or a cup of coffee.

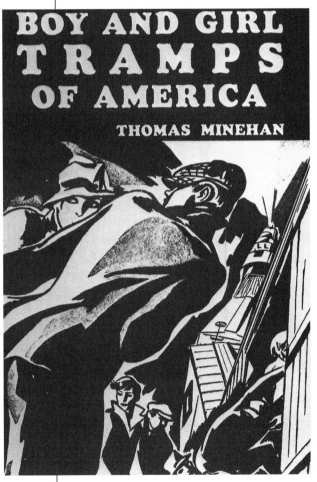

The cover of Minehan's Boy and Girl Tramps of America *provides some indication of the book's contents. During the depression, books and movies concerning the "down and out" attracted large audiences.*

Grown-up Worries

The depression forced many children to grow up quickly, often taking over adult responsibilities and being burdened with adult concerns.

Mr. and Mrs. Roosevelt.
Wash. D. C.

Dear Mr. President:
I'm a boy of 12 years. I want to tell you about my family My father hasn't worked for 5 months He went plenty times to relief, he filled out application. They won't give us anything. I don't know why. Please you do something. We haven't paid 4 months rent, Everyday the landlord rings the door bell, we don't open the door for him. We are afraid that will be put out, been put out before, and don't want to happen again. We haven't paid the gas bill, and the electric bill, haven't paid grocery bill for 3 months. My brother goes to Lane Tech. High School. he's eighteen years old, hasn't gone to school for 2 weeks because he got no carfare. I have a sister she's twenty years, she can't find work. My father he staying home. All the time he's crying because he can't find work. I told him why are you crying daddy, and daddy said why shouldn't I cry when there is nothing in the house. I feel sorry for him. That night I couldn't sleep. The next morning I wrote this letter to you. in my room. Were American citizens and were born in Chicago, Ill. and I don't know why they don't help us Please answer right away because we need it. will starve Thank you.

God bless you.
[Unsigned, 1936]
Chicago, Ill.

Travel interferes with meals. A youth shivers all night in a gondola. Next day he falls asleep on a hillside and sleeps the sleep of exhaustion until dusk. On awakening he is hungry, but where can he get food? The bread lines are closed. The police have, in one of their weekly raids, cleaned out the jungles. At none of the customary places are there friends or food. The youth can beg on the streets, walking miles perhaps before he gets a nickel. A boy can steal, but the chances are that he will be caught. A girl can offer her body, but as likely as not she will find nobody in the market with desire and a dime. The usual course is to remain hungry until breakfast at a mission for a boy, or until breakfast can be begged by a girl. If the boy is very hungry, he may glom a grub from garbage cans.

The breakfast at the mission, if he remains there, is a thin bowl of gruel containing too few vitamins and calories to replace the energy lost on a twenty-four-hour fast. In one day's fast the boy's body has been definitely robbed of much strength. With work and walking, sleeping out of doors, and riding in box cars, it may be a long time before that lost energy can be replaced. Yet, unlike the adult tramp, all the time the boy is growing. He needs enough food not only for the repair and replacement of tissue oxidized in daily activity, but for growth, development, and future use. He does not get it.

Not only does he fail to receive food enough for a growing, healthy boy, but because he is constantly calling upon reserves he is definitely undernourished. The signs of malnutrition may not be so evident to the casual observer. A dozen child tramps in a shower room or swimming hole appear merely a group of lean and lanky boys. But if the observer is critical, he will note the too-prominent ribs, an abdomen too concave, and legs and arms on which the skin, strange phenomenon in the young, is loose and baggy as if there were not enough muscle and flesh underneath. He will notice, too, the tired, hungry eyes, the nervous mannerisms, and the habitual posture of weariness and want.

Communities differ in their systems of caring for all transients. Almost all, however, give one free meal, work for the second meal, a bed on the floor, and eviction before a second or third day. . . .

. . . The soup is invariable—I write from experience—thin, watery, lukewarm, tasteless, and served without even stale bread, and never with soda crackers. A portion equals about a small cupful. No second bowl is ever given, no matter how tired and hungry the boy.

Meals vary from city to city, but the two old reliables are stew and beans. Stew and beans, beans and stew. Sandwiches are sometimes given instead—usually cheese or peanut butter. Once a week, perhaps, a boiled vegetable dinner or hash is on the bill. Bread accompanies the meal. The bread is almost always bakery returns, stale and unpalatable, or Red Cross flour bread baked by the missions in their own ovens. Fresh, wholesome and appetizing, the latter bread is good—but there isn't enough of it.

. . . Meat is something that was served yesterday or last week, or is to be served next Sunday. For myself, after scores of mission and relief station meals, I must say, so far as the young tramp's meals are concerned, I have tasted it but once—meat loaf in a sandwich. . . . Mission stew served to boy tramps always has in it a hint of meat. There is an inevitable sliver of bone that sticks between your teeth and small diced squares of tripe, but of flesh-and-blood meat, of muscle and sinew, I have tasted none. . . . But when a boy is hungry and unable to obtain food by begging or working he must steal or starve.

To date, stealing has not developed many complicated techniques among the young tramps. In summer, the farmer's gardens and orchards are raided regularly. Chickens, turkeys, ducks, and even small pigs are picked up when they stray from the farm yard into a grove. They are run down, snared, or caught in any convenient fashion with as little noise and fuss as possible. Seldom, I suspect, do farmers miss the fowl. If they are missed, the farmer most likely blames a skunk or a fox.

Farmer John, it is true, is the most frequent and common victim of the young tramp's thievery, but there are others. Bakery trucks parked early in the morning before stores, vegetable trucks on the way to market before dawn, all furnish the youthful vagrant with some of his needed food. Sidewalk counters and tables inside stores are raided but not often. Produce trucks going to market early in the morning are the boy's best regular supply. Boys hiding in the culverts at grade crossings rush out, board the truck and are gone with an armful of supplies before the driver realizes he is being raided. . . .

This 1935 photograph of the children of the Mulhalls, an Ozark mountaineer family, was taken by Ben Shahn. Clinging to pets and a doll, these poor white children represent a universal theme of children's simple aspirations.

The relief stations for transients in the large cities feed but do not clothe the young tramps. Clothing is for the local homeless, not for the travelers. A boy or girl tramp must be not only in rags but half-naked to obtain a patched and dirty shirt or a worn cap.

"Will Women Lose Their Jobs?"

The assertion that women were taking jobs that might otherwise go to men was frequently made—and quite often acted upon in state legislatures—during the depression. Here Norman Cousins shows how mistaken these arguments were. His 1939 article says as much about gender stereotyping of occupations in the thirties as it does about the injustice and impracticality of replacing women workers with men.

Here is the latest depression cure-all, results guaranteed by its supporters:

"There are approximately 10,000,000 people out of work in the United States today. There are also 10,000,000 or more women, married and single, who are job-holders. Simply fire the women, who shouldn't be working anyway, and hire the men. Presto! No unemployment. No relief rolls. No depression."

Some women responded to the common demands that women, especially if married, give up their jobs so men could have work. Here, "forgotten women," unemployed and single, march to demand jobs.

This is the general idea behind the greatest assault on women's rights in two decades. Its supporters include not only the some-thing-for-nothing groups which can always be depended upon to support chain-letter movements and share-the-wealth plans, but a large section of public opinion—as yet unacquainted with all the facts—which finds it hard to resist the supposed logic of millions of unemployed men replacing millions of employed women. Impetus to the drive—at least psychologically—is lent by the fact that the payrolls of many communities and private organizations are open only to males.

The first move toward the complete defeminizing of public and private jobs is discrimination against the married woman. Having thus inserted its foot in the door, the oust-women cam-paign seeks eventually to enter and hang up the verboten [German for "forbidden"] sign to all women, married or single, employed or seeking employment. . . .

Of such concern is this trend to the nation's women leaders that it has been called the greatest issue to affect women since their victorious fight for suffrage. In its recent convention at Kansas City, the National Federation of Business and Professional Women's Clubs announced a frontal attack on what it considers the most serious problem it has faced in twenty years. In the eyes of Federation leaders the legislation already introduced is a por-tent of even more widespread attacks to come. . . .

There are, of course, many familiar "moral" arguments against the working wife: woman's place is in the home, the management of which is enough work for any person; her first allegiance is to the bearing and raising of children; there is a direct relationship between the increase of women in business and the declining birth rate. . . .

The Women's Bureau of the Department of Labor reports that in recent years the majority of married women at work have been working not because of a desire for a career or for economic inde-pendence but because of the need to provide or supplement the family income. . . .

Analysis of these figures prompts the Department of Labor to point out that competition in industry is between one man and another, rather than between men and women. At most, not more than 1,000,000 jobs now held by women could pass to men. And of the 3,000,000-odd jobs held by women who admittedly are married, probably no more than 300,000 could be satisfactorily or willingly filled by males. This would "create" new jobs for only 3 per cent of the men now out of work.

Married women are just as much free citizens of this country as unmarried women or men. They have the same right to pursue their own lives and to be employed in any occupation they can find, as men. To deny them this right is an abridgement of their con-stitutional rights.

—Massachusetts Supreme Court (1939)

The belief that married women should be discriminated against in the matter of jobs fails to take account of certain basic principles. One of these is that except in a relief program jobs must be awarded on qualifications and not on need. Thus where married women hold jobs in private or public employment it is because they are qualified for such types of work. Any wholesale or arbitrary move to oust them would be upsetting to their employers as well as to the women themselves. This is especially true since many married women are often doing work for which they are better suited than men, or which men do not want except as a makeshift in an emergency.

The very considerable and necessary attention given to work projects for the needy in recent years tends to influence people's thinking in a way unknown prior to the depression. They stress unduly the need factor in normal employment, particularly in regard to married women. But in some instances they would even apply this theory to the family, and thus imply that one wage earner per family is adequate. This is a wholly unsound, unrealistic, and unfortunate approach to our unemployment problems. Moreover, it is un-American.

—Secretary of Labor Frances Perkins, quoted in Norman Cousins, "Will Women Lose Their Jobs?"

Fundamentally, the unemployment of men is not caused by women who hold jobs but by the infirmities of the economic structure itself. Nor is the depression an affliction visited exclusively upon the male; the woman must bear her part of the burden, as more than 2,000,000 unemployed women can attest. . . .

In answer to all of which the oust-women-from-jobs group may say that, yes, we are living in changing times and that, indeed, this is an emergency. And that, they may add, is precisely why extreme measures are needed and justified. Millions of men, many of them with families, are out of work. Most of them would be satisfied with salaries now paid to women. The ouster should begin with the working married woman because she should be dependent upon the man. After that, single women should be withdrawn from jobs. And who will look after them? Well, someone will; someone always does. Besides, unemployment with women is a matter of relative hardship at worst. But with men— especially family men—the hardship is absolute and complete. The state should have the right to step in and, for the greater benefit of all, say who shall work and who shall not.

An intriguing but hardly a practical thought. Because the more you study the figures of the various occupations which would be involved in the taking over of women's jobs by men, the more preposterous the scheme becomes. Imagine an average day in an America without working women:

John Citizen arrives at his office to be greeted by a male receptionist, a male switchboard operator and a male private secretary who opens his mail, arranges his appointments and takes dictation. At lunch his favorite waitress is missing, her place taken by a young man. At three o'clock he visits his dentist and is greeted by a male nurse. At four-thirty Mrs. Citizen calls to complain about Harry, who has taken the place of the part-time maid, and who refuses to wash the baby's clothes.

At the dinner table, Mary, who has just entered kindergarten, complains about Mr. Mann, the new teacher. Mrs. Citizen resents the personal questions asked by the new male salesclerk when she went shopping for underwear. She also resents the husky baritone voice that moans "Number, please," every time she picks up the phone.

Ridiculous? Certainly. But this is what a general purge of all women in industry would mean. It is impossible to carry through a large-scale replacement of one large bloc of labor for another unless there is an identity of functions all along the line. Approximately 3,500,000 men out of work are manual laborers.

Which places vacated by women can they take? Approximately 3,100,000 women are employed as domestics. Which men want to take their places? There are about 920,000 salesgirls, whose replacement by men in most cases would be ludicrous. . . .

But even outside the economic sphere, arguments against the working wife reveal weakness. There is much talk about the mother's place in the home, very little about the fact that the home has changed. Housekeeping for the average family today is no longer a full-time job. We are no longer living in the days when families numbered a dozen or more, and, what with cooking, baking, canning, washing, spinning, sewing and mending, woman's work was never done. The average American family today numbers three children or less, who are away from home at least five hours a day. Inexpensive, modern gadgets simplify what were once long, tedious household tasks. In short, the home has changed from a producing to a consuming unit.

This change is reflected not only in employment of married women but in the growth of social and church work, and in the spread of adult education, of culture and entertainment groups. In these circumstances, it is difficult to blame the married woman who is not content to remain a semi-idle dependent, but who seeks in business an outlet for her talents and energies. Dr. Richard Cabot, of Boston, recently noted that many of his nervous patients were women suffering for want of serious occupational interest.

Nazi Germany thought it could casually disregard these important questions when it decided to oust its 900,000 women workers from industrial and governmental life. For years Germany had been looked upon as the foremost example of a nation in which, to the benefit of the state, equal rights for women were scrupulously upheld. The Nazi regime waved the women out of their jobs and herded them back to the home, where they were told to bear children.

However as Clifford Kirkpatrick revealed in *Nazi Germany: Its Women and Family Life*, the Nazi conception of woman as a biological instrument soon changed when it was realized that no such large bloc of labor could be displaced—or even replaced—without severely upsetting the national economy. "The 'sacred' mothers went back to the machine," observed Dr. Kirkpatrick, "and the employment of women even increased." . . .

. . . [I]n the final analysis this question of women and jobs will be fought out on the issue of equal rights and opportunities for men and women alike.

Many women, after marriage, find plenty of work in the home. They have no time, no inclination or no ability for any other kind of work. The records show that very few married women work from choice, that they are working only because a husband is ill or had deserted them, or there are special expenses caused by illness or educational requirements in the home. There may even be fathers, mothers, sisters or brothers to be supported. It seems to me that it is far more important for us to think about creating more jobs than it is for us to worry about how we are going to keep any groups from seeking work.

—Eleanor Roosevelt, *Current History and Forum*, September 1939

Chapter Nine

"The Negro Was Born in Depression"

Race and Ethnicity in the Thirties

Members of minority groups who had long suffered from discrimination faced a double burden in the depression. The other side of the coin, however, was that the New Deal provided the 20th century's first positive, though very limited, federal action that affected minorities.

I t would, obviously, be a mistake to think that the depression had the same effect on people of different classes (rich and poor). We have seen in the preceding chapter that the depression affected children and adults and women and men in distinct ways. The same is true for people of different races and ethnic groups. The depression was different for minorities in many ways, but three aspects stand out in particular. First, suffering and deprivation were nothing new to many ethnic groups. Second, minorities were the first to be fired when members of the majority found themselves in need of jobs. Finally, minorities were the first choice when people were looking for scapegoats.

In this 1938 poem, Langston Hughes gives voice to those who had been left out of the American Dream. He points out that if the promise of America is to be realized, more is needed than simply restoring the conditions that existed before the depression began. There was no good place in that America for African Americans, for many other racial and ethnic groups, or for the poor in general.

Let America Be America Again

Let America be America again.
Let it be the dream it used to be.

Let it be the pioneer on the plain
Seeking a home where he himself is free.

(America never was America to me.)

Let America be the dream the dreamers dreamed—
Let it be that great strong land of love
Where never kings connive nor tyrants scheme
That any man be crushed by one above.

(It never was America to me.)

0, let my land be a land where Liberty
Is crowned with no false patriotic wreath,
But opportunity is real, and life is free,
Equality is in the air we breathe.

(There's never been equality for me,
Nor freedom in this "homeland of the free.")

Say who are you that mumbles in the dark?
And who are you that draws your veil across the stars?

I am the poor white, fooled and pushed apart,
I am the Negro bearing slavery's scars.
I am the red man driven from the land,
I am the immigrant clutching the hope I seek—
And finding only the same old stupid plan.
Of dog eat dog, of mighty crush the weak.
I am the young man, full of strength and hope,
Tangled in that ancient endless chain
Of profit, power, gain, of grab the land!
Of grab the gold! Of grab the ways of satisfying
  need!
Of work the men! Of take the pay!
Of owning everything for one's own greed!

I am the farmer, bondsman to the soil.
I am the worker sold to the machine.
I am the Negro, servant to you all.
I am the people, humble, hungry, mean—
Hungry yet today despite the dream.
Beaten yet today—O, Pioneers!

I am the man who never got ahead,
The poorest worker bartered through the years.
Yet I'm the one who dreamt our basic dream
In that Old World while still a serf of kings,
Who dreamt a dream so strong, so brave, so true,
That even yet its mighty daring sings
In every brick and stone, in every furrow turned
That's made America the land it has become.
0, I'm the man who sailed those early seas
In search of what I meant to be my home—
For I'm the one who left dark Ireland's shore,
And Poland's plain, and England's grassy lea,
And torn from Black Africa's strand I came
To build a "homeland of the free."

The free?

Who said the free? Not me?
Surely not me? The millions on relief today?
The millions shot down when we strike?
The millions who have nothing for our pay?
For all the dreams we've dreamed
And all the songs we've sung
And all the hopes we've held
And all the flags we've hung,
The millions who have nothing for our pay—
Except the dream that's almost dead today.

O, let America be America again—
The land that never has been yet—
And yet must be—the land where every man is free.
The land that's mine—the poor man's, Indian's, Negro's, ME—
Who made America,
Whose sweat and blood, whose faith and pain,
Whose hand at the foundry, whose plow in the rain,
Must bring back our mighty dream again.

Sure, call me any ugly name you choose—
The steel of freedom does not stain.
From those who live like leeches on the people's
    lives,
We must take back our land again,
America!

O, yes,
I say it plain,
America never was America to me,
And yet I swear this oath—
America will be!

Out of the rack and ruin of our gangster death,
The rape and rot of graft, and stealth, and lies,

We, the people, must redeem
The land, the mines, the plants, the rivers,
The mountains and the endless plain—
All, all the stretch of these great green states—
And make America again!

A New Pattern of Life for the Indian

The depression saw a radical shift in government policy toward Native Americans. This "Indian New Deal" was largely the work of Roosevelt's Commissioner of Indian Affairs, John Collier. In Collier's description of what the new policy is intended to accomplish, there is a distinct foretaste of the ethnic pride movements (e.g., "Black is beautiful") that arose in the 1960s: "If he happens to be a blanket Indian, we think he should not be ashamed of it." The following article was written by Frank Ernest Hill in 1935.

Although the "Indian New Deal" represented an improvement in federal policy toward Native Americans, Indians remained the poorest of all ethnic groups in the United States. This Navajo family in St. Michael's, Arizona, is waiting for government-supplied food in 1937.

More than a mile above the sea level, on a plateau of the American Southwest, two hundred and fifty men are building a new capitol. It is not the capitol of a State. Its stone walls rise in shapes that are strange to most Americans; its name—Nee Alneeng—falls with a strange accent. Nee Alneeng belongs to a world far from Manhattan and Main Street. It is an Indian world, and the capitol belongs to the Navajo, now the largest of the North American tribes.

This little centre is symbolic of a new way of life among the Navajo: in fact, a new way of life for the 340,000 Indians of the United States. A year ago the Wheeler-Howard Act gave to the tribes the right to decide whether they would accept important privileges in education, self-determination and self-government. A popular vote was asked; the essential question was: "Do you want to help save yourselves?" . . .

Thus the Wheeler-Howard Act embodies an Indian policy far different from that pursued in the past. The Federal Government could have conferred self-government upon the American Indian without asking him if he wanted it. To understand why he was asked, one must take a brief but discriminating glance at American history as it has affected the Red man. . . .

The third stage may be said to have begun with the growing conviction among thoughtful Americans that Indian life had latent strength and important cultural values and that the Indian if given the right opportunities could do what the government had failed to do: he could arrange a place for himself and his customs in this modern America. The appointment of John Collier as Commissioner of Indian Affairs in April, 1933, brought into power a leader of this trend of opinion. . . .

Mr. Collier, slight, almost scholarly in appearance, at his desk in Washington describes what the administration is trying to do for the Indian and why he believes the new policy to be enlightened.

"In the past," he says, "the government tried to encourage economic independence and initiative by the allotment system, giving each Indian a portion of land and the right to dispose of it. As a result, of the 138,000,000 acres which Indians possessed in 1887 they have lost all but 47,000,000 acres, and the lost area includes the land that was the most valuable. Further, the government sought to give the Indian the schooling of the whites, teaching him to despise his old customs and habits as barbaric. Through this experiment the Indian lost much of his understanding of his own culture and received no usable substitute. In many areas such efforts to change the Indian have broken him economically and spiritually.

"We have proposed in opposition to such a policy to recognize and respect the Indian as he is. We think he must be so accepted before he can be assisted to become something else, if that is desirable. It is objected that we are proposing to make a 'blanket Indian' of him again. That is nonsense. But if he happens to be a blanket Indian we think he should not be ashamed of it. We believe further that while he needs protection and assistance in important ways, these aids should be extended with the idea of enabling him to help himself. We are sure that he can and will do this. But he must have the opportunity to do it in his own way. This is what we have been trying to extend to him. It is an oppor-

A Cherokee Woman Recalls the Depression Years

I was born in 1920 in Claremore, Oklahoma, and I went to the public schools with my seven brothers and sisters. My father was a farmer, and my family always had a member on the tribal government. . . .

By 1934 I was in high school and working hard to graduate. A lot of Indians went to that high school . . . but no issue was made of it. They "painted us white." The Indian world knew who we were, and the white world knew who we were, and we just didn't get out of line. We dressed white and acted white and did everything we could to give up the Indian culture.

My father tried to teach us about our ways . . . not my mother . . . she was too frightened. You know she went to Carlisle Indian School when Jim Thorpe [the Sauk-Fox football, track, and baseball star often hailed as the greatest all-around athlete in U.S. history] was there, and she was punished for speaking Cherokee. I used to try to get her to teach my younger sisters and brothers, and she would not. "I would not want to see them punished," she would say.

. . . My father would not take government handouts during the Depression. He was mad at the government because of their broken treaties. I remember my father . . . because of a bad snowstorm . . . going out with his legs wrapped in gunnysacks to kill rabbits with a stick. We ate them baked or fried as long as the fat lasted. Then it was gone, and finally the corn and flour, as well.

My father loved to tell stories; this is also a big part of our Indian culture. In the evening when the work was done and he felt like talking, he would retell the legends. But he could tease, too. I remember he told about this family—a family much like ours—with eight children who were hungry and the food was gone and a storm was on . . . they had nothing to eat but shoe soup. So they found the newest pair of shoes and they boiled them, carefully taking out the shoestrings because there were no nutrients in cotton fibers. They boiled the shoes and spooned out the shoe soup.

Now in Indian stories they leave spaces so the listener can fill in. I filled in that story: I got up and hid my new shoes—my only pair of shoes. Then I brought back my brother's shoes. How they laughed and teased, about how much I wanted to eat my brother's shoe soup.

—Sarah Hutchinson

FROM AN INDIAN PAINTING ON ELKSKIN · GREAT PLAINS

INDIAN COURT
FEDERAL BUILDING
GOLDEN GATE INTERNATIONAL EXPOSITION
SAN FRANCISCO 1939

The resurgent democratic values of the 1930s produced a great revival of interest in folk culture, particularly that of Native Americans, that was both reflected in and stimulated by the WPA arts projects. This WPA poster promotes a 1939 exhibit of Indian art in San Francisco.

tunity that he has not had since he entered the reservations, where he has been discouraged from thinking and acting for himself.

". . . Our design is to plow up the Indian soul, to make the Indian again the master of his own mind. If this fails, everything fails; if it succeeds, we believe the Indian will do the rest." . . .

The people whom the commissioner is trying to reanimate, and to incite to this crusade for self-survival, are in one sense heterogeneous. There is no typical Indian but rather a hundred different types. These are scattered. The 230 tribes that comprise the race are to be found here and there in twenty-two States. They are of many different stocks physically and they speak dozens of different languages.

Their cultures vary, and so does the degree to which they have adopted the white man's ways. . . .

Underneath all their differences lie identical, unifying instincts, habits, aptitudes and spiritual feelings. Fine qualities are to be observed in almost any Indian group: artistic cleverness, tenacity, courage, dignity, and a decent pride. Under the parochial control of the past, with its effort to make the Indian a white man, these qualities have shown but little. They have come out best where the Indian, as in the Southwest, has lived his own life. . . .

The new policy has already started a renaissance in Indian arts. Young Indians are painting murals on the walls of school houses and government buildings. They are studying the ancient pottery of their tribes in museums, and devising new designs and textures in their workshops. The young people are flocking to the ceremonial dances, which for a time they had avoided. This cultural revival goes hand in hand with an interest in self-government and economic independence. In Mr. Collier's opinion, it is equally valuable.

"The Indian," he says, "can use white technologies and remain an Indian. Modernity and white Americanism are not identical. If the Indian life is a good life, then we should be proud and glad to have this different and native culture going on by the side of ours. Anything less than to let Indian culture live on would be a crime against the earth itself. The destruction of a pueblo is a barbarous thing. America is coming to understand this, and to know that in helping the Indian to save himself we are helping to save something that is precious to us as well as to him."

Getting By

In the following interview (around 1969) with radio host and author Studs Terkel, Clifford Burke, a 68-year-old retiree and volunteer in Chicago, provides insight into the effects of the depression on African Americans.

The Negro was born in depression. It didn't mean too much to him, The Great American Depression, as you call it. There was no such thing. The best he could be is a janitor or a porter or shoeshine boy. It only became official when it hit the white man. If you can tell me the difference between the depression today and the Depression of 1932 for a black man, I'd like to know it. Now, it's worse, because of the prices. Know the rents they're payin' out here? I hate to tell ya.

We had one big advantage. Our wives, they could go to the store and get a bag of beans or a sack of flour and a piece of fat meat, and they could cook this. And we could eat it. Steak? A steak would kick in my stomach like a mule in a tin stable. Now you take the white fella, he couldn't do this. His wife would tell him: Look, if you can't do any better than this, I'm gonna leave you. I seen it happen. He couldn't stand bringing home beans instead of steak and capon. And he couldn't stand the idea of going on relief like a Negro.

You take a fella had a job paying him $60, and here I am making $25. If I go home taking beans to me wife, we'll eat it. It isn't exactly what we want, but we'll eat it. The white man that's been making big money, he's taking beans home, his wife'll say: Get out. (Laughs.)

Why did these big wheels kill themselves? They weren't able to live up to the standards they were accustomed to, and they got ashamed in front of their women. You see, you can tell anybody a lie, and he'll agree with you. But you start layin' down the facts of real life, he won't accept it. The American white man has been superior so long, he can't figure out why he should come down.

I remember a friend of mine, he didn't know he was a Negro. I mean he acted like he never knew it. He got tied downtown with some stock. He blew about twenty thousand. He came home and drank a bottle of poison. A

This Scene in the Negro Quarter of Atlanta, taken by Walker Evans in 1936, makes no attempt at putting a positive face on the conditions under which most African Americans lived, whether or not the rest of the country was experiencing a depression.

A Plea against Racism

Marion Ark
Feb 3, 1935

Pres Roosevelt
of Washington DC

Dear sir if every eny body need you we poor peoples need you here at marion we are all sufing mody bad the drauf [drought] come and cut off the corn and white peoples took all the cotton and wont give us a day work at in the marion cort House mrs miller and mrs nomen and mr mace ant doing nottien for the poor negores at all wont give them no work and just robing the Govement and mr abry Kooser is roobing all the negroes one the farm he wont furnish the peoples untell the last of april and the wont furnish nothen but a little som-tom to eat and dont car how large your family is he just you 2 sack of flour and one sack of meal and 8 lbs of lard for weeks if you got 13 in family that is what he give dont even gave a rag of clothen and shoes. and all of his peoples that is got large family has made from 11 to 17 bales of cotton and come out in deat over 300 hirndraw dellers in dat. you aught send a man around one his farm just talk with his negores and see how they is suffen and that money all the otheres white men has pay thay negroes he did not gives his negroes but 5 dollers and mad them sine on the second day of this month and told all that dident sine to give him his house and move please send a man here one orbry Kooser plase at marion ark and dont send the letter back here he will have every negro on his place put in jail please come here at marion ark and helpe the poor negrous and stop them peoples at the cort house frome Robing the govment dont send this back here do these white peoples will kill all the negroes in marion some of us have been here one this man place fore 10 to 17 years and all over 3 hundrew dollars in deat yet

bottle of iodine or something like that. It was a rarity to hear a Negro killing himself over a financial situation. He might have killed himself over some woman. Or getting in a fight. But when it came to the financial end of it, there were so few who had anything. (Laughs.)

I made out during that . . . Great Depression. (Laughs.) Worked as a teamster for a lumber yard. Forty cents an hour. Monday we'd have a little work. They'd say come back Friday. There wasn't no need to look for another job. The few people working, most all of them were white.

So I had another little hustle. I used to play pool pretty good. And I'd ride from poolroom to poolroom on this bicycle. I used to beat these guys, gamble what we had. I'd leave home with a dollar. First couple of games I could beat this guy, I'd put that money in my pocket. I'd take the rest of what I beat him out of and hustle the day on that. Sometimes I'd come home with a dollar and half extra. That was a whole lot of money. Everybody was out trying to beat the other guy, so he could make it. It was pathetic.

I never applied for PWA or WPA 'cause as long as I could hustle, there was no point in beating the other fellow out of a job, cuttin' some other guy out.

The Mexican-American Dream

During the 1920s, Mexican immigrants had often been brought into the United States as contract laborers. They were lured from their homes, as so many earlier immigrants from many lands had been, by promises of "big money." As this folk song indicates, these promises were hollow, especially after the depression began, and many Mexicans decided to return home.

El Enganchado (The Hooked One)

Desde Morelia vine enganchado
ganar los dólars fué mi ilusión
compré zapatos, compré
    sombrero
y hasta me puse de pantalón.

Pues me decían que aquí los
    dólars
se pepenaban y de a montón

que las muchachas y que los
   teatros
y que aquí todo era vacilón.

Ahora me encuentro ya sin
   resuello . . .

Ya estoy cansado de esta tonteada
yo me devuelvo para Michoacán
hay de recuerdo dejo a la vieja
a ver si alguno se la quiere armar.

[I came under contract from
   Morelia
To earn dollars was my dream
I bought shoes and I bought a
   hat
And even put on trousers.

For they told me that here the
   dollars
Were scattered about in heaps;
That there were girls and
   theaters
And that here everything was
   good fun.

Now I'm overwhelmed . . .

I am tired of all this nonsense
I'm going back to Michoacán
As a parting memory I leave the
   old woman
To see if someone else wants to
   burden himself.]

While some Mexican Americans chose to return to their native land when they found conditions unsatisfactory in the United States, many more were forced out in "repatriation" programs designed to open jobs for "real" Americans (that is, Anglos). What follows is a 1931 publicity release for one such "repatriation" effort in Los Angeles.

Russell Lee photographed these Mexican-American pecan workers in a San Antonio union hall in 1939. Earlier in the decade, many people of Mexican extraction (theoretically only those who were not citizens of the United States, but in fact including some citizens) were sent across the border to create job opportunities for "real Americans."

Incident to the present unemployment conditions, official Washington is deeply concerned over the number of aliens now in the United States, illegally, who are holding jobs that rightfully should be available to those having a legal status here; and also over the number of aliens now abroad, who will no doubt seek entry to this country if some additional barriers are not placed in the way of their coming.

Legislation is now before Congress for consideration, looking not only to a complete cessation of immigration for a period of at least two years, but also to the appropriation of sufficient funds to render possible the immediate deportation of aliens who are now here without a legal status.

Los Angeles authorities concerned in Unemployment Relief have wired Secretary Doak, Department of Labor, for help from the surrounding districts. The plan is that trained members of the Immigration Department's Deportation Squad in Nogales, San Francisco, and San Diego be sent to Los Angeles to cooperate with Mr. W. E. Carr, Chief of the Immigration Service here. These men should be here in about ten days.

Chief R. E. Steckel of the Los Angeles Police force and Capt. Hines [W. J. Hynes, chief of the Los Angeles Police Department's controversial "Red Squad"] promise their cooperation in rounding up the deportable aliens as fast as the Immigration Department calls for them.

Sheriff Wm. Traeger in the County, in conference accompanied with his chief deputies, is very much interested that deportable aliens leave the County, and has promised that his force will be called to constructively help clean up Los Angeles County.

The status of a deportable alien is one who is in this country illegally and subject to deportation by law. These people here are of all races and nationalities. We have some aliens who are not deportable under the law.

The U.S. Immigration law is very definite and inflexible as to the status of a deportable alien and as to the methods of rejecting from the United States.

Deportable aliens include Chinese, Japanese, Europeans, Canadians, Mexicans, and in fact peoples of every nation in the world.

It so happens that many of the deportable aliens in this district are Mexicans; on the other hand, a large majority of Mexicans are not deportable. This article deals only with those who are deportable aliens.

1,200 Mexicans Return to Homeland

LOS ANGELES, Oct, 29. (AP) — Twelve hundred Mexican repatriates left today in two special trains for Juarez and Nogales. The trains were chartered by the Los Angeles County Board of Supervisors, which has aided in repatriating 1,547 others during the last few months. Between 60,000 and 80,000 Mexicans have returned to Mexico since Jan. 1, officials said, principally because of economic troubles.

—*New York Times*, October 30, 1931

Captain J. F. Lucey, Southwestern Representative of the President's Emergency Committee on Unemployment Relief, is responsible for the following:

The Mexican Government is helping greatly in the situation. They want their people to come home and stay there. They welcome them and are glad to get them back.

The Mexican Government offers to pay railroad fare from the Mexican border to their homes for any returning Mexicans who apply. They even notified their Consul to look out for unemployed Mexicans in some instances. Particularly from Dallas, Texas, the Mexican Government has paid the fare this side of the border as well as south of the Rio Grande. The action of the Mexican government has helped materially to alleviate this situation.

Mary Tsukamoto's Story

Americans of Asian ancestry, who were most numerous on the West Coast and especially in California, experienced their own brand of hardships during the depression. These are some of the recollections of a Japanese American's girlhood during the twenties and thirties.

In 1925 my father brought us from Fresno to a farm in Florin. I was ten years old. We had always attended school with Caucasian children; Fresno had been more of a melting pot, with Armenians and Italians. I'd never encountered discrimination—oh, there were embarrassing moments when people made unthinking remarks, but somehow, I didn't see it as my personal problem.

All this changed when I went to the Florin grammar school where I soon found out that everybody had a Japanese face. Of course, I spoke English but many of my classmates were aliens— their parents spoke only Japanese—and they were growing up in a strange bicultural world.

At recess they would speak Japanese. They were scolded for that, as it was bad to speak Japanese at Florin grammar school.

It's kind of hard to explain just what I felt. I remember feeling a little bit ashamed, a little bit bewildered. And at that moment I began to feel for the first time that maybe there was something the matter with me.

Many children were held in the lower grades for two years until they learned to read and write English; there was no such thing as a bilingual program then. All the teachers were Caucasian.

250,000 Mexicans Repatriated

MEXICO CITY, July 8 [1932].—More than 250,000 Mexicans have been repatriated from the United States, where they were almost starving, according to General Juan José Rios, Minister of the Interior. He appealed to all employers in Mexico to do their utmost to find work for those returned, the majority of whom he says are skilled operatives.

—*New York Times,* July 9, 1932

So you see, in 1929 when I graduated from the segregated school, it was quite a shock to go to the Elk Grove High School which was mixed with all kinds of people.

At the same time, I was interested in my education. Among Japanese families, education is important. My parents felt they had suffered by missing their education in Japan because of poverty. My father felt a powerful need to educate his children and was always willing to give us a lot of time to study although he had to work even harder on our strawberry farm.

To be fair, I think the teachers tried their best to involve us in high school activities. They encouraged us and yet we were shy. I felt inadequate. I tried to go to the class parties and things, but it was hard. I was always aware that I was Japanese.

Of course, I was especially aware of the people who didn't care for Japanese, as you could sense they didn't want us there—even some teachers—so we were careful not to tread on anybody's toes. I was always apologetic about being around.

We knew of the Depression. It became harder and harder for my father to eke out a living. As the time approached for me to graduate, there seemed little chance that I could go on to college.

It's really a long story, but during my last years at Elk Grove I had a wonderful English teacher, Mrs. Mabel Barren. She also taught public speaking. Now, I don't know why I took public speaking, but I did. One time the assignment was to prepare an oration on California history and the best speech was to win a prize. I was told I won. I was called to the principal's office and he told me that because of my background, I'd been refused the prize by the Elk Grove Native Sons and Daughters of the Golden West.

I was innocent. I did my assignment. I had no ambition to win—no plans to be part of an oratorical contest where they didn't want me. My teacher, Mrs. Barren, was upset about all this, more shocked and hurt, I think, than I was.

But there was nothing she could do. I knew then that there would be places where I couldn't go, where doors would be closed to me.

After that, Mrs. Barren made up her mind she was going to get me into college. She went to Stockton and

In some parts of the country, especially portions of California, Americans of Asian ancestry performed the lowest levels of work and were often scapegoats for problems, much like African Americans, Native Americans, and Latinos in other areas. Dorothea Lange photographed these Filipinos working in a California lettuce field in 1935.

talked about me with Dr. Towlie Knowles at College of the Pacific, and got me a fifty dollar scholarship for my first semester. And that same spring—during Easter vacation—this wonderful woman begged and borrowed clothes from people, cut them down, and sewed a wardrobe for me. And she did that on her vacation.

Then she came home with me one day and talked with my father and got his permission for me to go to college.

I helped on the farm that summer in '33, and then went to college. Things I could major in were limited because counselors told me I wouldn't be able to find jobs in many fields. I was religious, and so I told them I would be a missionary. They agreed I could minor in that, but that I should major in social work. At that point, I really didn't know what I wanted except a college education. I was sure of that.

The college got me a job working in a home for my room and board. It was the Depression, remember, and tuition was high. But now and then there would be an anonymous gift for a worthy student. So, when my tuition was due, I would get a call from the dean's office that a gift had come which I could have. I was able to finish all but the last year of college this way.

All the time Mrs. Barren helped when she could. But she had two children of her own and her husband was sick, so things were hard on her. She came to see me every now and then. She'd find out I needed shoes and would buy me a pair. Another teacher, Miss Helen Householder, who had been my high school domestic science teacher, contributed ten dollars a month so that I would have spending money.

You know, I have always felt that if there is anything good in me, it's because women like these made it that way.

Another job at Pacific came as an NYA grant. I worked in the infirmary for forty cents an hour, dusting furniture and sweeping rooms. It was a doctor there who first discovered my arthritis when I was nineteen.

COP was a wonderful learning experience for me. And for the first time I became involved in student activities. During my sophomore year, I discovered interpretive dancing; and the class really made me feel welcome. I would wear my kimono and interpret Japanese dance for them. I think I contributed to their appreciation of Japanese culture.

There were many warm friends I made there, and my wonderful teachers helped to heal the wounds.

My father had a farm in southern California. I remember the *Grapes of Wrath* kind of people. They used to work for us, pick crops. It amazed me. They'd say, "Let the Jap boy count it." They'd come in from the fields, and I'd tally up the totals for the day. I'd weigh them on the scale. I didn't feel I was qualified. I was just a little kid. But I could count. They would honor my counting. It was a tremendous trust. It seems the less affluent you are, the more you are able to trust people, the more you are able to give to others.

—Kiko Konagamitsu, interviewed by Studs Terkel

Chapter Ten

Down on the Farm
The Rural Depression

The experiences of the depression by rural Americans differed in some important respects from those of their urban counterparts. In one regard, many of those living on farms were better off. They could grow at least some of their own food and so survive without much cash income. But other factors greatly reduced this seeming advantage. The land of many small farmers was heavily mortgaged. Others were tenants or sharecroppers and had no legal claim to their land. When deeply indebted farmers could not meet their mortgage payments, they were likely to be forced off their land. Even when they had a successful crop, farmers could not obtain good prices for their products because the supply exceeded the demand created by consumers. In addition to all this, weather conditions in much of the country combined with the depression to make it impossible for farmers to continue their way of life. The worst drought in the recorded history of the United States gripped the Great Plains and parts of the South during the depression years, transforming vast areas of formerly bountiful farmland into a gigantic dust bowl.

Rebellion in the Corn Belt

Seeing overproduction as a major source of their problems, some farmers formed organizations, such as the Farmers' Holiday Association, designed to raise the prices farmers received by decreasing the supply of farm products. Other farmers helped each other by organizing "penny auctions," in which groups of armed farmers would come to the auction of a dispossessed farmer's land,

Grant Wood's American Gothic (1930) is one of the best-known of American paintings. Casual observers often mistake it as a tribute to hard-working farm families. A more careful look reveals it to be a pointed critique of what Wood saw as the narrow-minded, puritanical intolerance of many rural and small-town Americans. In that sense, it runs against the trend in the depression of celebrating community in the face of hardship, often thought of during the 30s as the essence of small-town life.

throw a rope with a noose on the end over a beam or tree limb, and intimidate all in attendance so that no one would bid more than a penny (or a similarly tiny sum); the land would then be returned to the previous owner. In the following 1932 article, journalist Mary Heaton Vorse describes some of the activities of organized farmers in Iowa.

Suddenly the papers were filled with accounts of highway picketing by farmers around Sioux City. A Farmers' Holiday Association had been organized by one Milo Reno, and the farmers were to refuse to bring food to market for thirty days or "until the cost of production had been obtained."

"We have issued an ultimatum to the other groups of society," they proclaimed. "If you continue to confiscate our property and demand that we feed your stomachs and clothe your bodies we will refuse to function. We don't ask people to make implements, cloth, or houses at the price of degradation, bankruptcy, dissolution, and despair."

Reno, their first leader, was crying to them, "Agriculture as we know it has come to a parting of the ways. We will soon have no individually owned and operated farms. We have come to the place where you must practice what every other group does—strike! Or else you're not going to possess your homes."

This is literally true. In no group of farmers can you find anyone who is secure, and this is what has brought the farmers out to the roads and into action. . . .

As farmers faced the impossible situation of the prices their crops could fetch on the market being lower than what it cost to produce them, the Farmers' Holiday Association attempted to force prices up by declaring a farmer's "holiday"—withholding their produce from the market until prices rose to a level at which they could make enough to survive. Members of the association, like these in Iowa in 1932, blocked highways to prevent trucks carrying farm products from reaching markets.

Like industrial workers, many American farmers saw concerted action with others in their occupation as the only way to combat an economic system that seemed to have failed them. In many cases they saw a higher law applying that superseded their customary adherence to federal, state, and local laws. Nooses hang ominously at this 1936 "penny auction," reminding anyone tempted to make a bid that would deprive the foreclosed farm family of their livelihood what the consequences for the bidder might be.

Highway No. 20, leading to Sioux City, has been the scene of some of the sharpest clashes between deputies and farmers. It has won itself the proud name of "Bunker Hill 20." On the night we visited No. 20 a score of men were sitting round a campfire. A boy was sprawled out on an automobile cushion asleep. Everyone was in overalls. Their sunburned faces shone red in the firelight.

A lamp in a smaller tent glowed in the darkness. A trestle table stood near at hand. The Ladies' Aid bring substantial meals to the picketers. The irregular circle round the fire, the high moonlit poplar trees, the lighted tent were like a stage set for a play. There was an air of immense earnestness about the farmers. They had been swung completely out of their usual orbit, but they are absolutely sure of the righteousness of their cause. An old man with white mustache said:

"They say blockading the highway's illegal. I say's, 'Seems to me there was a Tea-party in Boston that was illegal too. What about destroying property in Boston Harbor when our country was started?'" He sets the note of the evening.

"If we farmers go down bankrupt," says one of the younger men, "everything in this country goes down. If we get enough to live on, everybody's going to go to work again."

"When we can't buy," says another, "there can't be any prosperity. We ain't been buying nothing, not for four years."

"My binder's fallen apart so, don't know how I'm going to get through this year." The conversation moves slowly from one man to another with quiet deliberation. There is a cry:

This song by Bob Miller captures the farmers' economic dilemma: the prices they received for their crops were much lower than those they had to pay for other necessities.

Seven Cent Cotton and Forty Cent Meat

Seven cent cotton and forty cent meat.
How in the world can a poor man eat?
Flour up high and cotton down low;
How in the world can we raise the dough?
Clothes worn out, Shoes run down,
Old slouch with a hole in the crown.
Back nearly broken and fingers all sore,
Cotton gone down to rise no more.

Seven cent cotton and forty cent meat.
How in the world can a poor man eat?
Mules in the barn, no crops laid by,
Corn crib empty and the cow's gone dry.
Well water low, nearly out of sight,
Can't take a bath on Saturday night.
No use talking, any man is beat
With seven cent cotton and forty cent meat

Seven cent cotton and eight dollar pants,
Who in the world has got a chance?
We can't buy clothes and we can't buy meat,
Too much cotton and not enough to eat.
Can't help each other, what shall we do?
I can't explain it so it's up to you.
Seven cent cotton and two dollar hose,
Guess we'll have to do without any clothes.

Seven cent cotton and forty cent meat.
How in the world can a poor man eat?
Poor getting poorer all around here,
Kids coming regular every year.
Fatten our hogs, take 'em to town,
All we get is six cents a pound.
Very next day we have to buy it back,
Forty cents a pound in a paper sack.

"Truck!"

They hurry out in the roadway. All of them carry heavy stakes, some made from axe handles. None of them is armed, though a young fellow pointed to a little mound of quarter bricks.

"Plenty of Irish confetti," he said cheerily. Beside the road, handy to use, are heavy spiked logs and planks bristling with spikes to throw in front of trucks. The truck is empty. There is a short conference. The truck passes on its way.

"Good-night, boys," calls the driver. "Good luck!" He is one of them, part of the movement that is just beginning to realize its power. We go back to the fire. . . .

As we went from picket line to picket line the talk harked back continually to 1776 when other farmers blockaded the highways. Up in James they had a "battle" with deputies last Wednesday. They liken it to a revolutionary battle. Over in Stevens in South Dakota, across the Missouri to Nebraska, we find similar groups of farmers who talk of "revolution." These farmers feel that they have a historic mission. The word "revolution" occurs often among them, but what they mean is a farmers' revolt. They do not understand revolution in the communist sense. They think of themselves as fighting the banking interests of the East or the "international bankers" about whom they are perpetually talking.

They have sat still for years and seen prices of food and animals which they raised slide down the hill to ruin. The bread lines in the cities grew, and the number of unemployed swelled to millions while their fruit rotted on the ground because there was no market for it. Now they are out to do something about it.

To them the solution of this evil situation seems simplicity and sense itself. In the slow shift of their talk there are no threats, there is no braggadocio.

These farmers who sat around campfires picketing highways, who came miles to meetings, have the serenity of faith. They feel the certainty and power of a young, vital movement, American and militant.

"Dust Bowl Diary"

As drought enveloped the nation's midsection, plants and animals alike died for lack of water, and the parched earth was swept up in huge, swirling dust storms that literally blackened the sky and made day seem like night. In her diary, Ann Marie Low describes the effects of this ecological disaster on her family in North Dakota.

The dust bowl was the subject of many of the most memorable of the Farm Security Administration photographs. This one that Arthur Rothstein took during a dust storm in Cimarron County, Oklahoma, in 1936 is one of the most striking images of the decade.

April 25, 1934, Wednesday

Last weekend was the worst dust storm we ever had. We've been having quite a bit of blowing dirt every year since the drought started, not only here, but all over the Great Plains. Many days this spring the air is just full of dirt coming, literally, for hundreds of miles. It sifts into everything. After we wash the dishes and put them away, so much dust sifts into the cupboards we must wash them again before the next meal. Clothes in the closets are covered with dust.

Last weekend no one was taking an automobile out for fear of ruining the motor. I road Roany to Frank's place to return a gear. To find my way I had to ride right beside the fence, scarcely able to see from one fence post to the next.

Newspapers say the death of many babies and old people are attributed to breathing in so much dirt.

May 7, 1934, Monday

The dirt is still blowing. Last weekend Bud [her brother] and I helped with the cattle and had fun gathering weeds. Weeds give us greens for salad long before anything in the garden is ready. We use dandelions, lamb's quarter, and sheep sorrel. I like sheep sorrel best. Also, the leaves of sheep sorrel, pounded and boiled down to a paste, make a good salve. . . .

May 21, 1934, Monday

. . . Saturday, Dad, Bud and I planted an acre of potatoes. There was so much dirt in the air I couldn't see Bud only a few feet in front of me. Even the air in the house was just a haze. In the evening the wind died down, and Cap came to take me to the movie. We joked about how hard it is to get cleaned up enough to go anywhere.

Painters as well as photographers and songwriters found the awesome natural and human disaster of the dust bowl to be a rich source of material for their art. The title of this 1936 painting by Joe Jones, juxtaposed with what it depicts, says a great deal about agricultural conditions in the 30s: Ameri-can Farm.

The newspapers report that on May 10 there was such a strong wind the experts in Chicago estimated 12,000,000 tons of Plains soil was dumped on that city. By the next day the sun was obscured in Washington, D.C., and ships 300 miles out of sea reported dust settling on their decks.

Sunday the dust wasn't so bad. Dad and I drove cattle to the Big Pasture. Then I churned butter and baked a ham, bread, and cookies for the men, as no telling when Mama will be back.

May 30, 1934, Wednesday

Ethel got along fine, so Mama left her at the hospital and came to Jamestown by train Friday. Dad took us both home.

The mess was incredible! Dirt had blown into the house all week and lay inches deep on everything. Every towel and curtain was just black. There wasn't a clean dish or cooking utensil. There was no food. Oh, there were eggs and milk and one loaf left of the bread I baked the weekend before. I looked in the cooler box down the well (our refrigerator) and found a little ham and butter. It was so late, so Mama and I cooked some ham and eggs for the men's supper because that was all we could fix in a hurry. It turned out they had been living on ham and eggs for two days.

Mama was very tired. After she fixed starter for bread, I insisted she go to bed and I'd do all the dishes.

It took until 10 o'clock to wash all the dirty dishes. That's not wiping them—just washing them. The cupboards had to be washed out to have a clean place to put them.

Saturday was a busy day. Before starting breakfast I had to sweep and wash all the dirt off the kitchen and dining room floors, wash the stove, pancake griddle, and dining room table and chairs. There was cooking, baking, and churning to be done for those hungry men. Dad is 6 feet 4 inches tall, with a big frame. Bud is 6 feet 3 inches and almost a big-boned as Dad. We say feeding them is like filling a silo.

Mama couldn't make bread until I carried water to wash the bread mixer. I couldn't churn until the churn was washed and scalded. We just couldn't do anything until something was washed first. Every room had to have dirt almost shoveled out of it before we could wash floors and furniture.

We had no time to wash clothes, but it was necessary. I had to wash out the boiler, wash tubs, and the washing machine before we could use them. Then every towel, curtain, piece of bedding, and garment had to be taken outdoors to have as much dust as possible shaken out before washing. The cistern is dry, so I had to carry all the water we needed from the well.

That evening Cap came to take me to the movie, as usual. Ixnay. I'm sorry I snapped at Cap. It isn't his fault, or anyone's fault, but I was tired and cross. Life in what the newspapers call "the Dust Bowl" is becoming a gritty nightmare.

Woody Guthrie on the Dust Bowl

Woody Guthrie, one of America's greatest songwriters, came to be a chief spokesman for the plight of dust bowl victims from his native Oklahoma and other areas. The following two songs are good examples of Guthrie's ability to convey a social message through music.

Goin' Down This Road (I Ain't Going to Be Treated This Way)

I'm blowin' down this old dusty road;
Yes I'm blowin' down this old dusty road;
I'm blowin' down this old dusty road, Lord, God,
And I ain'ta gonna be treated this a way.

Lost my farm down in old Oklahoma,
Lost my farm down in old Oklahoma,

Lost my farm down in old Oklahoma, Lord, Lord,
And I ain'ta gonna be treated this a way.

I'm a going where them dust storms never blow,
I'm a going where these dust storms never blow,
I'm a going where these dust storms never blow,
  Lord, Lord,
And I ain'ta gonna be treated this a way.

They say I'm a dust bowl refugee
They say I'm a dust bowl refugee
They say I'm a dust bowl refugee, Lord, Lord,
And I ain'ta gonna be treated this a way.

I'm a lookin' for a job at honest pay
I'm a lookin' for a job at honest pay
I'm a lookin' for a job at honest pay, Lord, Lord,
And I ain'ta gonna be treated this a way.

Takes a ten dollar shoe to fit my feet,
Takes a ten dollar shoe to fit my feet,
Takes a ten dollar shoe to fit my feet, Lord, Lord,
And I ain'ta gonna be treated this a way.

Your two dollar shoe hurts my feet,
Your two dollar shoe hurts my feet,
Your two dollar shoe hurts my feet, Lord, Lord,
And I ain'ta gonna be treated this a way.

I'm a goin' where them grapes and peaches grow,
I'm a goin' where them grapes and peaches grow,
I'm a goin' where them grapes and peaches grow,
  Lord, Lord,
And I ain'ta gonna be treated this a way.

I been living on cold navy beans,
I been living on cold navy beans,
I been living on cold navy beans, Lord, Lord,
And I ain'ta gonna be treated this a way.

Although he never became nearly as well known nation-ally, black farmer John L. Handcox of Arkansas spoke for rural southerners in the same way that Woody Guthrie spoke for the "Okies." This song expresses the troubles of depression-era farmers in simple but powerful terms.

Hungry, Hungry Are We

Hungry, hungry are we
Just as hungry as hungry can be,
We don't get nothin for our labor,
So hungry, hungry are we.
Raggedy, raggedy are we
Just as raggedy as raggedy can be,
We don't get nothin for our labor,
So raggedy, raggedy are we.

Homeless, homeless are we
Just as homeless as homeless can be,
We don't get nothin for our labor,
So homeless, homeless are we.

Landless, landless are we
Just as landless as landless can be,
We don't get nothin for our labor,
So landless, landless are we.

So Long, It's Been Good To Know Yuh (Dusty Old Dust)

I've sung this song but I'll sing it again,
Of the place that I lived on the wild windy plains.
In the month called April, the county called Gray,
And here's what all of the people there say:

Chorus:
So long, it's been good to know ye,
So long, it's been good to know ye,
So long, it's been good to know ye,
This dusty old dust is a getting my home,
and I've got to be drifting along.
(Repeat after each verse)

A dust storm hit and it hit like thunder;
It dusted us over, it covered us under;
blocked out the traffic, it blocked out the sun.
straight for home all the people did run
singing:

We talked of the end of the world and then
We'd sing a song and then sing it again;
We'd sit for an hour and not say a word,
And then these words would be heard:

The sweethearts sat in the dark and they sparked.
They hugged and kissed in that dusty old dark.
They sighed and cried, and hugged and kissed,
Instead of marriage they talked like this: Honey

Now, the telephone rang and it jumped off the wall;
That was the preacher a-making his call.
He said, "Kind friend, this may be the end,
You've got your last chance at salvation of sin":

The churches was jammed, the churches was packed,
And that dusty old dust storm blowed so black;
The preacher could not read a word of his text;
And he folded his specs, and he took up collection, said:

*Ben Shahn's 1936 gouache painting
Dust, created to promote the New
Deal's Resettlement Administration,
captures the human toll of the drought.*

Chapter Eleven

Art for the Millions

Culture in the Thirties

Cultural creations—especially in the realm of popular culture—always reflect, in one way or another, the time and place in which they are brought to life. Certainly this is true of culture in the United States during the Great Depression. The economic crisis and its moral meaning, the viability and morality of a profit-based economy, social values—these and many related themes and questions were the steady fare of depression-era cultural works.

It is an ill wind, they say, that blows no one some good, and the ill wind of economic collapse blew much good for American artists. "The Depression offered a bonanza for art and literature," as historian David Peeler has said. "Subjects were everywhere . . . scores of injustices needed rebuking." As artists were attacking greed and injustice, many of them were celebrating the revival of community spirit and the fortitude of the poor in the face of hardship.

Art in the United States in the 1930s was art with which the general public could readily identify. It was self-consciously "American"—so much so that the major art movement of the decade was called "the American Scene." The two most prominent genres within the American Scene were social realism and regionalism. Both favored more realistic depictions of people and things over the modernist trend towards abstraction. The problems in the depression as experienced by its victims were, after all, not abstract. Both expressed sympathy and respect for "the people." Yet when it came to portrayals of working people, the "realism" of many of these artists looks more like idealism, as can be seen in many of the examples of painting and sculpture throughout this book.

Thomas Hart Benton was one of the greatest American artists of the 20th century. His distinctive stylized human figures are evident in this panel, Steel. *Respect for the "common man" and glorification of industrial labor frequently appear in depression-era art.*

It may seem curious that the newly introduced board game Monopoly became a national craze in the midst of the Great Depression. The fact that a game whose object was to become "filthy rich" while putting all the other players into bankruptcy would catch on during hard times might suggest that many Americans had not abandoned the acquisitive attitudes of the 1920s. On the other hand, neither the riches nor the bankruptcies were real, and the game provided a great deal of fun and harmless diversion from the harsh realities of the decade.

Superman: New Deal Hero

First conceived in 1933 by Jerry Siegel and Joe Shuster, two 19-year-olds living in Cleveland, Superman finally made his public debut in 1938. As the selection reprinted here indicates, Superman was a champion of oppressed workers, racial minorities (in other early stories he stopped lynchings), and the downtrodden in general. He had no use for greedy businessmen. The comic-book Superman is nearly the opposite of Friedrich Nietzsche's 19th-century *Übermensch,* a concept translated into English as "superman." Whereas Nietzsche uses the term to describe someone with a will to power, Siegel and Shuster's Superman really is a "super mensch," in the Yiddish sense of the term—a generous individual who is always willing to "do the right thing" for others. Their Superman is, at the least, a New Deal liberal, a character who embodies the social values that were ascendent during the depression years. *Batman,* which debuted a year later, parallels Franklin Roosevelt even more, since he is a wealthy heir who takes on a different persona to fight for justice.

In this episode, Clark Kent is sent to report on a miner trapped by a cave-in. Superman rushes to the site, disguises himself as a miner, intentionally falls into the shaft, and rescues the miner. In the process, he discovers that safety devices in the mine do not work. The next day, as Kent, he interviews the mine owner:

Disguised again as a miner, Superman goes to the estate of the mine owner, where a party for very rich people is in progress. He is seized as a trespasser and the owner is about to have him thrown out when he gets an inspiration. He has the miner take him and his guests into the mine to continue the party there. Superman pulls out the tunnel supports, causing a cave-in that traps the wealthy revelers. They start to panic and the owner remembers the safety devices to call for help. Of course they do not work. The party guests start digging, quickly becoming exhausted. Finally, the mine owner says, "Oh, if I only had this to do over again!—I never knew— really knew—what the men down here have to face!" Hearing this, Superman slips away and clears the way out of the mine. When Kent again visits the mine owner, he has reformed:

Little Orphan Annie *presented comic readers with a somewhat different view of the rich from that seen in the greedy men against whom Superman often struggled. Unlike many businessmen who had risen from the lower ranks of society, Daddy Warbucks continued to identify with the common people. Yet Annie herself had run-ins with forces of evil, such as cheating businessmen, gangsters, crooked politicians, and fascists, almost as often as Superman did.*

Joe Louis Uncovers Dynamite

Music, like art, is prominently featured throughout this book, and we have frequently seen its connection with the mood of the times. "On the Sunny Side of the Street" is another example of the striving for optimism that prevailed during the early years of the depression. This popular song was written in 1930 by Dorothy Fields, with music by Jimmy McHugh.

On the Sunny Side of the Street

Grab your coat, and get your hat
Leave your worry on the doorstep
Just direct your feet
To the sunny side of the street—
Can't you hear a pitter-pat?
And that happy tune is your step
Life can be so sweet
On the sunny side of the street,

I used to walk in the shade
With those blues on parade
But I'm not afraid
This Rover crossed over,

If I never have a cent
I'll be rich as Rockefeller
Gold dust at my feet
On the sunny side of the street.

Sports were a very important part of American popular culture during the depression. Many of the great names of that era are still widely known today: Lou Gehrig, Mel Ott, Hank Greenberg, and Dizzy Dean in baseball; Knute Rockne, Sammy Baugh, and Red Grange in football; and many others.

But it was also during the thirties that sports began to play a larger role as a reformer, as well as reflector, of society. The impact of sports on race relations, for example, has been larger than many Americans realize. This was especially true in the late 1940s, when Jackie Robinson integrated major league baseball. But the process began with two key figures in the 1930s. When track star Jesse Owens won four gold medals at the Berlin Olympics in 1936, he did more than upset Adolf Hitler and his racist doctrines. He also inspired white Americans to cheer for a black athlete and treat him as a hero.

This phenomenon was even more evident in the case of longtime heavyweight boxing champion Joe Louis. In his two fights with the German Max Schmeling (a loss in 1936 and a one-round knockout in 1938), white American fight fans were obliged to choose between backing a black American or a white German. To be sure, the admiration expressed for Owens and Louis had little tangible effect on white attitudes toward blacks in general, but it did begin a process of change that would gather new momentum after World War II.

As the following 1935 article by Richard Wright makes clear, Louis's effect on African Americans was electrifying. The article was written for the Communist magazine *New Masses*, and at its conclusion Wright attempts (with limited success) to place the racial feelings he is describing in a class context.

"Wun-tuh-three-fooo-fiiive-seex-seven-eight-niine-thuun!" Then:"JOE LOUIS—THE WINNAH!"

On Chicago's South side five minutes after these words were yelled, and Joe Louis' hand was hoisted as victor in his four-round go with Max Baer, Negroes poured out of beer taverns, pool rooms, barber shops, rooming houses and dingy flats and flooded the streets.

"LOUIS! LOUIS! LOUIS!" they yelled and threw their hats away. They snatched newspapers from the stands of astonished Greeks and tore them up, flinging the bits into the air. They wagged their heads. Lawd, they'd never seen or heard the like of it before. They shook the hands of strangers. They clapped one another on the back. It was like a revival. Really, there was a religious feeling in the air. Well, it wasn't exactly a religious feeling, but it was *something*, and you could feel it. It was a feeling of unity, of oneness.

Two hours after the fight the area between South Parkway and Prairie Avenue on 47th Street was jammed with no less than twenty-five thousand Negroes, joy-mad and moving to they didn't know where. Clasping hands, they formed long writhing snake-lines and wove in and out of traffic. They seeped out of doorways, oozed from alleys, trickled out of tenements, and flowed down the street; a fluid mass of joy. White storekeepers hastily closed their doors against the tidal wave and stood peeping through plate glass with blanched faces.

Something had happened, all right. And it had happened so confoundingly sudden that the white in the neighborhood were dumb with fear. They felt—you could see it in their faces—that *something* had ripped loose, exploded. Something which they had long feared and thought was dead. Or if not dead, at least so safely buried under the pretence of good-will that they no longer had need to fear it. Where in the world did it come from? And what was worst of all, how far would it go? Say, what's got into these Negroes?

And the whites and the blacks began to *feel* themselves. The blacks began to remember all the little

Joe Louis became a hero without peer in the African-American community during the 1930s. The fact that he could punch white men, often knock them out, and get away with it gave many long-oppressed blacks enormous vicarious pleasure. Here he is shortly before his 1938 victory over Max Schmeling.

Following the example of such Mexican muralists as Diego Rivera, Federal Art Project painters produced murals in many public buildings across the country. Although this brought art to a wide public, the pro-union, leftist orientation of many of the works—such as City Life, *painted by Victor Arnautoff in San Francisco's Coit Tower, a portion of which is shown here— brought criticism from political conservatives.*

slights, and discriminations and insults they had suffered; and their hunger too and their misery. And the whites began to search their souls to see if they had been guilty of something, some time, somewhere, against which this wave of feeling was rising.

As the celebration wore on, the younger Negroes began to grow bold. They jumped on the running boards of automobiles going east or west on 47th street and demanded of the occupants:

"Who yuh fer—Baer or Louis?"

In the stress of the moment it seemed that the answer to the question marked out friend and foe.

A hesitating reply brought waves of scornful laughter. Baer, Huh? That was funny. Now, hadn't Joe Louis just whipped Max Baer? Didn't think we had it in us, did you? Thought Joe Louis was scared, didn't you? Scared because Max talked loud and made boasts. We ain't scared either. We'll fight too when the time comes. We'll win, too.

A taxicab driver had his cab wrecked when he tried to put up a show of bravado.

Then they began stopping street cars. Like a cyclone sweeping through a forest, they went through them, shouting, stamping. Conductors gave up and backed away like children. Everybody had to join in this celebration. Some of the people ran out of the cars and stood, pale and trembling, in the crowd. They felt it, too.

In the crush a pocketbook snapped open and money spilled on the street for eager black fingers.

"They stole it from us, anyhow," they said as they picked it up.

When an elderly Negro admonished them, a fist was shaken in his face. Uncle Tomming, huh?

"Whut in hell yuh gotta do wid it?" they wanted to know.

Something has popped loose, all right. And it had come from deep down. Out of the darkness it had leaped from its coil. . . .

You stand on the border-line, wondering what's beyond. Then you take one step and feel a strange, sweet tingling. You take two steps and the feeling becomes keener. You want to feel some more. You break into a run. You know it's dangerous, but you're impelled in spite of yourself.

Four centuries of oppression, of frustrated hopes, of black bitterness, felt even in the bones of the bewildered young, were rising to the surface. Yes, unconsciously they had imputed to the brawny image of Joe Louis all the balked dreams of revenge, all the secretly visualized moments of retaliation, AND HE HAD WON! Good Gawd Almighty! Yes, by Jesus, it could be done! Didn't Joe do it? You see, Joe was the consciously-felt symbol. Joe was the concentrated essence of black triumph over white. And it comes so seldom, so seldom. And what could be sweeter than long nourished hate vicariously gratified? From the symbol of Joe's strength they took strength, and in that moment all fear, all obstacles were wiped out, drowned. They stepped out of the mire of hesitation and irresolution and were free!

Invincible! A merciless victor over a fallen foe! Yes, they had felt all that—for a moment. . . .

Say, Comrade, here's the wild river that's got to be harnessed and directed. Here's that *something*, that pent up folk consciousness. Here's a fleeting glimpse of the heart of the Negro, the heart that beats and suffers and hopes—for freedom. Here's that fluid something that's like iron. Here's the real dynamite that Joe Louis uncovered!

Federal Patronage of the Arts

The following selection, taken from a 1937 *Fortune* magazine article, analyzes the success of the WPA arts projects during their first two years.

The difficulty is to judge this Project objectively. For, whatever else may be said of the government's flyer in art, one statement is incontrovertible. It has produced, one way and another, a greater human response than anything the government has done in generations. In the first fifteen months of the Federal Music Project, while orchestras were still being put together and halls arranged and programs prepared, over 50,000,000 people, not counting radio listeners, heard WPA concerts. In the first year of WPA Theatre approximately sixteen millions in thirty states saw performances, and the weekly attendance by the end of the period had reached half a million.

In the first few months of the Federal Painters' Project (The WPA Arts Project devoted to painters, sculptors, etchers, etc. is called in Washington The Federal Art Project—as though theatre, music, and writing were not also arts. For clarity that project is referred to in this article as the Painters' Project.) twenty-eight federal art

The Federal Arts Projects were enormously successful, but also highly controversial. The Art Project both presented works by its artists on relief and produced the posters to advertise such shows. Posters, which often have the purpose of swaying opinion, were among the more controversial products of the Art Project.

THE DIVISION OF WOMENS AND PROFESSIONAL PROJECTS OF THE WORKS PROGRESS ADMINISTRATION

PRESENTS

AN EXHIBITION
OF THE SKILLS OF THE UNEMPLOYED
ON NON-MANUAL PROJECTS

NATIONAL MUSEUM
10th STREET & CONSTITUTION AVENUE, N.W.
WASHINGTON D.C.

JANUARY 10th to 31st

WEEKDAYS 9:30 A.M. TO 4:30 P.M.
SUNDAYS 1:30 P.M. TO 4:30 P.M.

One of the achievements of the Federal Theatre Project was its opening, in its Harlem unit under the direction of John Houseman, of non-traditional roles to black actors. The Harlem unit's production of Voodoo Macbeth, *directed by Orson Welles, was a great hit.*

galleries and art centers were established in towns in the Carolinas, Tennessee, Alabama, Virginia, Oklahoma, Florida, Utah, Wyoming, and New Mexico where art galleries had never existed before. And by the end of the year more than a million people had attended classes in these galleries or listened to lectures or come in to look at travelling exhibits.

What the government's experiments in music, painting, and the theatre actually did, even in their first year, was to work a sort of cultural revolution in America. They brought the American audience and the American artist face to face for the first time in their respective lives. And the result was an astonishment needled with excitement such as neither the American artist nor the American audience had ever felt before. Down to the beginning of these experiments neither the American audience nor the American artist had ever guessed that the American audience existed. The American audience as the American artist saw it was a small group of American millionaires who bought pictures not because they liked pictures but because the possession of certain pictures was the surest and most cheaply acquired sign of culture. Since all pictures, to qualify, must necessarily have been sold first for a high price at Christie's in London this audience did not do much for American painters.

The same thing was true of the American audience as the American composer saw it. The American audience as the American composer saw it was something called the concertgoer: a creature generally female and ordinarily about sixty years of age who . . . prided herself on never hearing anything composed more recently than 1900 or nearer than Paris, France. This audience also was little help to the American composer. From one end of the range to the other, American artists, with the partial exception of the popular novelists and the successful Broadway playwrights, wrote and painted and composed in a kind of vacuum, despising the audience they had, ignoring the existence of any other.

It was this vacuum which the Federal Arts Projects exploded. In less than a year from the time the program first got under way the totally unexpected pressure of popular interest had crushed the shell which had always isolated painters and musicians from the rest of their countrymen and the American artist was brought face to face with the true American audience. One example, the most extreme, may be taken to stand for many. A Federal Theatre Project in New York City produced in the spring of 1936 T. S. Eliot's verse play, *Murder in the Cathedral.* This play by an anglicized American poet had run for some time in a small theatre in London and was recognized by competent critics to be the first important verse play in this generation. Its excellence was in no doubt. But it was a "difficult" play in an experimental form and its verse was very far from the Broadway idea of verse for the theatre. It was almost the last play on earth any commercial producer would have brought to New York. And yet *Murder in the Cathedral* ran to crowded houses for the full term permitted by the contract and was seen by a total of over 40,000 people who paid up to fifty-five cents for the privilege. . . .

On the record of accomplishment since the fall of 1935, then, there can be little question of the general success of the Federal Arts Projects either in terms of their respective arts or in terms of their services to the public. Ford Madox Ford, an eminent British novelist and critic with a considerable knowledge of America, told New York newspapermen last fall: "Accidentally WPA has dug up an extraordinary amount of talent. The level of the work is astonishingly high. Art in America is being given its chance and there has been nothing like it since before the Reformation. . . " Erich Wolfgang Korngold, the Austrian composer, who heard WPA music units a year ago, told American musicians that "Nowhere in Europe is there anything to compare with it. Of course we have state subsidized opera but no country in Europe has anything to equal this."

On the one hand there is equally little doubt that the Arts Project cost the government $46,000,000 down to December 31, 1936—a life of about fourteen months. The question, therefore, is accurately posed. Granted that the Art Projects are good, are they that good? The answer is fairly clear. As relief projects they are very definitely that good. They have not only carried 40,000 artists but they have permitted those 40,000 artists to share in one of the most thoroughly useful and exciting jobs ever done in America. As long therefore as the number of unemployed artists remains as large as it is now there will be very little doubt in anyone's mind that the Projects should be continued.

In addition to bringing live orchestral music to numerous smaller cities that had never before had such performances available, the Federal Music Project provided instruction for aspiring young musicians, as in this violin class in 1936.

Chapter Twelve

Cinema in the Depression

Movies were a major feature of American life during the depression. The thirties were, in some respects, the Golden Age of Hollywood. At the time of the stock market crash, sound was still a novelty in movie houses, "talkies" having been introduced only two years earlier, beginning with *The Jazz Singer*. By the end of the 1930s, audiences could thrill to such color extravaganzas as *Gone with the Wind* and *The Wizard of Oz*.

Of course, the depression had an adverse financial effect on the film industry. In the early thirties ticket sales fell off sharply, and admission prices had to be lowered. (Even with the drop, however, more than 60 million tickets were bought each week in the early thirties. Movies, like automobiles and radios, had by this time come to seem a virtual necessity to most Americans—so much so that they did all they could to avoid giving them up entirely, even in hard times.) In 1934, giving in to pressure from religious groups, the movie studios established a stringent production code that enforced morality and prohibited subject matter that was deemed indecent.

By the second half of the decade, Hollywood was thriving once again. An average of some 80 million movie tickets were sold each week during the last few years of the depression.

As in earlier times, people went to movie theaters in the thirties to escape from their troubles for a couple of hours—during the depression this need was more intense than ever before. But if that was all there was to it, movies could not reveal very much about the depression and its effects on Americans' thinking and values.

In fact, a large number of 1930s films reflected the changing values of the United States under the impact of the depression. Movies during the depression were, as historian Arthur Schlesinger, Jr., once noted, "near the operative center of the nation's consciousness."

Golddiggers of 1933 was one of several musicals that became big box-office successes during the New Deal's first year. The mood of renewed hope of 1933 was reflected in these musicals as much as the total hopelessness of the preceding year had been evident in I Am a Fugitive from a Chain Gang. *In* Golddiggers, *a show is forced by the depression to close, and a new show about the depression is planned.*

Little Caesar (1930)

Gangster films became enormously popular in the early thirties. One of the best examples is Mervyn LeRoy's *Little Caesar*. In it, Caesar "Rico" Bandello, played by Edward G. Robinson, represents a completely self-centered man-on-the-make. Rico embodies the characteristics that many Americans were coming to see as typical of ruthless, ambitious businessmen of the 1920s. This is one gangster with whom audiences feel little identification. Rico even refers to his criminal activities "this business." He frequently expresses contempt for the humane, compassionate values that were coming to the fore in depression-era America, dismissing them as "love, soft stuff!"

Dracula (1931)

Whether there was any direct connection between the depression and the popularity of horror movies in the early thirties is an open question. Both James Whale's *Frankenstein* and Tod Browning's *Dracula* were released in 1931, and Ernest B. Schoedsack's *King Kong* hit theaters the following year. Whether or not one sees a link between monsters and the economic demons devouring jobs and livelihoods, it is hard to doubt that there was some connection between the impact of these movies and people's fears of powerful, mysterious forces threatening their lives. The final triumph over the evil monstrosities (in the case of *Dracula*, a bloodsucker who might be linked in some viewers' minds with the sort of businessman represented by Rico in *Little Caesar*) provided a bit of hope in a very dark time.

I Am a Fugitive from a Chain Gang (1932)

It is probable that no movie has ever better captured the mood of a particular year than Mervyn LeRoy's *I Am a Fugitive from a Chain Gang*. In the film, World War I veteran James Allen (played by Paul Muni) hopes for a better life—"a man's job"—but is unable to find work. After an acquaintance attempts to rob a diner, Allen is unjustly arrested and sentenced to 10 years of hard labor. The chain gang on which he finds himself becomes a metaphor for society in the early depression: those in power are cruel, while the inmates are basically good people who help each other. Allen escapes, changes his name, and goes on to great success. When he is betrayed by his former wife, he accepts the promise of the authorities that he will only have to serve three months of "easy time" if he will return voluntarily. It turns out that the state has lied to him (which reflects the general view of government in 1932), and he is sent back to the chain gang. After a second escape, Jim Allen is an outcast—dirty, hungry, a hunted animal unable to find work. He clearly symbolizes depression victims. At the movie's end, he is asked how he lives. He whispers from the dark, "I steal!" No happy endings here.

Gabriel over the White House (1933)

One of the most extraordinary movies made during
the depression has been largely forgotten. Prior
to Roosevelt's inauguration, publisher William
Randolph Hearst's Cosmopolitan Studios produced
a film, directed by Gregory La Cava, called *Gabriel
over the White House*. Released three days before FDR
took office, the movie presents a President, Judson
Hammond, who is an old-style, corrupt politician
with no interest in the well-being of the people.
Following a car crash that nearly (or perhaps actually) kills him, President Hammond is transformed
through divine intervention. The result is a compassionate President who embarks on a program that
eerily foreshadows the New Deal: feeding the
unemployed, creating an "Army of Construction"
much like what the WPA would become, providing
aid to farmers, and a host of other measures. But
Gabriel went far beyond the New Deal. President
Hammond also assumes dictatorial powers (for the
public good, of course) and his actions point toward
some of the events beginning to unfold with the
Nazi regime in Germany.

Our Daily Bread (1934)

Only one major movie during
the depression was completely
open in its advocacy of a collective way of life. King Vidor's *Our
Daily Bread* depicts the establishment of a cooperative farm that
takes in unemployed people
who pass by. The people on the
farm have to overcome obstacles
caused both by nature and their
own competitive ways. Vidor's
transparent purpose is to show
that cooperation works better
than competition. The movie
was praised by some (including
the League of Nations), but was
labelled as "pinko" (that is, semi-
Communist) by some papers,
including those owned by
William Randolph Hearst.

Bullets or Ballots (1936)

Hollywood's view of government changed dramatically (as did that of much of the American public) with the New Deal. By the middle of the decade, the inept, corrupt, and uncaring government of the gangster movies in the Hoover years had been replaced by an efficient, powerful government that was an effective champion of the people. Many of the "gangsters" themselves had gone over to the other side. James Cagney, who had been a hard-boiled thug in *Public Enemy* in 1931, was an FBI star in *G-Men* in 1935. Perhaps an even more striking example came the following year, when Rico himself, Edward G. Robinson, appeared as a police agent in *Bullets or Ballots*. "There is just as much excitement in law enforcement as there is in racketeering," Robinson said in the Warner Brothers press release for the movie. "The activities of G-Men in recent months have proved that."

Duck Soup (1933)

The Marx Brothers had become great favorites of movie audiences years before the release of *Duck Soup*. Here Groucho Marx, as Rufus T. Firefly, becomes the dictator of an imaginary country, Freedonia, and is totally inept and utterly self-serving. Although it was certainly one of their best and funniest films, *Duck Soup* did not go over well with audiences at the time of the early New Deal. The reason is apparent: it ridicules government and political leaders at just the moment when many Americans had had their faith in both restored by Franklin D. Roosevelt. Had *Duck Soup* been released a year earlier, while Herbert Hoover was still in the White House, it probably would have enjoyed a much friendlier reception. In 1933, most Americans were not much amused by a satirical farce in which Rufus T. Firefly could be seen as a mocking portrait of FDR.

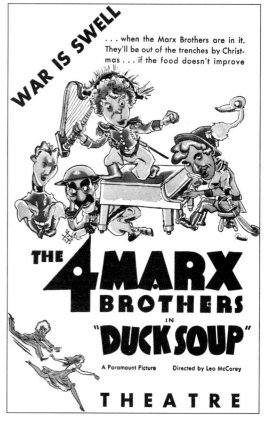

Mr. Smith Goes to Washington (1939)

Frank Capra's populist films, most notably *Mr. Deeds Goes to Town* (1936) and *Mr. Smith Goes to Washington,* struck a chord with depression-era audiences. Capra celebrated traditional small-town American values and has, therefore, often been classified as a conservative. But Capra's everyman heroes, such as Jefferson Smith—a wholesome and naive leader of a boys' club who is tapped by a political boss to be a United States senator because he will be so easy to fool—are very much opposed to the marketplace values of the business world. Jeff Smith may be an everyman, but he certainly does not embrace the "every man for himself" philosophy. Nor does Capra indicate that small-town life is necessarily good. He leaves viewers with the understanding that small-town folks can be led astray if they don't follow traditional values.

The Wizard of Oz (1939)

Although certainly regarded by generations of viewers as a delightful and entertaining piece of fantasy,
Victor Fleming's screen adaptation of L. Frank Baum's
1900 novel *The Wonderful Wizard of Oz* also carried
some serious messages for depression-era moviego-
ers. Certainly the idea that happiness was not really
to be found in the works of a wizard "somewhere
over the rainbow" but had to be worked for at home
had strong connections with the revival of community and small-town values in the depression. A
dream world to be reached through some magic
might be colorful, but in the end, there really is "no
place like home," even if home is a drab black-and-
white Kansas. That the wizard is a phoney who
achieves his illusions with smoke, mirrors, and levers
suggests a possible criticism of the Wizard of
Washington, FDR. And the ability of the lion, tin
man, and scarecrow to finally find what they are
looking for within themselves can be seen as a message in support of individualism and self-reliance.
This message is balanced by the fact that Dorothy
and her new friends must nonetheless cooperate in
order to triumph over the wicked witch.

The Grapes of Wrath (1940)

Like Frank Capra, John Ford was
a prolific champion of traditional
cooperative values. He condemned self-seeking and greed
and often (as, for example, in his
1939 film *Stagecoach*) portrayed
social outcasts as the truly good-
hearted people. Ford was the
ideal director to bring John
Steinbeck's *Grapes of Wrath* to the
screen. His film version is faithful
to the novel in most respects and
served to bring the book's powerful message and cooperative values to an even wider audience
than had been reached by
Steinbeck's best-seller.

Chapter Thirteen

The Mother and Father of the Nation?

Attitudes toward the Roosevelts

Franklin Roosevelt dominated the American scene during the depression years as few people have ever dominated any era in the nation's history. He was a polarizing figure; most people had strong feelings about him. A significant minority of Americans hated him; a far larger number loved him as no president had ever been loved, with the possible exception of Washington (for very different reasons) and Lincoln (for the most part after his death). Some of the contrasting views of FDR are evident in this chapter.

Eleanor Roosevelt was unlike any first lady who had come before her—and unlike most who have followed her. She took an active public role and expressed her opinions on controversial subjects, including racial equality. She traveled far and wide, personally investigating working conditions and the effects of New Deal programs. She became extremely controversial. Many people loved and respected her to a degree previously unknown among Presidents' wives. But many other Americans hated her. This was certainly true of most of the vehement opponents of the New Deal, who saw her as the "power behind the throne," constantly urging liberal ideas on her husband. But a significant number of New Deal supporters also disliked Mrs. Roosevelt. This was because she was carving out new roles for women and openly advocating more important positions for women in society.

Although hardly the ideal married couple in their private lives, Franklin and Eleanor Roosevelt were seen by vast numbers of Americans as the nearly ideal President and First Lady to lead the nation during the economic crisis. Here they celebrate on election night, 1932.

"Another Home Run"

Mr. Roosevelt stepped to the microphone last night and knocked another home run.

His message was not only a great comfort to the people, but it pointed a lesson to all radio announcers and public speakers [on] what to do with a big vocabulary—leave it at home in the dictionary.

Some people spend a lifetime juggling with words, with not an idea in a carload.

Our President took such a dry subject as banking—(and when I say "dry" I mean dry, for if it had been liquid he wouldn't have had to speak on it at all).

Well, he made everybody understand it, even the bankers.

Yours,
Will Rogers

—*New York Times*, March 14, 1933.

Prior to his election in 1932, Franklin Roosevelt had been dismissed by many critics as a lightweight. By 1940, when he was photographed here campaigning for an unprecedented third term, his extraordinary political and leadership skills were no longer in doubt.

Like her husband, Eleanor Roosevelt was born into the American aristocracy. Indeed, she was born into the same family. As the niece of former President Theodore Roosevelt, Eleanor Roosevelt was her husband's fifth cousin, once removed. She had experienced a traumatic childhood, virtually rejected by her mother, who considered Eleanor ugly and referred to her as "Granny." When she was only 10, she had to cope with the death of her beloved father, who had been an alcoholic. Her self-confidence developed only slowly and remained fragile throughout her life.

A Pre-Election View

Walter Lippmann was the preeminent political columnist and commentator in the United States during much of the first half of the 20th century. In this famous column he expresses the skepticism many observers felt toward FDR before he won the nomination and election in 1932.

It is now plain that sooner or later some of Governor Roosevelt's supporters are going to feel badly let down. For it is impossible that he can continue to be such different things to such different men. He is, at the moment, the highly preferred candidate of left-wing progressives like Senator Wheeler of Montana, and of Bryan's former secretary, Representative Howard of Nebraska. He is, at the same time, receiving the enthusiastic support of the *New York Times*.

Senator Wheeler, who would like to cure the depression by debasing the currency, is Mr. Roosevelt's most conspicuous supporter in the West, and Representative Howard has this week hailed the Governor as "the most courageous enemy of the evil influences" emanating from the international bankers. The *New York Times*, on the other hand, assures its readers that "no upsetting plans, no Socialistic proposals, however mild and winning in form," could appeal to the Governor.

The Roosevelt bandwagon would seem to be moving in two opposite directions.

There are two questions raised by this curious situation. The first is why Senator Wheeler and the *Times* should have such contradictory impressions of their common candidate. The second, which is also the more important question, is which has guessed rightly.

The art of carrying water on both shoulders is highly developed in American politics, and Mr. Roosevelt has learned it. His message to the Legislature, or at least that part of it devoted to his Presidential candidacy, is an almost perfect specimen of the balanced antithesis. . . .

The message is so constructed that a left-wing progressive can read it and find just enough of his own phrases in it to satisfy himself that Franklin D. Roosevelt's heart is in the right place.

. . . On the other hand, there are all necessary assurances to the conservatives. "We should not seek in any way to destroy or to tear down"; our system is "everlasting"; we must insist "on the permanence of our fundamental institutions."

That this is a studied attempt to straddle the whole country I have no doubt whatever. Every newspaper man knows the whole bag of tricks by heart. He knows too that the practical politician supplements these two-faced platitudes by what are called private assurances, in which he tells his different supporters what he knows they would like to hear. Then, when they read the balanced antithesis, each believes the half that he has been reassured about privately and dismisses the rest as not significant. . . .

In the case of Mr. Roosevelt, it is not easy to say with certainty whether his left-wing or his right-wing supporters are the most deceived. The reason is that Franklin D. Roosevelt is a highly impressionable person, without a firm grasp of public affairs and without very strong convictions. He might plump for something which would shock the conservatives. There is no telling. Yet when Representative Howard of Nebraska says that he is "the most dangerous enemy of evil influences," New Yorkers who know the Governor know that Mr. Howard does not know the Governor. For Franklin D. Roosevelt is an amiable man with many philanthropic impulses, but he is not the dangerous enemy of anything. He is too eager to please. The notion, which seems to prevail in the West and South, that Wall Street fears him, is preposterous. Wall Street thinks he is too dry, not that he is too radical. Wall Street does not like some of his supporters. Wall Street does not like his vagueness, and the uncertainty as to what he does think, but if any Western Progressive thinks that the Governor has challenged directly or indirectly the wealth concentrated in New York City, he is mightily mistaken.

Mr. Roosevelt is, as a matter of fact, an excessively cautious politician. He has been Governor for three years, and I doubt whether anyone can point to a single act of his which involved any political risk. . . .

. . . For Franklin D. Roosevelt is no crusader. He is no tribune of the people. He is no enemy of entrenched privilege. He is a

Eleanor Roosevelt overcame a traumatic childhood, an affluent upbringing, an unfaithful husband, and a physical appearance (especially in photographs) that led to frequent nasty comments to become an extraordinarily effective spokeswoman for oppressed people and the most successful First Lady in American history.

She was tall, five feet eleven I'd guess, and of a generation that did not run to tall women nor approve of them. She must have suffered as a girl from her lack of prettiness and her height. She had a delightful little turned-up nose and warm eyes and when she laughed her face took on an expression of surprised happiness, almost like a child's. . . . No one seeing her could fail to be moved; she gave off light, I cannot explain it better.

She possessed the rarest human quality; she was always kind. She was without any affectation; her modesty or humility was genuine, and staggering. . . . Because she happened to be the wife of the President, she had special opportunities to serve; no more than that. . . . With Mrs. Roosevelt, empathy reached the rank of genius; nothing in the human condition—the good, the fine, the tragic, the pitiful, the mean and base—was beyond her understanding. In Depression America, in America at war, her power of empathy was a national asset. She had a clear and constant sense of justice and injustice.

—Martha Gellhorn

pleasant man who, without any important qualifications for the office, would very much like to be President.

A Letter from Wisconsin

"Ordinary" Americans wrote to Franklin Roosevelt in completely unprecedented numbers. Many seem to have felt, in part because of the personal connection he established with them in his radio "fireside chats," that he was their friend and that they could confide in him and appeal to him as they could to no other President before. Many of the literally millions of letters addressed to Franklin and Eleanor Roosevelt echoed the example below by praising the President in truly extraordinary terms.

Cedarburg, Wis.
1045 A.M. Mar. 5, 1934
Mrs. F. D. Roosevelt
Washington D.C.

My dear Friend:
Just listened to the address given by your dear husband, our wonderful President. During the presidential campaign of 1932 we had in our home a darling little girl, three years old. My husband + I were great admirers of the Dem. candidate and so Dolores had to listen to much talk about the great man who we hoped and prayed would be our next Pres. We are Lutherans and she is a Catholic so you'll get quite a thrill out of what I'm to tell you now. That fall Judge Karel of Mil. sent me a fine picture of our beloved President, which I placed in our Public Library. When I received this fine picture my dear mother (who has since been called Home) said to Dolores "Who is this man?" and Dolores answered without any hesitation "Why who else, but Saint Roosevelt!" The old saying goes fools and children often tell the truth and indeed we all feel if there ever was a Saint. He is one. As long as Pres. Roosevelt will be our leader under Jesus Christ we feel no fear. His speech this morning showed he feels for the "least of these" I am enclosing a snap shot of the dear little girl who acclaimed our President a Saint and rightly so.

Mrs. L. K. S.

In the eyes of many Americans, Franklin Roosevelt seemed to have almost magical—or perhaps divine—powers. That viewpoint is evident in this 1934 cartoon by Rollin Kirby in the New York World Telegram, *"The Sower."*

Memorandum on "Court Packing"

Soon after FDR's overwhelming reelection in 1936, fears that he might be trying to assume too much personal power were raised anew. The immediate cause was a proposed bill that would allow the President to increase the membership of the Supreme Court (and lower federal courts as well) if justices over the age of 70 did not retire. Roosevelt's plan was inspired by three main considerations: a series of Supreme Court decisions making it appear that the Court was likely to invalidate most of the major legislation of the New Deal; the lack of any Supreme Court vacancies to fill during Roosevelt's first term; and the endorsement the voters had given the New Deal at the polls.

The ill-conceived "court-packing" plan placed the President's supporters in a difficult position. Many sincerely feared that it would upset the constitutional balance of power and (especially given the backdrop of a world replete with such dictators as Hitler, Stalin, and Mussolini) create the possibility of a Presidential seizure of power—if not by Roosevelt, then by some future President.

These fears are clearly evident in the following 1937 memorandum written by North Carolina Democratic congressman Lindsay Warren after FDR announced his plan.

Speaker W. B. Bankhead called me at my Office this morning at 10 a.m. saying he was on his way to the Capitol and wished to talk with me privately. He thought it best that we not go to the Speaker's Office or to my Office, but to use the room known in the Garner days as the "Board of Education." The Speaker arrived at 10:30 a.m. He told me that he had called me as his closest and most dependable friend, and that our conversation must be strictly confidential.

He said that he was alarmed and worried over the President's message on the Supreme Court, that inwardly he was burnt up about it, but that outwardly he must show calm and reserve. He said he didn't know who he could talk to. He was furious about the action of Maury Maverick of Texas who rushed down to the well of the House and snatched the bill from the message and introduced it. And yet, he said that men like Hatton Sumners of Texas and John O'Connor of New York by their violent opposition to the President could cause reaction in favor of the bill. I told the

Every home I visited—mill worker or unemployed—had a picture of the President. These ranged from newspaper clippings (in destitute homes) to large coloured prints, framed in gilt cardboard. The portrait holds a place of honour over the mantel; I can only compare this to the Italian peasant's Madonna. And the feeling of these people for the president is one of the most remarkable emotional phenomena I have ever met. He is at once God and their intimate friend; he knows them all by name, knows their little town and mill, their little lives and problems. And, though everything else fails, he is there, and will not let them down.

—Martha Gellhorn, Report to Harry Hopkins on South and North Carolina, November 11, 1934

"Mother, Milfred wrote a bad word!": This 1938 Esquire cartoon by Dorothy McKay sums up the attitudes of the Roosevelt haters with a succinctness that is only possible in a cartoon. Few political figures in American history have evoked both adoration and hatred to the degree that Roosevelt did.

Speaker that on Friday night (the day of the message) that I had talked over long distance to one of the best friends I had (Ed Flanagan, Greenville) and had told him I would rather be defeated than to vote for the President's bill. The Speaker reached over and took me by the hand and said "Lindsay, they are exactly my sentiments. You and I are steeped in the tradition of the separation of powers under the Constitution as well as respect for the Supreme Court and while it may be my political life, I shall not vote for it." We both agreed that if the vote was taken the next week it would pass by large majorities in both Houses. I told him as of today Senator Bailey and I would be the only two from North Carolina who would vote against it but that I believed if delay could be had that Lambeth, Umstead and Clark, all of whom were now noncommittal would wind up against it. We agreed that we had strong reasons to be against the Court—the declaring of the Bankhead Cotton Bill, the Tobacco Bill and the Warren Potato Bill unconstitutional—and that the Court had steeled itself against the President. Both of us stated that we hated to break with the President, as we were two of his assistant floor managers in the 1932 convention. The Speaker urged me not to give out any statement and not to write any strong condemning letters, saying that I would be much more effective if I didn't. He said he had already lost sleep over the matter and that he was going to tell Garner [Vice President John Nance Garner] and Senator Joe Robinson in confidence that this was one matter that the Senate act first. He said that the burden for just about everything was always put on the House—that as the Senate had to confirm appointments he was going to insist that the Senate act first. He said he knew the President would be after him tomorrow for House action and if we did act first it would mean the defeat of many House members. He urged me to begin talking immediately with as many House Democrats as possible saying that the Senate should act first. I told him I would. He said, "Lindsay, wouldn't you have thought that the President would have told his own party leaders what he was going to do. He didn't because he knew that hell would break loose." The Speaker said he already knew that Sam Rayburn would be with the President and that nearly every northern Democrat would follow him. We talked over an hour and he left greatly perturbed.

"My Day"

At the end of 1935, Eleanor Roosevelt began writing a newspaper column in a form similar to the letters she was in the habit of writing to close friends, describing what she was doing and thinking. These "My Day" columns provide many insights into Mrs. Roosevelt's feelings, thoughts, and beliefs.

The first column reprinted below is the first she wrote for publication. It provides an example of how far removed some of Mrs. Roosevelt's experiences were from those of many of her readers (see sidebar). The second column, from 1938, is vintage Eleanor Roosevelt. In reacting to speeches she heard at a dinner given to support the Léon Blum Colony Mrs. Roosevelt alludes to the various groups in the United States (plainly including African Americans, although she never says this explicitly) who were not enjoying the freedoms that most Americans like to associate with their country. (Léon Blum, a French Socialist leader, had become France's first Jewish prime minister in 1936 but later had been forced out of the country because of his opposition to any alliance between France and Nazi Germany; the Blum Colony was set up as a haven for refugees from Hitler's oppression.)

In the third selection from "My Day," the first lady refers obliquely to her resignation from the Daughters of the American Revolution (DAR) in protest of that organization's refusal to allow a performance by black contralto Marian Anderson in the DAR-controlled Constitution Hall in Washington. Secretary of the Interior Harold Ickes, who ranked with Mrs. Roosevelt as one of the New Deal's two most prominent advocates of civil rights for blacks, arranged for Anderson to give a free concert on the Mall in front of the Lincoln Memorial.

Washington, December 30 [1935]—I wonder if anyone else glories in cold and snow without and an open fire within and the luxury of a tray of food all by one's self in one's room. I realize that it sounds extremely selfish and a little odd to look upon such an occasion as festive. Nevertheless, Saturday night was a festive occasion, for I spent it that way.

A Reader Responds

Columbus, Ind.
[January 1936]

Dear Mrs. Roosevelt,
I would give ten years of my life to be able to have the luxury of an open fire just one evening, as you write about in the Indianapolis Times.

N. T. [female]

To the Editor of the *New York Times*

BEVERLY HILLS, Cal., June 7 [1933].—Aviation developed another Lindbergh, Jimmie Mattern and Amelia Earhart last night when Mrs. Franklin D. Roosevelt finished a transcontinental flight. There is a real boost for aviation.

But here is what she really takes the medal for: Out at every stop, day or night, standing for photographs by the hour, being interviewed, talking over the radio, no sleep. And yet they say she never showed one sign of weariness or annoyance of any kind. No maid, no secretary—just the first lady of the land on a paid ticket on a regular passenger plane.

If some of our female screen stars had made that trip they would have had one plane for secretaries, one for maids, one for chefs and chauffeurs and a trailer for "business representatives" and "press agents."

Yours,
Will Rogers

—*New York Times*, June 8, 1933.

Eleanor Roosevelt's level of activity and particularly her extensive travels were astounding to many observers. Even in the decade in which Amelia Earhart dazzled people by flying across the Atlantic and Pacific Oceans before disappearing on a 1937 attempt to fly around the world, few women traveled nearly as much as Eleanor Roosevelt did.

The house was full of young people, my husband had a cold and was in bed with milk toast for his supper, so I said a polite good night to everyone at 7:30, closed my door, lit my fire and settled down to a nice long evening by myself. I read things which I had had in my briefcase for weeks—a report on educational work in the CCC camps, a copy of "Progressive Education" dealing with the problems of youth, the first copy of a magazine edited by a group of young people, a chapter in manuscript and I went to sleep at 10:30. Because I haven't been to bed for weeks before 1 A.M. and often later, this was so unusual that I work this morning with a feeling that I must have slept for several years.

Yesterday was a grand contrast, with sixteen for lunch. My guest on my right was Mr. Regan of Groton School, who long watched over our boys and the boys of many other people and who is, I think, one of the best beloved masters in the school.

New York, December 8 [1938]—As I listened to the speeches last night at a dinner given for the support of the Léon Blum Colony again, I could not help thinking how much all human beings like to fool themselves.

Mr. William Green, President of the American Federation of Labor, a kindly gentleman with a rightful pride in his achievements, told me of his son practicing law, and how he had been able to give him and his five sisters college educations when he, himself, had had to leave school and spend twenty years in the mines. Natural enough that he should feel that this is a grand country. He knows that some things are not just as we might wish, but nevertheless this is the land of the free. He told us this in his speech and that we can pat ourselves on the back that we are lucky enough to live here.

Almost every other speaker gave us the same kind of pat and made us feel that, as a whole we were more virtuous than any other people in the world. Of course, I concede this, and I feel for me it is true, for I have been free and fortunate all my life. While I listened, however, I could not help thinking of some of the letters which pass through my hands.

Are you free if you cannot vote, if you cannot be sure that the same justice will be meted out to you as to your neighbor, if you are expected to live on a lower level than your neighbor and to work for lower wages, if you are barred from certain places and from certain opportunities? It seems from my mail that there are people in this country who do not feel as I do about having

There was no telling where Eleanor Roosevelt might show up. Here she is in one of the most surprising settings in which she ever appeared, visiting a West Virginia coal mine in 1933. "Ladies," first or otherwise, just did not do things like this in the 1930s.

personal freedom, even though they might agree that they are better off than they might be somewhere else.

I think of the little girl who wrote me not long ago: "Why do the other children call me names and laugh at my talk? I just don't live in this country very long yet."

Are you free when you can't earn enough, no matter how hard you work, to feed and clothe and house your children properly? Are you free when your employer can turn you out of a company house or deny you work because you belong to a union?

There are lots of things which make me wonder whether we ever look ourselves straight in the face and really mean what we say when we are busy patting ourselves on the back.

Somewhere someone must have a quiet laugh, I think, if there is a place where real truth is dealt in.

Washington, February 27 [1939]—I am having a peaceful day. I drove my car a short distance out of the city this morning to pilot some friends of mine who are starting off for a vacation in Florida. I think this will be my only excursion out of the White House today, for I have plenty of work to do on the accumulation of mail,

Eleanor Roosevelt had come to act as her husband's eyes and ears as she traveled around the country from the 1920s onward, after polio had largely immobilized the President. She also acted as his conscience, especially on matters of race, where she was constantly pressuring him to do the right thing. Here the First Lady is pictured at the dedication of the Southside Arts Center in Chicago in 1941.

and I hope to get through in time to enjoy an evening of uninterrupted reading. I have been debating in my mind for some time, a question which I have had to debate with myself once or twice in my life. Usually I have decided differently from the way in which I am deciding now. The question is, if you belong to an organization and disapprove of an action which is typical of a policy, should you resign or is it better to work for a changed point of view within the organization? In the past, when I was able to work actively in any organization to which I belonged, I have usually stayed until I had at least made a fight and had been defeated.

Even then, I have, as a rule, accepted my defeat and decided I was wrong or, perhaps, a little too far ahead of the thinking for the majority at that time. I have often found that the thing in which I was interested was done some years later. But in this case, I belong to an organization in which I can do no active work. They have taken an action which has been widely talked of in the press. To remain as a member implies approval of that action, and therefore I am resigning.

Praise for Eleanor Roosevelt

Eleanor Roosevelt made a special effort to encourage people to write to her. That effort, combined with the widespread

public impression that she was someone who really cared about the problems of "ordinary" people, produced a totally unprecedented flood of mail addressed to the First Lady. Many of these letters, like this one, expressed an extraordinary affection and admiration for Mrs. Roosevelt.

[Ridley Park, Pennsylvania]
9/1/34

Dear Mrs. Roosevelt.

I was delighted but I dont believe I was very much surprised when I received your letter. Just to look at your picture and that of our President seems to me like looking at the picture of a saint. So when you answered my letter and promised to have some one help me it only proved you are our own Mrs Roosevelt. I have told everyone what you done for me. I want them to know you are not too busy to answer our letters and give us what help and advice you can you hold the highest place any woman can hold still you are not to proud to befriend the poorer class, well your just big and fine enough to be the wife of our beloved president Thank you and God bless you both.

Respctfull

M. M. [female]

This memoir, from "an Idaho Republican," shows how Eleanor Roosevelt challenged and helped to transform people's opinions about what a woman's role should be.

That Mrs. Roosevelt—she was a magnificent woman. I remember there was a lot of criticism of her, but it was due to jealousy. People were jealous because she stepped out to give the people encouragement. We never had a First Lady who ever stepped out like her.

She organized groups and got people interested in helping themselves. To me, she's one of the fantastic women of our country.

I was proud of her, but at the time I just thought she was helping her husband. You see, in those days I wasn't used to looking to a woman as great and powerful, with a lot of guts.

There was a feeling on the part of some people that she was taking advantage because she was the president's wife—but that wasn't it at all. It was just because she was a great woman.

Granny and I went off to the movies. The film was H. Rider Haggard's *She,* which I assumed would be a newsreel about Mrs. Roosevelt. (I had grown up hearing: "it's not his fault, she made him do it. She got them all stirred up, she thinks they're just as good as she is.") I sat through the film waiting for the First Lady to appear. Finally, when the withered old woman died in the snows of Tibet, I asked Granny: "Is that Mrs. Roosevelt?"

She snorted and said: "Would that it were."

. . . Now I understood how it was possible for my family to worship FDR despite all the things he had done during his administration that enraged them. They had used Southern logic to "straighten everything out just fine." It was very simple: Credit Franklin, better known as He, for all the things you like, and blame Eleanor, better known as She or "that woman," for all the things you don't like. This way, He was cleared, She was castigated, and We were happy.

—Florence King, *Southern Ladies and Gentlemen*

Chapter Fourteen

"Social Values More Noble Than Mere Monetary Profit"

The Great Depression and American Values

Perhaps the most significant impact of the depression was on the values embraced by the citizens of the United States. At no other time in 20th-century U.S. history was the trend toward social disintegration and hyperindividualism reversed. The collapse of the economy went a long way toward discrediting the acquisitive "more, more, more" attitude that had been so popular in the twenties. The consumption ethic that had become so powerful in the 1920s had, of necessity, to be curtailed during hard times. Franklin Roosevelt gave voice to the resurgent community-oriented values of the depression decade in his first inaugural address when he spoke of applying "social values more noble than mere monetary profit" and the need to "minister to ourselves and to our fellow men."

The social values that gained acceptance during the depression formed the basis of much of the New Deal approach. A government that restored morality to economic considerations, a government that offered protections for its people against the ravages of an amoral economy, a government that was informed by a kind of "maternalism" (see

President Roosevelt's New Deal programs proved him to be the friend of the "forgotten man," as he is depicted in this 1936 Batchelor cartoon. Remembering the people who had been largely forgotten during the money-mad 1920s was one of the more important manifestations of depression-era values.

Remember My Forgotten Man

Remember my forgotten man,
You put a rifle in his hand,
You sent him far away,
You shouted, "Hip Hooray!"
But look at him today.
Remember my forgotten man,
You had him cultivate the land,
He walked behind a plow,
The sweat fell from his brow,
But look at him right now.

And once he used to love me,
I was happy then,
He used to take care of me,
Won't you bring him back again?

'Cause ever since the world began,
A woman's got to have a man,
Forgetting him, you see,
Means you're forgetting me,
Like my forgotten man.

—Song from film *Gold Diggers of 1933*. Lyrics by Al Dublin, music by Harry Warren

chapter 8)—that was what many Americans sought during the thirties, and it was what, at least to a degree, the New Deal gave them.

"Forgotten Man" Radio Address

None of Franklin Roosevelt's 1932 campaign speeches better reflected the emerging—or reemerging—values of the depression-era United States than his "Forgotten Man" radio address of April 7, 1932.

Although I understand that I am talking under the auspices of the Democratic National Committee, I do not want to limit myself to politics. I do not want to feel that I am addressing an audience of Democrats or that I speak merely as a Democrat myself. The present condition of our national affairs is too serious to be viewed through partisan eyes for partisan purposes.

. . . The generalship of that moment [World War I] conceived of a whole Nation mobilized for war, economic, industrial, social and military resources gathered into a vast unit capable of and actually in the process of throwing into the scales ten million men equipped with physical needs and sustained by the realization that behind them were the united efforts of 110,000,000 human beings. It was a great plan because it was built from bottom to top and not from top to bottom.

In my calm judgment, the Nation faces today a more grave emergency than in 1917.

It is said that Napoleon lost the battle of Waterloo because he forgot his infantry—he staked too much on the more spectacular but less substantial cavalry. The present administration in Washington provides a close parallel. It has either forgotten or it does not want to remember the infantry of our economic army.

These unhappy times call for the building of plans that rest upon the forgotten, the unorganized but the indispensable units of economic power, for plans like those of 1917 that build from the bottom up and not from the top down, that put their faith once more in the forgotten man at the bottom of the economic pyramid. . . .

. . . A real economic cure must go to the killing of the bacteria in the system rather than to the treatment of external symptoms. . . .

Such objectives as these three, restoring farmers' buying power, relief to the small banks and home-owners and a reconstructed tariff policy, are only a part of ten or a dozen vital factors.

But they seem to be beyond the concern of a national administration which can think in terms only of the top of the social and economic structure. It has sought temporary relief from the top down rather than permanent relief from the bottom up. It has totally failed to plan ahead in a comprehensive way. It has waited until something has cracked and then at the last moment has sought to prevent total collapse.

Memories of a Southern White Girl

In the following interview, conducted in Chicago at the end of the 1960s by Studs Terkel, a southerner named Peggy Terry who grew to womanhood during the depression describes some of the values she discovered during hard times in Oklahoma, Kentucky, and Texas. "There was a feeling of together," she recalls.

I first noticed the difference when we'd come home from school in the evening. My mother'd send us to the soup line. And we were never allowed to cuss. If you happened to be one of the first ones in line, you didn't get anything but water that was on top. So we'd ask the guy that was ladling out the soup into the bucket— everybody had to bring their own bucket to get the soup—he'd dip the greasy, watery stuff off the top. So we'd ask him to please dip down to get some meat and potatoes from the bottom of the kettle. But he wouldn't do it. So we learned to cuss. We'd say: "Dip down, God damn it."

Then we'd go across the street. One place had bread, large loaves of bread. Down the road just a little piece was a big shed, and they gave milk. My sister and me would take two buckets each. And that's what we lived off for the longest time.

I can remember one time, the only thing in the house to eat was mustard. My sister and I put so much mustard on biscuits that we got sick. And we can't stand mustard till today.

There was only one family around that ate good. Mr. Barr worked at the ice plant. Whenever Mrs. Barr could, she'd feed the kids. But she couldn't feed 'em all. They had a big tree that had fruit on it. She'd let us pick those. Sometimes we'd pick and eat 'em until we were sick.

Her two daughters got to go to Norman [the University of Oklahoma] for their college. When they'd talk about all the good things they had at the college, she'd kind of hush 'em up because

It's surprising how little money we can get along on. Let the banks never open. Let script never come. Just everybody keep on trusting everybody else.

Why, it's such a novelty to find that somebody will trust you, that it's changed our whole feeling toward human nature. Why, never was our country so united, never was a country so tickled with poverty.

For three years we have had nothing but "America is fundamentally sound." It should have been "America is fundamentally cuckoo."

The worse off we get the louder we laugh, which is a great thing. And, every American international banker ought to have printed on his office door, "Alive today by the grace of a nation that has a sense of humor."

Yours,
Will Rogers

—*New York Times*, March 9, 1933

The value of collective effort was reflected in many ways during the depression. Busby Berkeley created elaborate choreography in which large numbers of performers (usually attractive young women who look almost identical) were brought together to create a whole, as in this scene from the movie Footlight Parade (1933).

there was always poor kids that didn't have anything to eat. I remember she always felt bad because people in the neighborhood were hungry. But there was a feeling of together. . . .

When they had food to give to people, you'd get a notice and you'd go down. So Daddy went down that day and took my sister and me. They were giving away potatoes and things like that. But they had a truck of oranges parked in the alley. Somebody asked them who the oranges were for and they wouldn't tell 'em. So they said, well, we're gonna take those oranges. And they did. My dad was one of the ones that got up on the truck. They called the police, and the police chased us all away. But we got the oranges.

It's different today. People are made to feel ashamed now if they don't have anything. Back then, I'm not sure how the rich felt. I think the rich were as contemptuous of the poor then as they are now. But among the people that I knew, we all had an understanding that it wasn't our fault. It was something that had happened to the machinery. Most people blamed Hoover, and they cussed him up one side and down the other—it was all his fault. I'm not saying he's blameless, but I'm not saying either it was all his fault. Our system doesn't run by just one man, and it doesn't fall by just one man either.

[Interviewer] You don't recall at any time feeling a sense of shame?

I remember it was fun. It was fun going to the soup line. 'Cause we all went down the road, and we laughed and we played. The only thing we felt is that we were hungry and we were going to get food. Nobody made us feel ashamed. There just wasn't any of that. . . .

My husband and me just started traveling around, for about three years. . . .

I was pregnant when we first started hitchhiking, and people were really very nice to us. Sometimes they would feed us. I remember one time we slept in a haystack, and the lady of the house came out and found us and she said, "This is really very bad for you because you're going to have a baby. You need a lot of milk." So she took us up to the house.

She had a lot of rugs hanging on the clothesline because she was doing her house cleaning. We told her we'd beat the rugs for her giving us the food. She said, no, she didn't expect that. She just wanted to feed us. We said, no, we couldn't take it unless we worked for it. And she let us beat her rugs. I think she had a million rugs, and we cleaned them. Then we went in and she had a beautiful table, full of all kinds of food and milk. When we left, she filled a gallon bucket full of milk and we took it with us.

You don't find that now. I think maybe if you did that now, you'd get arrested. Somebody'd call the police. The atmosphere since the end of the Second War—it seems like the minute the war ended, the propaganda started. In making people hate each other.

I remember one night, we walked for a long time, and we were so tired and hungry, and a wagon came along. There was a Negro family going into town. Of course, they're not allowed to stop and eat in restaurants, so they'd cook their own food and brought it with 'em. They had the back of the wagon filled with hay. We asked them if we could lay down and sleep in the wagon, and they said yes. We woke up, and it was morning, and she invited us to eat with 'em. She had this box, and she had chicken and biscuits and sweet potatoes and everything in there. It was just really wonderful. . . .

This may sound impossible, but if there's one thing that started me thinking, it was President Roosevelt's cuff links. I read in the paper how many pairs of cuff links he had. It told that some of them were rubies and precious stones—these were his cuff links. And I'll never forget, I was sitting on an old tire out in the front yard and we were poor and hungry. I was sitting out there in the hot sun, there weren't any trees. And I was wondering why it is that one man could have all those cuff links when we couldn't even have enough to eat. When we lived on gravy and biscuits. That's the first time I remember ever wondering why.

And when my father finally got his bonus, he bought a secondhand car for us to come back to Kentucky in. My dad said to us kids: "All of you get in the car. I want to take you and show you something." On the way over there, he'd talk about how life had been rough for us, and he said: "If you think it's been rough for us, I want you to see people that really had it rough." This was in Oklahoma City, and he took us to one of the Hoovervilles, and that was the most incredible thing.

Here were all these people living in old, rusted-out car bodies. I mean that was their home. There were people living in shacks made of orange crates. One family with a whole lot of kids were living in a piano box. This wasn't just a little section, this was maybe ten-miles wide and ten-miles long. People living in whatever they could junk together.

And when I read *Grapes of Wrath*—she bought that for me (indicates young girl seated across the room)—that was like reliving my life. Particularly the part where they lived in this Government camp. Because when we were picking fruit in Texas, we lived in a Government place like that. They came around, and they helped

John Steinbeck's The Grapes of Wrath *encapsulated the experiences of many people during the depression. Even more important, the 1939 novel captured the community-minded values that had regained much support in the 1930s.*

the women make mattresses. See, we didn't have anything. And they showed us how to sew and make dresses. And every Saturday night, we'd have a dance. And when I was reading *Grapes of Wrath* this was just like my life. I was never so proud of poor people before, as I was after I read that book.

I think that's the worst thing that our system does to people, is to take away their pride. It prevents them from being a human being. . . .

I don't think people were put on earth to suffer. I think that's a lot of nonsense. I think we are the highest development on the earth, and I think we were put here to live and be happy and to enjoy everything that's here. I don't think it's right for a handful of people to get ahold of all the things that make living a joy instead of a sorrow. You wake up in the morning, and it consciously hits you—it's just like a big hand that takes your heart and squeezes it—because you don't know what that day is going to bring: hunger or you don't know.

The Changed Social Life of a Migrant Camp

John Steinbeck brilliantly captured the values of the depression era in *The Grapes of Wrath*. In the selection below, he discusses the community-minded ethics that were developed among the migrant "Okies."

In the evening a strange thing happened: the twenty families became one family, the children were the children of all. The loss of home became one loss, and the golden time in the West was one dream. And it might be that a sick child threw despair into the hearts of twenty families, of a hundred people; that a birth there in a tent kept a hundred people quiet and awestruck through the night and filled a hundred people with the birth-joy in the morning. A family which the night before had been lost and fearful might search its goods to find a present for a new baby. In the evening, sitting about the fires, the twenty were one. They grew to be units of the camps, units of the evenings and the nights. A guitar unwrapped from a blanket and tuned—and the songs, which were all of the people, were sung in the nights. Men sang the words, and women hummed the tunes. . . .

The families learned what rights must be observed—the right of privacy in the tent; the right to keep the past black hidden in the heart; the right to talk and to listen; the right to refuse help or to accept, to offer help or to decline it; the right of son to court daughter and daughter to be courted; the right of the hungry to be fed; the rights of the pregnant and the sick to transcend all other rights.

And the families learned, although no one told them, what rights are monstrous and must be destroyed: the right to intrude upon privacy, the right to be noisy while the camp slept, the right of seduction or rape, the right of adultery and theft and murder. These rights were crushed, because the little worlds could not exist for even a night with such rights alive.

And as the worlds moved westward, rules became laws, although no one told the families. It is unlawful to foul near the camp; it is unlawful in any way to foul the drinking water; it is unlawful to eat good rich food near one who is hungry, unless he is asked to share.

And with the laws, the punishments—and there were only two—a quick and murderous fight or ostracism; and ostracism was the worst. For if one broke the laws his name and face went with him, and he had no place in any world, no matter where created.

In the worlds, social conduct became fixed and rigid, so that a man must say "Good morning" when asked for it, so that a man might have a willing girl if he stayed with her, if he fathered her children and protected them. But a man might not have one girl one night and another the next, for this would endanger the worlds. . . .

There grew up government in the worlds, with leaders, with elders. A man who was wise found that his wisdom was needed in every camp; a man who was a fool could not change his folly with his world. And a kind of insurance developed in these nights. A man with food fed a hungry man, and thus insured himself against hunger. And when a baby died a pile of silver coins grew at the door flap, for a baby must be well buried, since it had nothing else of life. An old man may be left in a potter's field, but not a baby.

. . . The families, which had been units of which the boundaries were a house at night, a farm by day, changed their boundaries. In the long, hot light, they were silent in the cars moving slowly westward; but at night they integrated with any group they found.

Thus they changed their social life—changed as in the whole universe only man can change.

The populist sentiments that saw "the big men," "the interests," or "Wall Street" as the mortal enemies of the people and of traditional American values could be found in the most unexpected places during the depression, as this Dorothea Lange photo demonstrates.

Ma fanned the air slowly with her cardboard. "You been frien'ly," she said. "We thank you."

The stout woman smiled. "No need to thank. Ever'body's in the same wagon. S'pose we was down. You'd give us a han'."

"Yes," ma said, "we would."

"Or anybody."

"Or anybody. Use' ta be the fambly was fust. It ain't so now. It's anybody. Worse off we get, the more we got to do."

—John Steinbeck, *The Grapes of Wrath*

"Oh, Auntie Em, there's no place like home."

—Dorothy, in *The Wizard of Oz* (1939)

"What is there that matters?" —Scarlett O'Hara

". . . The land's the only thing that matters; it's the only thing that lasts . . ." —voice of Gerald O'Hara

"Tara. Home. I'll go home. Then I'll think of some way to get him back. After all, tomorrow is another day." —Scarlett

—*Gone With the Wind* (1939)

During the prosperity of the 20s, writers such as Sinclair Lewis had ridiculed the narrow-minded provincialism they associated with small-town life. In the midst of the depression, however, the better side of small-town values was emphasized, as in Thornton Wilder's 1938 Pulitzer Prize–winning play, Our Town.

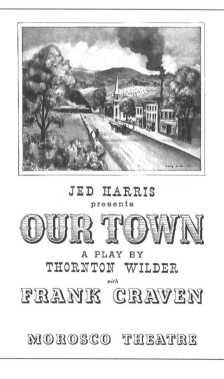

JED HARRIS
presents

OUR TOWN

A PLAY BY
THORNTON WILDER
with
FRANK CRAVEN

MOROSCO THEATRE

"Middletown in Transition"

In *Middletown* (1929), Robert and Helen Merrell Lynd produced a sociological classic. They studied the beliefs, habits, mores, and values of what they took to be a typical small American city (Muncie, Indiana), employing the same techniques anthropologists were using to study "primitive" peoples in far-off lands. The Lynds returned to Muncie a decade after their initial visit to see what effect the depression had had on the lives and values of these Middle Americans. In the following selection from *Middletown in Transition* (1937), they summarize their findings, which indicated that some important social and economic attitudes had changed under the impact of the depression.

Loudly as Middletown affirms and reaffirms all its hopeful, ameliorative beliefs, the "Down here under our vests we're scared to death" note was heard again and again in 1935 when business-class or working-class people were talking unofficially. Some of its tensions it had been unable to overlook, to sloganize away, or to brush aside as merely personal frailties subject to correction as men became "better." The long pull of the depression had even prompted occasional rare questions as to whether the system itself was as sound as Middletown liked to believe. An editorial in mid-1933 on "Machines and the human equation" had stated:

We have been making society mechanical instead of making machinery social. We have to humanize our mechanized industries by putting human values above material values and the real welfare of all above the false welfare of the few. What is needed here is social engineering.

An even bolder editorial (in the afternoon paper—it could hardly have appeared in the morning paper) about the same time, remarking on the suicide of an unemployed man, had said under the unfamiliar caption, "The Right to Live by Work":

Why should anybody wipe himself out of existence because he has no money? Have we set up some kind of false standard of value? . . . Someday and somehow, finally, we are going to straighten these things out. You may call the new order by anything you please, but it is coming. The inherent right of every man and woman who is willing to do his part to maintain reasonable social conditions, which means to live decently, cannot be gainsaid by any system. That is basic. Let us not fool ourselves by thinking the old systems are to be continued indefinitely. . . . The right of a willing man to work and live by his labor is paramount. There is nothing else important.

Although the official front had recovered its flawless exterior by 1935, Middletown people knew that they had been living for a while in a world that made more natural the raising of such questions. The acute concerns of the depression were dropping somewhat behind, but over the contours of the city stood out the bench marks of depression experience. And Middletown was afraid, even as it whooped things up over "the return of prosperity"; and perhaps whooped things up the more just because it was afraid.

Week after week during 1935 the outside radio was bringing in talks by men like Father Coughlin and Huey Long. Over the air came into the cottages and even into many business-class homes points of view not allowed to appear in a favorable light in the local press. "I'm surprised," commented a businessman, "at the number of people who listen to Father Coughlin and believe he talks sense. Curiously, too, people don't seem to resent his being a Catholic." Down at Pop Alexander's South Side beer hall men talked freely and favorably of Father Coughlin, and some South Side families had his emblems in their homes. On the South Side, too, Huey Long's slogan, "Share the wealth," elicited loyalty. Some working people expressed their willingness to "follow any kind of man who stands for that."

"A Spirit of Charity"

In his 1933 inaugural address, FDR had hit upon the main themes of depression-era morality. Those values came increasingly to the fore during his reelection campaign in 1936. He expressed them best in his acceptance speech that year, at the Democratic National Convention in Philadelphia.

America will not forget these recent years, will not forget that the rescue was not a mere party task. It was the concern of all of us. In our strength we rose together, rallied our energies together, applied the old rules of common sense, and together survived.

In those days we feared fear. That was why we fought fear. And today, my friends, we have won against the most dangerous of our foes. We have conquered fear.

But I cannot, with candor, tell you that all is well with the world. Clouds of suspicion, tides of ill-will and intolerance gather

Ballad of Pretty Boy Floyd

There's many a starving farmer the
    same old story told
How the outlaw paid their mortgage
    and saved their little home.
Others tell you 'bout a stranger that
    come to beg a meal
And when the meal was finished left
    a thousand dollar bill.

It was in Oklahoma City, it was on
    Christmas Day,
There come a whole carload of
    groceries with a note to say:
"You say that I'm an outlaw, you
    say that I'm a thief.
Here's a Christmas dinner for the
    families on relief."

Yes, as through this world I ramble,
    I see lots of funny men.
Some will rob you with a 6 gun, and
    some with a fountain pen.
But as through your life you'll travel,
    wherever you may roam.
You won't never see an Outlaw drive
    a family from their home.

—Woody Guthrie

Public Opinion Poll

Do you think that the federal government should follow a policy of taking money from those who have much and giving money to those who have little?

	YES	YES, IF IT DOESN'T GO TOO FAR	NO	DON'T KNOW
National total:				
	30.1%	23.5%	40.7%	5.7%
By Economic Status:				
Prosperous	18.4%	20.1%	60.0%	1.5%
Poor	42.8%	21.6%	28.9%	6.7%

—*Fortune*, October 1937

Michael Lantz captures the spirit of the New Deal in his sculpture, Man Controlling Trade, *in front of the Federal Trade Commission in Washington, D.C. Trade—the free market—had turned on humans with a vengeance at the end of the twenties, when it had been left almost completely unfettered. The New Deal placed some restraints on the free market, to tame it in the interests of the common good.*

darkly in many places. In our own land we enjoy indeed a fullness of life greater than that of most Nations. But the rush of modern civilization itself has raised for us new difficulties, new problems which must be solved if we are to preserve to the United States the political and economic freedom for which Washington and Jefferson planned and fought. . . .

Throughout the Nation, opportunity was limited by monopoly. Individual initiative was crushed in the cogs of a great machine. The field open for free business was more and more restricted. Private enterprise, indeed, became too private. It became privileged enterprise, not free enterprise.

An old English judge once said: "Necessitous men are not free men." Liberty requires opportunity to make a living—a living decent according to the standard of the time, a living which gives man not only enough to live by, but something to live for.

For too many of us the political equality we once had won was meaningless in the face of economic inequality. A small group had concentrated into their own hands an almost complete control over other people's property, other people's money, other people's labor—other people's lives. For too many of us life was no longer free; liberty no longer real; men could no longer follow the pursuit of happiness.

Against economic tyranny such as this, the American citizen could appeal only to the organized power of Government. The collapse of 1929 showed up the despotism for what it was. The election of 1932 was the people's mandate to end it. Under that mandate it is being ended.

The royalists of the economic order have conceded that political freedom was the business of the Government, but they have maintained that economic slavery was nobody's business. They granted that the Government could protect the citizen in his right to vote, but they denied that the Government could do anything to protect the citizen in his right to work and his right to live.

Today we stand committed to the proposition that freedom is no half-and-half affair. If the average citizen is guaranteed equal opportunity in the polling place, he must have equal opportunity in the market place.

These economic royalists complain that we seek to overthrow the institutions of America. What they really complain of is that we seek to take away their power. Our allegiance to American institutions requires the overthrow of this kind of power. In vain they seek to hide behind the Flag and the Constitution. In their blindness they forget what the Flag and the Constitution stand for. Now, as always, they stand for democracy, not tyranny; for freedom, not subjection; and against a dictatorship by mob rule and the overprivileged alike. . . .

We seek not merely to make Government a mechanical implement, but to give it the vibrant personal character that is the very embodiment of human charity. . . .

Governments can err, Presidents do make mistakes, but the immortal Dante tells us that divine justice weighs the sins of the cold-blooded and the sins of the warm-hearted in different scales.

Better the occasional faults of a Government that lives in a spirit of charity than the consistent omissions of a Government frozen in the ice of its own indifference.

There is a mysterious cycle in human events. To some generations much is given. Of other generations much is expected. This generation of Americans has a rendezvous with destiny.

"Over the Rainbow"

Much as "Blue Skies" speaks the voice of 1927 and "Stormy Weather" that of 1933, "Over the Rainbow" says much about popular feelings in 1939, as the depression entered a second decade. The music was composed by Harold Arlen, with lyrics by E. Y. Harburg.

Somewhere over The Rainbow way up high,
There's a land that I heard of once in a
   lullaby.

Somewhere over The Rainbow skies are blue,
and the dreams that you dare to dream really
   do come true.

Someday I'll wish upon a star and wake up
   where the clouds are far behind me,
Where troubles melt like lemon drops, away,
   above the chimney tops that's where you'll find
   me.

Somewhere over The Rainbow bluebirds fly,
Birds fly
Over The Rainbow, why then, oh why can't I?

Feelings similar to those in "Over the Rainbow" are evident in Rockwell Kent's 1936 lithograph, And Now Where? *The future is, of course, always uncertain, but depression conditions left people especially wistful.*

Timeline

1927
Irving Berlin writes "Blue Skies"

1928
Herbert Hoover elected President in November

1929
Stock market prices collapse in October

1930
Tenyear drought, which will eventually produce the dust bowl, begins in the Great Plains and the Southwest; "repatriation" programs to deport Mexican immigrants begin; Mervyn LeRoy's film *Little Caesar* opens; HawleySmoot Tariff enacted

1931
Florence Reese composes "Which Side Are You On?" in Harlan County, Kentucky

1932
Mervyn LeRoy's film *I Am a Fugitive from a Chain Gang* is released; Farmers' Holiday Association organized; Bonus Army arrives in Washington during the summer; Franklin D. Roosevelt elected President in November

1932–33
Depression hits bottom; onequarter of U.S. workforce unemployed during winter

1933
First New Deal unfolds, March–June; Civilian Conservation Corps (CCC) created in March; Federal Emergency Relief Act (FERA), Agricultural Adjustment Act, and Tennessee Valley Authority (TVA) are established in May; National Industrial Recovery Act (NIRA) passed in June; Busby Berekely creates lavish, collective choreography in films; Dr. Francis Townsend's letter launches "Townsend Plan" in September; John Maynard Keynes publishes "An Open Letter to President Roosevelt" in December

1934
King Vidor's *Our Daily Bread* is released; WheelerHoward (Indian Reorganization) Act is passed in June; major strikes erupt, including San Francisco general strike, spring–summer; Southern Tenant Farmers Union formed in July; American Liberty League formed in August; Upton Sinclair's End Poverty in California (EPIC) campaign spreads, summer–fall

1934–35
"Thunder on the left": radical ideas of Huey Long and Father Coughlin enjoy growing popularity

1935

"Second New Deal" unfolds, spring–summer; Emergency Relief Appropriation Act creates Works Progress Administration (WPA) in April; Supreme Court decision in *Schechter Poultry Corp.* v. *U.S.* overturns National Recovery Administration in May; Wagner (National Labor Relations) Act passed in July; Social Security Act passed in August; Congress of Industrial Organizations (CIO) formed in October

1935–45

Farm Security Administration (FSA) commissions historic photographs of depression and other American conditions

1936

Charlie Chaplin's film *Modern Times* is released; publication of Dale Carnegie's self-help book, *How to Win Friends and Influence People,* and Margaret Mitchell's novel, *Gone with the Wind;* Jesse Owens wins four gold medals at Berlin Olympics; Roosevelt is reelected in November; sit-down strike against General Motors begins in Flint, Michigan, in December

1937

FDR submits "court packing" plan in February; strikers are shot down at Republic Steel in Chicago on Memorial Day; "Roosevelt Recession" begins in August as economy slumps

1938

Opening of Thornton Wilder's play *Our Town;* Joe Louis knocks out Max Schmeling; Fair Labor Standards Act establishes minimum wage and 40-hour work week in June

1939

Marian Anderson, denied the use of Constitution Hall, sings at the Lincoln Memorial; release of Frank Capra's film *Mr. Smith Goes to Washington;* John Steinbeck's novel *The Grapes of Wrath* is published; film versions of *The Wizard of Oz* and *Gone with the Wind* are released

1940

Richard Wright's novel *Native Son* is published; John Ford's film version of *The Grapes of Wrath* opens; Roosevelt is elected to an unprecedented third term in November

1941

Stimulation of the economy by spending in preparation for U.S. entry into World War II ends the Great Depression

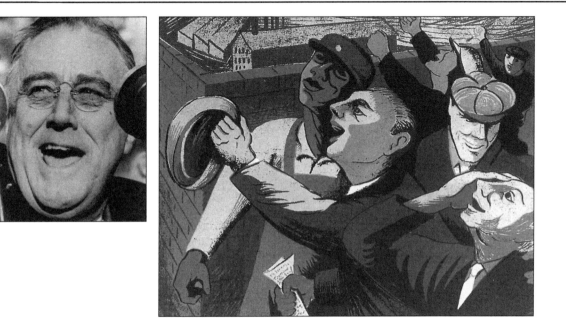

Further Reading

Overviews

Allen, Frederick Lewis. *Since Yesterday: The Nineteen-thirties in America.* New York: Perennial, 1986.

Biles, Roger. *A New Deal for the American People.* DeKalb: Northern Illinois University Press, 1991.

Kennedy, David M. *Freedom from Fear: The American People in Depression and War.* New York: Oxford University Press, 1999.

Leuchtenburg, William E. *The FDR Years.* New York: Columbia University Press, 1995.

————. *Franklin D. Roosevelt and the New Deal.* New York: Columbia University Press, 1995.

McElvaine, Robert S. *The Great Depression: America, 1929–1941.* New York: Times Books, 1993.

Schlesinger, Arthur M., Jr. *The Age of Roosevelt.* 3 vols. Boston: Houghton Mifflin, 1957–60.

Origins of the Great Depression

Bordo, Michael D., Claudia Goldin, and Eugene N. White, eds. *The Defining Moment: The Great Depression and the American Economy in the Twentieth Century.* Chicago: University of Chicago Press, 1998.

Galbraith, John Kenneth. *The Great Crash: 1929.* (1954, 1972); Boston: Houghton Mifflin, 1997.

Temin, Peter. *Did Monetary Forces Cause the Great Depression?* New York: Norton, 1976.

Depression Life

Banks, Ann. *First Person America.* New York: Vintage, 1981.

Bird, Caroline. *The Invisible Scar.* New York: D. McKay, 1966.

Lowitt, Richard, and Maurine Beasley. *One Third of a Nation.* Urbana: University of Illinois, 1981.

McElvaine, Robert S., ed. *Down and Out in the Great Depression: Letters from the "Forgotten Man."* Chapel Hill: University of North Carolina Press, 1983.

Terkel, Studs. *Hard Times: An Oral History of the Great Depression.* New York: Pantheon, 1986.

The Hoover Years

Burner, David. *Herbert Hoover.* New York: Knopf, 1979.

Daniels, Roger. *The Bonus March: An Episode of the Great Depression.* Westport, Conn.: Greenwood, 1971.

Romasco, Albert U. *The Poverty of Abundance: Hoover, the Nation, the Depression.* New York: Oxford University Press, 1965.

Smith, Richard Norton. *An Uncommon Man: The Triumph of Herbert Hoover.* New York: Simon & Schuster, 1984.

Wilson, Joan Hoff. *Herbert Hoover: Forgotten Progressive.* Boston: Little, Brown, 1975.

Franklin and Eleanor Roosevelt

Burns, James MacGregor. *Roosevelt: The Lion and the Fox.* New York: Harcourt, Brace, 1956.

Cook, Blanche Wiesen. *Eleanor Roosevelt, Volume 1, 1884–1933.* New York: Viking, 1992.

————. *Eleanor Roosevelt, Volume 2, 1933–1938.* New York: Viking, 1999.

Davis, Kenneth S. *FDR.* 4 vols. New York: Random House, 1972–93

Lash, Joseph. *Eleanor and Franklin.* New York: Norton, 1971.

Freidel, Frank. *Franklin D. Roosevelt: A Rendezvous with Destiny.* Boston: Little, Brown, 1990.

Maney, Patrick J. *The Roosevelt Presence: The Life and Legacy of FDR.* Berkeley: University of California Press, 1998.

Minorities

Carter, Dan. *Scottsboro: A Tragedy of the American South.* Rev. ed. Baton Rouge: Louisiana State University Press, 1979.

Deutsch, Sarah. *No Separate Refuge: Culture, Class, and Gender on an AngloHispanic Frontier in the American Southwest, 1880–1940.* New York: Oxford University Press, 1987.

Hoffman, Abraham. *Unwanted Mexican Americans in the Great Depression.* Tucson: University of Arizona Press, 1974.

Philp, Kenneth R. *John Collier's Crusade for Indian Reform, 1920–1954.* Tucson: University of Arizona Press, 1977.

Ruiz, Vicki. *Cannery Women, Cannery Lives: Mexican Women, Unionization, and the California Food Processing Industry, 1930–1950.* Albuquerque: University of New Mexico Press, 1987.

Sullivan, Patricia. *Days of Hope: Race and Democracy in the New Deal Era.* Chapel Hill: University of North Carolina Press, 1996.

Trotter, Joe William, Jr. *From a Raw Deal to a New Deal? African Americans 1929–1945.* New York: Oxford University Press, 1996.

Weiss, Nancy. *Farewell to the Party of Lincoln: Black Politics in the Age of FDR.* Princeton, N.J.: Princeton University Press, 1983.

Zangrando, Robert. *The NAACP Crusade Against Lynching 1909–1950.* Philadelphia: Temple University Press, 1980.

Women

Deutsch, Sarah Jane. *From Ballots to Breadlines: American Women 1920–1940.* New York: Oxford University Press, 1994.

Gordon, Linda. *Pitied But Not Entitled: Single Mothers and the History of Welfare 1890–1935.* New York: Free Press, 1994.

Scharf, Lois. *To Work and to Wed: Female Employment, Feminism, and the Great Depression.* Westport, Conn.: Greenwood, 1980.

Wandersee, Winifred D. *Women's Work and Family Values, 1920–1940.* Cambridge, Mass.: Harvard University Press, 1981.

Ware, Susan. *Beyond Suffrage: Women in the New Deal.* Cambridge, Mass.: Harvard University Press, 1981.

———. *Holding Their Own: American Women in the 1930s.* Boston: Twayne, 1982.

Westin, Jeane. *Making Do: How Women Survived the '30s.* Chicago: Follett, 1976.

Rural Life and Farm Policy

Agee, James, and Walker Evans. *Let Us Now Praise Famous Men.* 1941. Reprint, Boston: Houghton Mifflin, 1988.

Gregory, James. *American Exodus: The Dust Bowl Migration and Okie Culture in California.* New York: Oxford University Press, 1989.

Hamilton, David E. *From New Day to New Deal: American Farm Policy from Hoover to Roosevelt.* Chapel Hill: University of North Carolina Press, 1991.

Stock, Catherine McNicol. *Main Street in Crisis: The Great Depression and the Old Middle Class on the Northern Plains.* Chapel Hill: University of North Carolina Press, 1992.

Worster, Donald. *Dust Bowl: The Southern Plains in the 1930s.* New York: Oxford University Press, 1979.

Thunder on the Left (and Elsewhere)

Brinkley, Alan. *Voices of Protest: Huey Long, Father Coughlin, and the Great Depression.* New York: Vintage, 1983.

Holtzman, Abraham. *The Townsend Movement.* 1963. Reprint, New York: Octagon, 1975.

Klehr, Harvey. *The Heyday of American Communism: The Depression Decade.* New York: Basic Books, 1984.

Mitchell, Greg. *The Campaign of the Century: Upton Sinclair's Race for Governor of California and the Birth of Media Politics.* New York: Random House, 1992.

Williams, T. Harry. *Huey Long.* 1969. Reprint, New York: Vintage, 1981.

Labor

Bernstein, Irving. *The Lean Years: A History of the American Worker, 1920–1933.* 1960. Reprint, New York: Da Capo, 1983.

———. *Turbulent Years: A History of the American Worker, 1933–1941.* Boston: Houghton Mifflin, 1970.

Fraser, Steve. *Labor Will Rule: Sidney Hillman and the Rise of American Labor.* Ithaca, N.Y.: Cornell University Press, 1993.

Hall, Jacquelyn Dowd, et. al. *Like a Family: The Making of a Southern Cotton Mill World .* Chapel Hill: University of North Carolina Press, 1987.

Zieger, Robert H. *The CIO, 1935–1955.* Chapel Hill: University of North Carolina Press, 1995.

Culture and Values

Baigell, Matthew. *The American Scene: American Painting of the 1930s.* New York: Praeger, 1974.

Baxter, John. *Hollywood in the Thirties.* New York: A. S. Barnes, 1968.

Bergman, Andrew. *We're in the Money: Depression America and Its Films.* New York: New York University Press, 1971.

Bindas, Kenneth J. *All of This Music Belongs to the Nation: The WPA's Federal Music Project and American Society.* Knoxville: University of Tennessee Press, 1995.

Contreras, Belisario R. *Tradition and Innovation in New Deal Art.* Lewisburg, Pa.: Bucknell University Press, 1983.

Lomax, Alan, Woody Guthrie, and Pete Seeger, eds. *Hard Hitting Songs for Hard-Hit People.* New York: Oak Publications, 1967.

Marling, Karal Ann. *Wall-to-Wall America: A Cultural History of Post Office Murals in the Great Depression.* Minneapolis: University of Minnesota Press, 1982.

De Hart, Jane Sherron. *The Federal Theatre, 1935–1939: Plays, Relief, and Politics.* 1967. Reprint, New York: Octagon, 1980.

Stott, William. *Documentary Expressionism and Thirties America.* Chicago: University of Chicago Press, 1986.

Twelve Southerners. *I'll Take My Stand: The South and the Agrarian Tradition.* 1930. Reprint, Baton Rouge: Louisiana State University Press, 1977.

van Rijn, Guido. *Roosevelt's Blues: African-American Blues and Gospel Songs on FDR.* Jackson: University Press of Mississippi, 1997.

The New Deal and the New Dealers

Barber, William J. *Designs Within Disorder: Franklin D. Roosevelt, the Economists, and the Shaping of American Economic Policy.* New York: Cambridge University Press, 1996.

Colin Gordon, *New Deals: Business, Labor, and Politics in America, 1920–1935* (1994);

Hawley, Ellis. *The New Deal and the Problem of Monopoly.* 1966. Reprint, New York: Fordham University Press, 1995

Karl, Barry. *The Uneasy State: The United States from 1915 to 1945.* Chicago: University of Chicago Press, c1983

Leuchtenburg, William E. *The Supreme Court Reborn: The Constitutional Revolution in the Age of Roosevelt.* New York: Oxford University Press, 1995.

Patterson, James T. *Congressional Conservatism and the New Deal.* 1967. Reprint, Westport, Conn.: Greenwood, 1981.

————. *The New Deal and the States.* Princeton, N.J.: Princeton University Press, 1969.

Rosenof, Theodore. *Economics in the Long Run: New Deal Theorists & Their Legacies.* Chapel Hill: University of North Carolina Press, 1997.

Schwarz, Jordan A. *The New Dealers: Power Politics in the Age of Roosevelt.* New York: Vintage, 1994.

The Legacy of the Depression and the New Deal

Brinkley, Alan. *The End of Reform: New Deal Liberalism in Recession and War.* New York: Knopf, 1995.

Fraser, Steve, and Gary Gerstle, eds. *The Rise and Fall of the New Deal Order.* Princeton, N.J.: Princeton University Press, 1989.

Leuchtenburg, William E. *In the Shadow of FDR.* 2nd ed. Ithaca, N.Y.: Cornell University Press, 1993.

Tobey, Ronald C. *Technology as Freedom: The New Deal and the Electric Modernization of the American Home.* Berkeley: University of California Press, 1996.

Credits

Text Credits

Main Text

p. 18–19: Charles Kettering, "Keep the Consumer Dissatisfied," *Nation's Business* (January 1929): 30–31, 79. Reprinted by permission. Copyright 1929, U.S. Chamber of Commerce.

p. 20–21: In *Public Papers of the Presidents of the United States—Herbert Hoover, 1929* (Washington, D.C.: Government Printing Office, 1974), 1–12.

p. 22–23: "Stocks Collapse in 16,410,030-Share Day," *New York Times*, October 30, 1929. Reprinted by permission.

p. 23–25: William T. Foster, "When a Horse Balks," *North American Review* (July 1932).

p. 27–28: Harold Arlen and Ted Koehler, "Stormy Weather." © 1933 (Renewed) EMI Mills Music, Inc. Rights for Extended Renewal Term in U.S. controlled by Ted Koehler Music, administered by Fred Ahlert Music Corporation and SA Music. All rights outside the U.S. administered by EMI Mills Music, Inc. All Rights Reserved. Warner Bros. Publications U.S. Inc., Miami, FL, 33014.

p. 28–30: Charles L. Walker, "Relief and Revolution," *The Forum* LXXXVIII (1932): 73–74.

p. 30–34: Meridel Le Sueur, "Women on Breadlines," *New Masses,* (January 1932): 5–7. Reprinted by permission. Reprinted in Harvey Swados, ed., *The American Writer and the Great Depression* (Indianapolis: Bobbs-Merrill, 1966), 181–190.

p. 34–36: Florence Converse, "Bread Line," *Atlantic Monthly* (January 1932): 55–56. Reprinted by permission.

p. 36–37: Arthur Garfield Hays, "Letters from a Kentucky Miner," *The Nation* (June 8, 1932). Reprinted with permission.

p. 37–39: Stephen Vincent Benét, "Ode to Walt Whitman," *Burning City* (New York: Farrar and Rinehart, 1936), 32–35. Copyright © 1935 by Stephen Vincent Benét. Copyright renewed © 1964 by Thomas C. Benét, Stephanie B. Mahin and Rachel Benét Lewis. Reprinted by permission of Brandt & Brandt Literary Agents, Inc.

p. 42–45: In Samuel I. Rosenman, ed., *The Public Papers and Addresses of Franklin D. Roosevelt*, vol. II (New York: Russell and Russell, 1938–1950), 11–16.

p. 45–48: Roosevelt, Franklin D. "An Intimate Talk with the People of the United States on Banking," in Rosenman, ed., *The Public Papers and Addresses of Franklin D. Roosevelt*, vol. II, 61–65.

p. 48–52: Adolf A. Berle, Jr., "The Social Economics of the New Deal," *New York Times Magazine*, October 29, 1933: 4–9, 19.

p. 52–54: John Maynard Keynes, "An Open Letter to President Roosevelt," *New York Times*, December 31, 1933. Copyright © 1933 by the *New York Times*. Reprinted by permission.

p. 54–56: Francis Perkins, radio address, September 2, 1935; reprinted in Howard Zinn, ed., *New Deal Thought* (Indianapolis: Bobbs-Merrill, 1966), 275–81.

p. 56–57: Jesse Stone, "W.P.A." Original release on Decca 3151; reissued on Classics CD 615, April 10, 1940; reproduced in Guido van Rijn, *Roosevelt's Blues: African-American Blues and Gospel Songs on FDR* (Jackson: University Press of Mississippi, 1997), 87–89.

p. 59–60: Jouette Shouse, "The American Liberty League," *New York Times*, August 23, 1934. Copyright © 1934 by the *New York Times*. Reprinted by permission.

p. 60–63: Edward Filene, "What Businessmen Think: See the New Deal Through," *The Nation* (December 9, 1934): 707–709. Reprinted with permission.

p. 63–65: As printed in the *New York Times*, May 28, 1935.

p. 65–67: In Rosenman, ed., *The Public Papers and Addresses of Franklin D. Roosevelt*, vol. V, 566–72.

p. 70: Florence Reece, "Which Side Are You On?" © Copyright 1946, 1966 by Stormking Music Inc. All Rights Reserved. Used by permission. Reprinted in Edith Fowke and Joe Glazer, *Songs of Work and Protest* (New York: Dover, 1973), 55.

p. 70–73: U.S. Statutes at Large, XLIX, 449; reprinted in Zinn, ed., *New Deal Thought*, 195–200.

p. 73–75: Report of the Proceedings of the Fifty-fifth Annual Convention of the American Federation of Labor (Washington, D.C., 1936), 534–38, 540–42.

p. 75–77: Carey McWilliams letter to Louis Adamic, October 3, 1937. Department of Special Collections, Charles E. Young Research Library, UCLA. Carey McWilliams Collection #1319, Louis Adamic File, Box 1. Reproduced in Vicki L. Ruiz, *Cannery Women—Cannery Lives: Mexican Women, Unionization and the California Food Processing Industry, 1930–1950* (Albuquerque: University of New Mexico Press, 1987), 135–36.

p. 77: George Jones, "Dis What de Union Done." In George Korson, *Coal Dust on the Fiddle* (Philadelphia: University of Pennsylvania Press, 1943), 302–03, 444–46; reprinted in Irving Bernstein, *Turbulent Years: A History of the American Worker, 1933–1941* (Boston: Houghton Mifflin, 1969, 1970), 768–69.

p. 79–83: Reprinted in Daniel Aaron and Robert Bendiner, eds., *The Strenuous Decade: A Social and Intellectual Record of the 1930s* (Garden City, N.Y.: Anchor, 1970), 290–300.

p. 83–85: Richard Wright, "I Have Seen Black Hands," *New Masses* (June 26, 1934). Reprinted by permission.

p. 85–88: Upton Sinclair, "End Poverty in Civilization," *The Nation* (September 26, 1934). Reprinted with permission.

p. 88–89: Langston Hughes, "The Ballad of Roosevelt," *The New Republic* (November 14, 1934). Copyright © 1994 by the Estate of Langston Hughes. Reprinted by permission of Alfred A. Knopf Inc., a Division of Random House, Inc.

p. 91–93: Reprinted in Francis E. Townsend, *New Horizons: An Autobiography*, ed. Jesse George Murray (Chicago: J.L. Stewart, 1943).

p. 93–96: Abridged, reprinted in Aaron and Bendiner, eds., *The Strenuous Decade*, 150–61.

p. 97–99: Abridged from the Congressional Record, 74th Congress, 1st session, vol. 70 (Washington, D.C.: Government Printing Office, 1935), 8040–43; reprinted in Hugh David Graham, ed., *Huey Long* (Englewood Cliffs, N.J.: Prentice-Hall, 1970) 69–75.

p. 102–103: Reprinted in Richard Lowitt and Maurine Beasley, *One Third of a Nation: Lorena Hickok Reports on the Great Depression* (Urbana: University of Illinois Press, 1981), 324–25.

p. 104–107: John Steinbeck, *The Grapes of Wrath*, (Reprint, New York: Penguin, 1976), 467–68, 500–502. Copyright 1939, renewed © 1967 by John Steinbeck. Used by permission of Viking Penguin, a division of Penguin Putnam Inc.

p.107–109: Thomas Minehan, *Boy and Girl Tramps of America* (New York: Farrar and Rinehart, 1934), 67–71, 78–83; reproduced in David A. Shannon, ed., *The Great Depression* (Englewood Cliffs, N.J.: Prentice-Hall, 1960), 61–65.

p. 110–113: Norman Cousins, "Will Women Lose Their Jobs?," *Current History and Forum* (September 1939).

p. 115–118: Langston Hughes, "Let America Be America Again," *A New Song* (New York: International Workers Order, 1938). Copyright © 1994 by the Estate of Langston Hughes. Reprinted by permission of Alfred A. Knopf, a Division of Random House, Inc.

p. 118–120: Frank Earnest Hill, "A New Pattern of Life for the Indian," *New York Times Magazine*, July 14, 1935: 10, 22. Copyright © 1935. Reprinted by permission.

p. 121–122: Studs Terkel, *Hard Times: An Oral History of the Great Depression* (New York: Pantheon, 1970), 82–83. Copyright © 1970 by Studs Terkel. Reprinted by permission of Pantheon Books, a division of Random House, Inc.

p. 122–123: From Paul S. Taylor, *Mexican Labor in the United States*, No. 2 (Berkeley: University of California Press, 1932), v–vii. © 1932, Regents of the University of California.

p. 123–125: Charles P. Visel, coordinator of the Los Angeles Citizens Committee on Coordination of Unemployment Relief, to Colonel Arthur Woods, national coordinator of the President's Emergency Committee for Employment, January 19, 1931, with publicity release attached; Record Group 73, entry 3, 040, PECE Papers, National Archives. Reproduced in Abraham Hoffman, *Unwanted Mexican Americans in the Great Depression: Repatriation Pressures, 1929–1939* (Tucson: University of Arizona Press, 1974), appendix.

p. 125–127: Jeane Westin, *Making Do: How Women Survived the '30s* (Chicago: Follett, 1976), 100–03.

p. 129–132: Mary Heaton Vorse, "Rebellion in the Cornbelt," *Harper's* (December 1932): 3–9. Copyright © 1932 by *Harper's* Magazine. All rights reserved. Reproduced by special permission.

p. 132–135: Ann Marie Low, *Dust Bowl Diary* (Lincoln: University of Nebraska Press, 1984), 95–98. Used by permission. Copyright 1984 by the University of Nebraska Press.

p. 135–136: Woody Guthrie, "Goin' Down This Road," in *Hard-Hitting Songs for Hard-Hit People*, ed. Alan Lomax, Woody Guthrie, and Pete Seeger (New York: Oak, 1967), 216–17. © Guthrie Children's Trust Fund.

p. 137: Woody Guthrie, "So Long, It's Been Good to Know Yuh," in *Hard-Hitting Songs for Hard-Hit People*, ed. Lomax, Guthrie, and Seeger, 226–27. © Folkways Music Publishers, New York, N.Y.

p. 142–145: Richard Wright, "Joe Louis Uncovers Dynamite," *New Masses* (October 8, 1935): 18–19. Reprinted by permission.

p. 145–147: "Unemployed Arts," *Fortune* (May 1937): 111–17, 172. Reprinted by special permission. Copyright © 1937, Time Inc.

p. 158–160: Walter Lippman, "Governor Roosevelt's Candidacy," *New York Herald-Tribune*, January 8, 1932. Reprinted with the permission of Simon & Schuster, Inc., from *Walter Lippman's Interpretations 1931–1932*, selected and edited by Allan Nevins. Copyright 1932 by Walter Lippman; copyright renewed © 1960 by Allan Nevins.

p. 160: Eleanor Roosevelt Papers, Box 2691, FDR Library; reproduced in Robert S. McElvaine, ed., *Down and Out in the Great Depression: Letters from the "Forgotten Man"* (Chapel Hill: University of North Carolina Press, 1983), 218–19.

p. 161–163: Memorandum by Lindsay Warren, 2 P.M., Sunday, February 7, 1937; Lindsay C. Warren Papers, Southern Historical Collection, Chapel Hill, N.C. Permission to reprint granted by Lindsay C. Warren, Jr. and the Manuscripts Department of the University of North Carolina at Chapel Hill Academic Libraries.

p. 163–166: Rochelle Chadakoff, ed., *Eleanor Roosevelt's My Day: Her Acclaimed Columns, 1936–1945* (New York: Pharos, 1989), 3–4, 105–06, 113.

p. 167: (top) Eleanor Roosevelt Papers, Box 2197, FDR Library, Hyde Park, N.Y.; reprinted in McElvaine, *Down and Out in the Great Depression*, 219.

p. 167: (bottom) Quoted in Westin, *Making Do.*

p. 170–171: In Rosenman, ed., *The Public Papers and Addresses of Franklin D. Roosevelt*, Vol. I, 624–27.

p. 171–174: Terkel, *Hard Times.* Copyright © 1970 by Studs Terkel. Reprinted by permission of Pantheon Books, a division of Random House, Inc.

p. 174–175: Steinbeck, *The Grapes of Wrath*, 213–15. Copyright 1939, renewed © 1967 by John Steinbeck. Used by permission of Viking Penguin, a division of Penguin Putnam Inc.

p. 176–177: From Robert S. Lynd and Helen M. Lynd, *Middletown in Transition: A Study in Cultural Conflicts* (New York: Harcourt Brace, 1937). Copyright 1937 by Harcourt, Inc. and renewed 1965 by Robert S. Lynd and Helen M. Lynd. Reprinted by permission of the publisher.

p. 177–179: In Rosenman, ed., *The Public Papers and Addresses of Franklin D. Roosevelt*, Vol. V, 230–36.

p. 179: Harold Arlen and E.Y. Harburg, "Over the Rainbow." ©1938 (Renewed) Metro-Goldwyn-Mayer Inc. © 1939 (Renewed) EMI Feist Catalog, Inc. Rights throughout the World controlled by EMI Feist Catalog, Inc. All rights reserved. Used by permission. Warner Bros. Publications U.S. Inc., Miami, FL 33014.

Sidebar Text

p. 13: In McElvaine, *Down and Out in the Great Depression*, 117.

p. 18: Robert S. Lynd, with the assistance of Alice C. Hanson, "The People as Consumers," in *Recent Social Trends in the United States: Report of the President's Research Committee on Social Trends*, Vol. II (New York: McGraw-Hill, 1933), chapter XVII.

p. 19: Lynd, "The People as Consumers."

p. 21: In *Public Papers of the Presidents of the United States—Herbert Hoover, 1929*, 355.

p. 28: E. J. Sullivan, "The 1932nd Psalm," *Seamen's Journal*, 1932.

p. 32: In McElvaine, *Down and Out in the Great Depression*, 164.

p. 33: "Homeless Women Sleep in Chicago Parks," *New York Times*, September 20, 1931; reproduced in Shannon, ed., *The Great Depression*, 14–15.

p. 36: Jay Gorney and E.Y. Harburg, "Brother, can you spare a dime?" © 1932 (Renewed) Warner Bros. Inc. Rights for extended Renewal Term in U.S. controlled by Glocca Morra Music and Gorney Music Publishers. Canadian Rights controlled by Warner Bros. Inc.

p. 37: Charlie Spand, "Hard Time Blues." Composer credit: Spand-Lamoore, Paramount 13112; reissued on Document DOCD 5108, Grafton, Wisconsin, c. September 1931; reproduced in van Rijn, *Roosevelt's Blues*, 26.

p. 39: "Beans, Bacon, and Gravy," in *American Folksongs of Protest*, ed. John Greenway (Philadelphia: University of Pennsylvania Press, 1953), 64–65.

p. 42: Milton Ager and Jack Allen, "Happy Days Are Here Again." ©1929 Advanced Music Corp. (ASCAP) All rights reserved. Used by permission.

p. 47: Will Rogers, *New York Times*, March 6, 1933.

p. 51: "N.R.A. Prosperity March," in *The New Deal and the Problem of Monopoly*, ed. Ellis W. Hawley (Princeton: Princeton University Press, 1966), 54. Copyright © 1965, renewed 1993, by Princeton University Press. Reprinted by permission of Princeton University Press.

p. 54: Joe Pullman, "C.W.A. Blues." Original issue on Bluebird B5534; reissued on Document DOCD 5393, San Antonio, Texas, April 3, 1934; reproduced in van Rijn, *Roosevelt's Blues*, 69–70.

p. 55: *Jackson Daily News*, June 20, 1935.

p. 70: National Industrial Recovery Act, Section 7(a) (1933).

p. 74: Maurice Sugarman, "Sit Down." ©1946, People's Songs, Inc.; in Edith Fowke and Joe Glazer, eds., *Songs of Work and Protest* (New York: Dover, 1973), 17–19.

p. 76: Woody Guthrie and the Almanac Singers, "Union Maid," in Lomax, Guthrie, and Seeger, eds., *Hard-Hitting Songs for Hard-Hit People*, 244–45.

p. 81: "Culture and Crisis" (1932), as quoted in Aaron and Bendiner, eds., *The Strenuous Decade*, 265.

p. 88: Floyd Olson, reprinted in Dan C. McCurry, ed., *The Farmer-Labor Party: History, Platform and Programs* (New York: Arno, 1975).

p. 93: Eleanor Roosevelt Papers, Box 2735, Franklin D. Roosevelt Library, Hyde Park, N.Y.: 207–08. From McElvaine, *Down and Out in the Great Depression*, 164.

p. 103: Westin, *Making Do*, 34.

p. 104: Albert Crews, *Professional Radio Writing* (Boston: Houghton Mifflin, 1946).

p. 106: *New York Times*, April 12, 1936. Reproduced in Shannon, ed., *The Great Depression*, 52.

p. 108: FERA Central Files, Box 87, National Archives; From McElvaine, *Down and Out in the Great Depression*, 117.

p. 111: Massachusetts Supreme Court (1939), quoted in Cousins, "Will Women Lose Their Jobs?"

p. 112: Frances Perkins, quoted in Cousins, "Will Women Lose Their Jobs?"

p. 113: Eleanor Roosevelt, *Current History and Forum* (September 1939).

p. 119: Westin, *Making Do.*

p. 122: FERA Central Files, Box 91, National Archives; From McElvaine, *Down and Out in the Great Depression*, 82.

p. 124: "1,200 Mexicans Returned to Homeland," *New York Times*, October 30, 1931.

p. 125: "250,000 Mexicans Repatriated," *New York Times*, July 9, 1932.

p. 127: Terkel, *Hard Times*, 51. Copyright © 1970 by Studs Terkel. Reprinted by permission of Pantheon Books, a division of Random House, Inc.

P. 132: Bob Miller, "Seven Cent Cotton and Forty Cent Meat," in Lomax, Guthrie, and Seeger, eds., *Hard-Hitting Songs for Hard-Hit People*, 38–39. © Bob Miller.

P. 136: H. L. Mitchell, *Mean Things Happening in This Land* (Montclair, N.J.: Allanheld, Osmun, 1979), 347.

P. 142: Dorothy Fields and Jimmy McHugh, "On the Sunny Side of the Street." Copyright 1930 by Shapiro, Bernstein & Co., Inc. Copyright renewed 1957 and assigned to Shapiro, Bernstein & Co., Inc., New York, N.Y. All Rights Reserved. Used by Permission.

p 158: Will Rogers, *New York Times*, March 14, 1933.

p. 159: Martha Gellhorn, introduction to Chadakoff, *Eleanor Roosevelt's My Day*, ix–x.

p. 161: Martha Gellhorn, Report to Harry Hopkins on South and North Carolina, November 11, 1934, Harry Hopkins Papers, Franklin D. Roosevelt Library, Hyde Park, N.Y.; as quoted in Bernstein, *Turbulent Years*, 171.

p. 164: Will Rogers, *New York Times*, June 8, 1933.

p. 167: From Florence King, *Southern Ladies and Gentlemen* (New York: Stein and Day, 1975), 12.

p. 170: Al Dublin and Harry Warren, "Remember My Forgotten Man." © 1933 (Renewed) Warner Bros. Inc. All Rights Reserved. Used by Permission, Warner Bros. Publications U.S. Inc., Miami, FL, 33014.

p. 171: Will Rogers, *New York Times*, March 9, 1933.

p. 175: Steinbeck, *The Grapes of Wrath*, 491.

p. 177: Woody Guthrie, "Ballad of Pretty Boy Floyd." © 1958 Sanga Music, Inc.; in Lomax, Guthrie, and Seeger, eds., *Hard-Hitting Songs for Hard-Hit People*, 115.

p. 178: From *Fortune* (October 1937); in Hadley Cantril and Mildred Strunk, *Public Opinion 1935–1946* (Princeton: Princeton University Press, 1951), 1041.

Picture Credits

20th Century Fox: 155; Collection of the Akron Art Museum (Gift of Miss Leona E. Prasse): 179; Archives of American Art: 57; The Art Institute of Chicago, Friends of American Collection, All rights reserved by The Art Institute of Chicago and VAGA, New York, New York, 1930.934, photograph © 1999, The Art Institute of Chicago, All Rights Reserved: 128; The Bancroft Library: 87; Courtesy of the Estate of Irving Berlin: 17; Margaret Bourke-White/*Life* Magazine © *Time* Inc.: 168; Brown University Library: 90–92; Carnegie Library of Pittsburgh: 29; *Chicago Tribune*: 49; Cleveland Public Library Photograph Collection: 165; Columbia Pictures Corporation: 154; Superman is a trademark of DC Comics © 1999. All rights reserved. Used with permission: 141–142; Collection of Christopher DeNoon: 77; Collection, the Equitable Life Assurance Society of the United States: 138;

By permission of *Esquire* magazine, © Hearst Communications, Inc., Esquire is a trademark of Hearst Magazines property, Inc., All Rights Reserved: 162; Federal Trade Commission, Washington, D.C.: 178; The Granger Collection: 22; Herbert Hoover Presidential Library Museum: 20, 22; Library of Congress: 15, 31, 34, 36, 37, 38, 39, 41, 56, 75, 95, 97, 102, 105, 109, 110, 114, 120, 121, 123, 126, 131, 133, 137, 143, 145, 147, 174, 175; Photo by Lito, courtesy Masha Zakheim: 144; The George Meany Memorial Archives: 72; Richard Merkin Collection: 96; Metro-Goldwyn-Mayer: 152, 155; Eudora Welty Collection, Mississippi Department of Archives & History: 84, 103; National Archives: 25, 100, 118; New York Public Library: 107; Copyright © 1933 by the New York Times Co., Reprinted by permission: 43; New York Tribune Inc. (1936): 63; Oldsmobile History

Center, Lansing, Michigan: 19; The *Oregonion* © 1938 Oregonian Publishing Co., All Rights reserved, Reprinted with permission: 66; Parker Brothers: 140; Philadelphia Museum of Art: 23; Photofest: 141, 176; Photofest/Universal Pictures: 153; Photofest/Walt Disney: 45; *Punch*: 64; *San Francisco News*: 164; Social Security Administration: 2; Courtesy State Historical Society of Iowa, Des Moines: 130; United Artists Television: 150, 152; Universal Pictures: 150; Collection of the University of Arizona Museum of Art, Tuscon (Gift of C. Leonard Pfeiffer): 28; Warner Brothers: 149, 153, 172; Archives of Labor and Urban Affairs, Wayne State University: 73, 82; Collection of Whitney Museum of American Art, New York: 12, 134; Williamson Music: 16.

Acknowledgments

I want to thank several people who provided assistance in the development of this book. Susan Ware, Anthony Badger, Lawrence Levine, and Julia Kirk Blackwelder generously offered suggestions on documents for inclusion in the book.

Special thanks are due to three people who helped with the preparation of the manuscript: Louise Hetrick, Ann McCord Diaz-Barriga, and Virginia Salter.

Sarah Deutsch, one of the academic editors of this series, and Nancy Toff and Lisa Barnett at Oxford University Press were extremely helpful with their suggestions (and their patience).

The staff of the Millsaps College Library, especially James F. Parks and Michele Guyer, aided greatly in tracking down documents.

My greatest debt, as always, is to my family. My parents, Edward and Ruth McElvaine, lived through the Great Depression and sparked my interest in it through their stories about their experiences. John and Anna Lee, to whom the book is dedicated, also survived the depression and told me about it. Their more important contribution to me was their daughter, Anne, who is the love of my life, the mother of Kerri, Lauren, Allison, and Brett, and the mother-in-law of Scott, my five other greatest loves (with another name to be added to that list by the time this book is published).

Index

About the Author

Robert S. McElvaine is Elizabeth Chisholm Professor of Arts and Letters and Chair of the Department of History at Millsaps College in Jackson, Mississippi. He is the author of five previous books: *Down and Out in the Great Depression: Letters from the "Forgotten Man"*; *The Great Depression: America, 1929–1941*; *The End of the Conservative Era*; *Mario Cuomo: A Biography*; and *What's Left?: A New Democratic Vision for America*. He served as historical consultant for the PBS television series *The Great Depression*. His writing has appeared frequently in such publications as the *New York Times*, *Washington Post*, *Los Angeles Times*, *Wall Street Journal*, *New York Times Book Review* and *Newsweek*.